Revolution and reaction
Europe 1789–1849

Andrew Matthews

CAMBRIDGE
UNIVERSITY PRESS

For Sarah, William and Emma and all my sixth-form students.

PUBLISHED BY THE PRESS SYNDICATE OF THE UNIVERSITY OF CAMBRIDGE
The Pitt Building, Trumpington Street, Cambridge, United Kingdom

CAMBRIDGE UNIVERSITY PRESS
The Edinburgh Building, Cambridge CB2 2RU, UK
40 West 20th Street, New York, NY 10011-4211, USA
477 Williamstown Road, Port Melbourne, VIC 3207, Australia
Ruiz de Alarcón 13, 28014 Madrid, Spain
Dock House, The Waterfront, Cape Town 8001, South Africa

http://www.cambridge.org

© Cambridge University Press 2001

This book is in copyright. Subject to statutory exception and to the provisions of relevant collective licensing agreements, no reproduction of any part may take place without the written permission of Cambridge University Press.

First published 2001
Third printing 2004

Printed in the United Kingdom at the University Press, Cambridge

Typeface 10.5pt Minion   *System* QuarkXPress®

A catalogue record for this book is available from the British Library

ISBN 0 521 56734 3   paperback

Text design by Newton Harris Design Partnership

Map illustrations by Kathy Baxendale

The cover shows the painting *Napoleon crossing the Alps*, by Jacques Louis David. (1748–1825) Reproduced courtesy of Peter Willi/Louvre, Paris/Bridgeman Art Library.

ACKNOWLEDGEMENTS
Archiv Gerstenberg, Wietze, Germany: pp.158, 179, 180; Bibliothèque nationale de France: p.56; *Louis XVI* (1754–93) by Antoine François Callet (1741–1823), Prado, Madrid/Bridgeman Art Library: p.16; *Marie Antoinette* (1755–93) *with a Rose*, 1783 (oil on canvas) by Louise Elisabeth Vigée-Lebrun (1755–1842), Château de Versailles, France/Lauros-Giraudon/BAL: p.31; *'A Versailles, A Versailles' March of the Women on Versailles, Paris*, 5th October 1789 (engraving) by French School (18th century), Musée Carnavalet, Paris, France/Giraudon/BAL: p.42; *Transporting corpses during the Revolution, c.1790*, (w/c) by Etienne Béricourt (18th century), Musée Carnavalet, Paris, France/Giraudon/BAL: p.53; *The Singer Chenard, a "Sans-Culotte"*, 1792 by Louis Léopold Boilly (1761–1845), Musée Carnavalet, Paris, France/Giraudon/BAL: p.71; *Napoleon Bonaparte visiting the plague stricken of Jaffa in 1799*, 1804 by Baron Antoine Jean Gros (1771–1835), Louvre, Paris, France/Giraudon/BAL: p.85;

Liberty Leading the People, 28 July 1830 (oil on canvas) by Delacroix (Ferdinand Victor), Eugène (1798–1863), Louvre, Paris, France/Peter Willi/BAL: p.131; *Les Poires*, caricature of King Louis-Philippe (1773–1850) from '*Le Charivari*' (engraving) (b/w photo) by French School (19th century), Private Collection/Roger Viollet, Paris/BAL: p.136; *Patience, my Lord, Your Turn is Coming*, 1790 (engraving) (b/w photo) by French School (18th century), Private Collection/Roger-Viollet, Paris/BAL: p.200; Soit © ARCH.PHOT.PARIS/CMN, Soit © CMN: p.128; Mary Evans Picture Library: pp.23, 79, 123; The Fotomas Index: pp.12, 22, 115, 142, 189; Peter Newark's Pictures: pp.17, 50, 64, 65, 86, 118, 167; The Royal Collection © 2000, Her Majesty Queen Elizabeth II: p.18; Österreichische Nationalbibliothek-Bildarchiv/Foto Leutner Fachlabor: p.165.

Picture Research by Sandie Huskinson-Rolfe of PHOTOSEEKERS.

Contents

Introduction

This study begins with arguably the most significant revolution of the modern era, the French Revolution of 1789, and ends with the failure of a whole series of revolutions that broke out across Europe in 1848. It encompasses a period of great social and economic development, from a massive expansion of population to a trend to urbanisation and the beginnings of industrialisation. The forces of change – ideological, political, social, economic and cultural – may, in the long view, seem irresistible, but their victory was not accepted stoically. Indeed, the failure of the 1848 revolutions seems to demonstrate that the forces opposed to change, the forces of reaction, were still potent, even supreme.

This book examines various aspects of the struggle between the forces of change and the forces of reaction at this crucial time in the development of modern Europe.

What were the forces of reaction?

The French Revolution of 1789 threatened the overthrow of the established order across Europe. However, despite the strength of the forces of change that became apparent then and over the succeeding 60 years, the established order remained remarkably resilient. Indeed, it appeared to have triumphed once again in 1849 after the 1848 revolutions had failed, as it had after the final defeat of Napoleon in 1815.

The forces of reaction included the institutions of absolute monarchy, landed aristocracy and church. These were later supported by the development of a conservative ideology to counter the new ideas of liberalism, nationalism and, in its infancy, socialism.

Absolute monarchy was the norm in Europe in 1789. Most states were ruled by hereditary rulers whose theoretical powers were unlimited, although in practice they governed within the established laws of the kingdom. They viewed their states more or less as personal property, acquired and disposed of through a combination of inheritance, marriage, treaty and war. The people within their states were subject to the king's law and the king's taxes. Monarchs were buttressed in their rule by a landed aristocracy whose authority and privileges were protected by the crown and on whom the crown relied to keep local order. This state of affairs was given religious sanction by the church, whose privileges and position the crown also protected. These institutions owned much of the land directly and could demand a range of dues and services from their peasantry. They also had the advantage of controlling all the levers of **power** within the state.

The French monarchy was toppled by the revolution in 1789 and Napoleon was to make and unmake kings and states. When the dust settled in 1815, monarchy, aristocracy and church remained. The upheavals and excesses of revolution and war had not destroyed them. Indeed, they helped them to develop a powerful ideology of conservatism with which to counter liberalism and nationalism. According to conservative political thinkers, revolutionary change upset the 'natural order' of society and one tampered with institutions hallowed by time and tradition at one's peril. New ideas should be resisted because, as the French Revolution demonstrated, if practised, their result was chaos, violence and bloodshed.

For example, the crown controlled the army, which was officered by the nobility, a major source of **power**.

What were the forces of change?

In this period the pace of development in a range of areas – ideological, political, scientific, technological, cultural, social, economic and others – was rapid. These changes were to have profound implications for the nature of society and politics and to produce stresses and tensions that sometimes found their outlet in revolution. The changes taking place were not all working in the same direction or at the same pace. However, society and states were forced to take note of them and react or adapt in some way. The areas of change can be broadly categorised as social, economic and political.

Social changes

Perhaps the key changes here were demographic. In this period the population of Europe expanded rapidly. Estimates vary, but between 1800 and 1850 it rose by some 50 per cent. The **rate of increase** varied across Europe. Such a rapid rise in population inevitably posed problems, the most obvious being one of food supply. Whilst there was some improvement in agricultural production and some alternative sources became available, food provision remained a key problem. Bad harvests created severe shortages and rapid inflation very quickly. The high price of basic foodstuffs left people little to spend on manufactured goods. A consequence of food scarcity was wider economic crisis as demand contracted. The unrest and problems food shortages caused were an important ingredient in the causes of revolutions throughout this period.

Examples of the **rate of increase** include the German states, where the population rose by a third, and Britain, where it doubled. The population of France rose from about 27 million to 37 million, and that of Austria-Hungary from about 23 million to 31 million.

The population explosion was also accompanied by a shift in population distribution. This period witnessed an explosion in the number and size of **towns**. Whilst in 1849 the majority of the population still lived and worked in the countryside, the proportion living in towns had increased more rapidly than the rate of growth of the population generally. Some towns grew from almost nothing into major centres.

Rapid urbanisation brought its own problems. In a time without significant town planning, house building was unable to keep up with the population growth, with resultant problems of increasing rents and overcrowding. Much of the urban population was also poor: unskilled workers and their families who were often unemployed. Such pressures resulted also in increased public health difficulties. Disease spread rapidly and cholera epidemics killed thousands. Infant mortality was higher and life expectancy lower in towns than in the countryside.

These and other developments, such as economic expansion, were also producing changes in social structure. The most notable development was the growth of the middle class. The term 'middle class' does not lend itself to easy definition – it may include everybody from small shopkeepers and workshop owners; through professionals like lawyers, journalists and government officials; to wealthy merchants, industrialists and financiers. The middle class across much of Europe in 1850 was still small, but it was growing and of increasing political and social importance, associated as it was with the new ideas of liberalism and nationalism that challenged existing social and political values.

This process of growth of **towns** is called 'urbanisation'. Examples include St Etienne in France, which more than trebled in size in the 1830s, whilst Paris grew from 785,000 in 1831 to over a million in 1840.

Economic changes

Whilst in 1850 Europe remained predominantly an agricultural continent, industrialisation was beginning to transform economics and society. Industrialisation had begun first in Britain and was at its most advanced there, but by 1850 no European state was completely immune to its effects. **Technological advances** in machinery and the application of steam power began to have an impact everywhere.

Advances by mechanising processes like weaving that were formerly the preserve of skilled workers created tensions in society. Skilled workers expressed their discontent through machine breaking and demanding economic protection. The application of steam power to manufacturing processes, like spinning, promoted the development of large-scale factory production with its vast numbers of unskilled, poorly paid workers, many of them women and children. However, whilst factory production began to appear in industrial cities, especially in France and Germany, the bulk of manufacturing still took place in small workshops in 1850.

Technological advances brought expansion in the textile, coal, iron and steel industries. Transport and communications were transformed by the development of metalled roads, canals, the telegraph and, most dramatically, by railways after 1830.

Improved communications not only reduced business costs, but also opened up new markets and allowed a freer flow of people, information and news. The world was becoming a smaller place. Improved communication facilitated the spread of ideas whilst the increase in literacy and the blossoming of journalism provided an ever-widening audience.

Political and ideological changes

The changing nature of society and economics was mirrored by the development of new ideas and approaches to social, economic and political problems. The eighteenth century had witnessed the Enlightenment, a loose intellectual movement which, building on the scientific revolution of the previous century, sought to apply logic and reason to try to understand politics, economics and society. The result was a critique of the existing situation that spawned a range of **ideas** that developed into liberalism, nationalism, democracy and later socialism. The thinkers and the ideas were not always opposed to the existing political, social and economic systems, but they did encourage a questioning of them and provided alternative approaches. Against a society based on privilege was posed one based on the equal natural rights of all men, against absolute monarchy the idea of constitutional government, against protectionist economic policy a doctrine of economic liberalism (free trade), against religious intolerance freedom of conscience, and so on.

Ideas emerged from thinkers like Voltaire, who attacked the superstition of the Catholic church. Montesquieu and Rousseau examined the nature of government, Adam Smith analysed economics and so on.

The success of the rebels in the American War of Independence (1776–83) – with their espousal of the doctrines of no taxation without representation, equal rights and war on tyranny – brought home some of the power of these ideas. The French Revolution was to make crowned heads and aristocracies across Europe take notice. It gave life to the ideas of liberalism, nationalism and democracy that were to shape the next century. The problems created by industrial society were also to spawn ideas that developed into socialism.

Liberalism was based around the idea that all men are equal in rights (such as freedom of speech and of the press, freedom of conscience and equality before the law). It attacked social privilege based on birth and advocated the idea of 'careers open to talents', or equality of opportunity. In place of absolute monarchy it proposed constitutional government, a government responsible in some way to the people (usually via an elected assembly).

Nationalism is linked to this last idea. The French Revolution adopted the idea that **sovereignty** resides in the nation, the citizens of a state. Governments are there to serve the nation and are answerable to the nation. Democracy offered one way in which this could be achieved, by suggesting that all men should have the vote. Such a solution was not always palatable to liberals, however, who feared the idea of 'mob rule'.

Sovereignty is ultimate political power.

As industrialisation gathered pace towards the end of the period covered by this book, another set of ideas developed: socialism. Socialism sought to address the evils of poverty and hardship created for many by industrialisation. At this time, socialist thinkers produced a range of solutions, from the reordering of society on communal lines to the provision of national workshops for the unemployed. Their influence before 1848, however, except in France and parts of Germany, was slight.

Revolutions: nature and causes

In this book we are principally concerned with political revolutions, although these certainly have social, economic and cultural ramifications. By revolution in this context we mean a decisive change in the nature of the political system. This is more than a change of government or a reform of the existing system. It implies something more fundamental. The French Revolution of 1789, for instance, overthrew an absolute monarchy and replaced it first with a constitutional monarchy and later (in the summer of 1792) with a republic. This revolution also resulted in huge social changes – a society based on privilege was replaced by one based on the civil equality of all men. Similarly, the revolutions of 1848 sought to replace absolute monarchies with either constitutional monarchies or republics. Furthermore, some sought a reorganisation of states on the basis of nationality.

The fundamental nature of such revolutions has led historians to consider whether there are common patterns to be found amongst them which will help to explain both why they occurred and why they succeeded or failed.

Features that help to explain why revolutions occur
Economic and social unrest
Those who examine the threat of revolution in Britain in the period 1815–20 or 1830–32 often quote **William Cobbett**'s dictum that you cannot agitate a man with a full stomach. At a time when the prime concern of the majority of the population was not politics or political systems, but acquiring enough resources to feed and shelter themselves and their family, Cobbett's conclusion was probably literally true. A man at work with sufficient wages was unlikely to prove useful for revolutionary activity. A hungry man, an unemployed man, a man threatened with future insecurity might be, however. It might be possible to persuade such a man that his problems had a political solution, that the blame for his misfortune lay in the political system, that politics was – as the English **Chartists** argued – a 'knife and fork' question. Additionally, at a time when most were illiterate, when most were living at or near the subsistence level, the only chance of getting mass support for revolution was economic hardship. The coincidence of revolutionary crises with economic crisis

William Cobbett (1763–1835) was an English social reformer and journalist. He exposed the shortcomings of early-nineteenth-century industrial society.

The **Chartists** were supporters of a movement for electoral reform in Britain, 1837–48. Their principles were set out in their manifesto, *The people's charter.*

or its immediate aftermath is startling. The revolution of 1789 was at a time of dear bread and high unemployment. The overthrow of the monarchy in 1792 coincided with severe economic difficulties. The revolution of 1830 occurred after years of economic depression and the 1848 revolutions followed two years of bad harvests and inflation. However, the relationship can be pushed too far. Revolution does not necessarily occur at the height of an economic crisis. If that were so, the revolutions of 1848 should have happened in 1847, during the 'year of dear bread'. There were 'bread riots' and 'potato riots' in this year but no revolution. Economic crisis alone, then, will not necessarily produce revolution.

The discrediting of the existing regime/system

Revolutions do not appear to be the result merely of a sudden or short-term disillusion with the existing regime, but rather are the result of longer-term criticism and problems. For example, arguably the reputation of the French monarchy had been in decline for decades before 1789. Its prestige had been damaged by defeat in war, the supposed debauchery of the court and later of Louis XVI's queen, Marie-Antoinette. Louis XVIII and, especially, Charles X did much to undermine their own fragile positions by their reluctance to accept the changes wrought by the revolution that toppled their brother.

Divisions or loss of nerve amongst the political elite

Other ingredients might help explain the groundswell of protest, but if the ruling classes remained united or held their nerve then the chances of protest proceeding to revolution were considerably reduced. It was noble opposition to the crown's reform plans in France that brought about the political crisis of 1789. Crucially, the combination of Louis XVI's indecisive leadership and the unreliability of the armed forces in the summer of 1789 contributed greatly to the success of the revolution. Loss of nerve by the emperor and his council led to Metternich's fall and revolution in Vienna in 1848. Arguably it was the relative unity of the English ruling class in opposing unrest that saw off the threat of revolution in the period 1815–20 and again during Chartist agitation after 1839.

The existence of an alternative political ideology

The presence of alternative ideas and political concepts can turn mere protest and rebellion into revolution. Such ideas provided a rationale for protest and a legitimate alternative to the status quo. The key ideas in this respect during the period 1789–1849 are liberalism and nationalism. These ideas provided protest with a vision of a better world, a new way of organising the state and politics. However, these ideas would be relatively insignificant if not supported by key groups who could lead and shape and exploit protest. So, for example, ideas of natural rights and constitutional government gained support amongst a significant proportion of the French nobility and bourgeoisie in the years before 1789, and nationalism and liberalism captivated the lesser Hungarian nobility before 1848.

A triggering event

There may be one or more events that allow the above factors to come into play. The calling of the Estates-General in 1789 was crucial. The issue of the Ordinances of Saint-Cloud in 1830 similarly brought unrest into the open. The fall of the French monarchy in February 1848 encouraged liberals, nationalists and radicals across Europe and created panic in the courts of princes.

Features that determine the success of a revolution

Decisive defeat of the old order

One reason why the 1848 revolutions failed in central Europe was perhaps that, although revolutionaries appeared to carry all before them initially, the old order remained relatively intact. In 1848 kings and princes tended to grant concessions rather than be toppled from power. They could then wait until the time seemed ripe for a counter-stroke. On the other hand, where the existing order was effectively toppled, as in France in 1848, there was no route back.

Popular support

Popular support was fickle and needed to be nurtured. In France in 1789 the revolution enjoyed great popular support and revolutionary leaders had to accept some popular demands (such as an end to feudalism) to maintain that support. In 1793 revolutionary leaders accepted demands for economic controls to maintain the support of the urban workers. In 1848 the revolutions in Germany and Austria succeeded initially on the back of popular unrest, but the failure to respond to popular demands saw that support wither. Indeed, in Germany the Frankfurt parliament seemed to turn on the lower orders when popular unrest threatened in the autumn of 1848. In Austria, the timely concession of the abolition of labour service by the emperor (although amongst the revolutionary demands) meant peasants had little further interest in revolution.

Relative unity amongst leaders

There is much truth in the adage 'United we stand, divided we fall!' In 1789 there was relative unanimity amongst the revolutionary leaders about what was required. The revolutionary consensus was to continue into 1790, when divisions over what to do about the Catholic church began to cause serious cracks to appear and contributed to renewed crisis and revolution in France.

In Germany in 1848 the revolutionary leaders gathered at Frankfurt agreed on very little and debated away their chance of creating a united Germany. Splits between radicals and liberals and nationalists of all kinds contributed to the failure of revolutions in the Austrian Empire in 1848.

The quick establishment of effective government

This was a key priority if revolution was to have a real chance of survival. It is significant, for instance, that the longest lasting and hardest to defeat of the revolutions in the Austrian Empire in 1848 was that in Hungary, where the nationalists were quick to establish their government and organise their state. Similarly, in France in 1830, the moderates acted quickly to secure Louis-Philippe on the throne and so avoid a potentially destructive confrontation with more radical elements. However, in Germany in 1848 a parliament was elected, but no effective system of government emerged.

The monopolisation of armed force within the state

A state without an army, without the means to see policies enforced and to defend itself against opposition, is unlikely to survive long. Louis XVI lost power in 1789 partly because he lost the support of the army. The French Revolution survived after 1792 partly because it was able to organise effective armed forces to deal with internal and external threats. The Hungarian bid for independence in 1848–49 lasted so long because the revolutionaries quickly organised their own army to defend their revolution. On the other hand, the Frankfurt parliament was rendered impotent by its lack of armed forces, and revolutions in the Austrian Empire were defeated in large measure because the emperor retained the loyalty of the armed forces, which were willing to act against revolutionaries – be they Italian, Czech or Viennese.

The list of factors identified above is not exhaustive or conclusive. Each revolution emerged out of unique and particular circumstances and if the above elements were present the exact mix of them in proportion and importance varied from place to place and time to time.

1

The coming of the French Revolution, 1783–89

Focus questions

◆ What was the nature of France before 1789?

◆ What happened in the period 1774–89?

◆ What were the political and ideological causes of the French Revolution?

◆ What were the social and economic causes of the French Revolution?

Significant dates

1774   Accession of Louis XVI.

1776–83   American War of Independence.

1778   French declare war on Britain in support of the Americans.

1783   Treaty of Versailles ends the American war.

1787   *February–May* Assembly of Notables fails to sanction royal tax reform package.

1788   *June–July* Revolt of the Nobles.
August Hailstorms destroy the harvest.

1789   *May* Meeting of Estates-General.
20 June Tennis Court Oath.
14 July Storming of the Bastille.
4 August Nobles give up their feudal privileges.
26 August Declaration of the Rights of Man and the Citizen.

Overview

On 14 July 1789 the people of Paris stormed the royal fortress of the Bastille. When news of the event was brought to Louis XVI, out hunting in the grounds of his palace at Versailles, he is reported to have asked: 'Is it a rebellion?' 'No,' came the reply, 'It is a revolution.' The significance of the event was apparent at the time to most observers, including the **earl of Dorset**, British ambassador in Paris.

The **earl of Dorset** reported: 'Thus, my lord, the greatest Revolution that we know anything of has been effected with . . . the loss of very few lives; from this moment we may consider France as a free country; the king a very limited monarch, and the nobility as reduced to a level with the rest of the nation.'

The taking of what had become a relatively insignificant royal fortress, used mainly as an arms depot and a prison – and defended by a few old men and a small number of Swiss mercenaries, has since been taken as the defining moment of the French Revolution, the moment at which absolute royal authority was overthrown. But this was just one event in a whole series that represented a fundamental political and social revolution, in which the whole structure of traditional government and society was overthrown and the foundations laid for a new order.

This chapter examines the causes of the French Revolution and the events of 1789. The starting point has to be an understanding of the nature of French society in the period before 1789.

What was the nature of France before 1789?

In 1788 the term *ancien régime* became current to describe the system of government and structure of society in France. In short, it described a state where the government was based on **absolute monarchy** and where society and social structure were based on privilege.

Social structure

Today we tend to talk about society in terms of classes or occupational groups. In eighteenth-century France society was divided by order or estate. There were three orders: the first was the clergy, the second the nobility, and the final order comprised everybody else and was collectively known as the Third Estate. What distinguished these orders was not necessarily wealth, but privilege. The first two orders enjoyed a range of privileges and the Third Estate none. The basic features of this social structure are important in understanding the social and political tensions that contributed to the French Revolution.

The clergy – the First Estate

There were about 130,000 clergy in France in the 1780s (about 1 for every 200 Frenchmen), ranging from the thousands of parish priests to the 143 bishops and archbishops. In many ways the clergy mirrored French society. Parish priests were generally poor and had much in common with the peasantry who attended their churches; bishops and abbots were all noble in background, wealthy and often servants of the crown. As an order, the clergy enjoyed a number of privileges:

- The clergy had their own courts.
- The clergy had their own assembly to control their affairs.
- The clergy enjoyed exemption from all direct taxes and many indirect taxes.
- The clergy collected their own tax – the tithe – from the rest of the population.

Absolute monarchy is a system in which the state is ruled by a monarch who claims absolute or total authority. Absolute monarchs were thereby theoretically answerable to no-one for their actions and their word was law. The basis of this authority was a mixture of divine right (the belief that kings were placed in authority by God) and hereditary right. Absolute monarchs had a duty to have paternal concern for their subjects.

What were the main features of the three orders or estates?

- The Catholic church had a monopoly over education and care of the sick.

In exchange for its privileged position in the state, the Catholic church generally supported the monarchy and voted through its assembly a ***don gratuit*** to the crown. The church was also a major landowner, owning about 10 per cent of the land in France. It enjoyed considerable income from this source in rents and other dues. Although the church was wealthy as an institution and had many ostentatiously wealthy and worldly bishops, most parish priests were poor and received only a fraction of the tithes levied supposedly for their maintenance.

The nobility – the Second Estate
There were between 100,000 and 400,000 people of noble status in France in the eighteenth century. What distinguished them was not necessarily their wealth – many provincial nobles were no more than small farmers – but their social status and privileges. These included:
- privileges under the law (they were not liable to some of the crueller punishments);
- exemption from the *taille* (the main direct tax);
- exemption from forced labour on the roads (*corvée royale*);
- the right to bear a sword and access to officer status in the army (for established nobility).

The nobility owned a considerable proportion of the land (over 10 per cent) and enjoyed **rights** as local lords of the manor.

There were many types of noble: rich and poor, court nobility and provincial nobility, old and new, **nobility of the sword**, **nobility of the robe** and the ***anoblis*** – those who had purchased noble status. Some nobles, especially amongst the wealthy and those based around Paris, were well educated and took a great interest in new ideas. Others, especially amongst the poor provincial nobility, were jealous of their privileges, which alone distinguished them from their fellow farmers.

The Third Estate
About 95 per cent of the 26 million population of France were neither clergy nor nobility. They were the Third Estate, ranging from wealthy bankers and financiers to lowly landless peasants. What they had in common was lack of the privileges enjoyed by the other two orders and the general disdain in which the nobility held them. There were three broad groups:
1 The bourgeoisie: probably between 4 and 10 per cent of the French population could be described as bourgeois, a term that refers to all from the shopkeeper and master craftsman; through writers, doctors and poorer lawyers; to the wealthy merchants, lawyers, officeholders and financiers. Education

The ***don gratuit*** was a gift of money, a lump sum raised largely through a levy on the lower clergy.

These were known as seigneurial **rights** and included hunting rights. As landlord a nobleman would also enjoy various feudal dues, such as the right to a proportion of a peasant's crop.

The **nobility of the sword** were the descendants of the old feudal nobility. The **nobility of the robe** had gained their status through the official post they held or had purchased in the law courts and royal administration. The *anoblis* had generally gained their status by the purchase of a royal office which, immediately or in time, conferred nobility. These venal offices included the position of royal secretary and could cost as much as 150,000 livres. Over two thousand were purchased during 1774–89, indicating the use of the sales to raise revenue for the crown and the high demand for them. Even Voltaire purchased a royal secretaryship.

What made someone a noble?

What did some members of the bourgeoisie have in common with some nobles?

and relative wealth made the bourgeoisie distinctive. The higher bourgeoisie – financiers, bankers, prosperous lawyers and officeholders – were as well off as the wealthier nobles and sought to transfer into the nobility through purchase of noble office or marriage. They invested their surplus wealth in land and property, and owned collectively over 12 per cent of the land. The lower bourgeoisie felt themselves above the peasants and workers, but were frustrated by the lack of opportunities for advancement.

2 The urban workers: perhaps 4 million Frenchmen lived in large towns, the vast majority of these being small shopkeepers, skilled workers (artisans) and unskilled manual workers. The first two groups especially formed the bulk of what became known as the ***sans-culottes***, who were to play a crucial role in the development of the revolution.

3 The peasantry: perhaps 20 million strong, the peasantry formed the vast majority of the population. They ranged from relatively wealthy peasant farmers to landless labourers and **sharecroppers**. Many peasants owned land but generally holdings were very small and subject to feudal and seigneurial dues. The dues and taxes with which the peasant was burdened limited their ability to do more than survive from year to year.

Sans-culottes means literally 'without breeches'. Members of the bourgeoisie and nobility wore breeches and could therefore be distinguished from the lower orders, who wore trousers.

A **sharecropper** was a peasant farmer who gave a share of his crop to his landlord in exchange for the right to farm his land. Sharecroppers were amongst the poorest of peasants.

Peasantry bowed down by the weight of the first and second orders, a contemporary cartoon. What point is being made by this picture? What kind of burdens are the peasants under?

The various dues and taxes included:

- money payments or labour on the lord's land (*corvée*);
- payments in kind on the crops grown (*c.*12 per cent of the harvest);
- a transfer tax on the sale or inheritance of land;
- a requirement to use the lord's mill, bake bread in the lord's oven and make wine in the lord's winepress;
- the lord's hunting rights meant special permission was needed to build walls or harvest hay before midsummer;
- payment of tithes to the church (on average about one twelfth of the crop);
- direct royal taxes – the *taille*, *vingtième* and *capitation*;
- indirect royal taxes, such as the hated *gabelle*;
- labour on the roads (*corvée royale*).

The incidence of these dues varied from peasant to peasant, village to village and region to region. Circumstances varied enormously and depended not just on the dues listed above but also on the amount of land held, the quality of the land, the size of the family, the talents of the farmer, the weather and so on. What is clear is that the demands made on the peasant were heavy and disproportionate.

Economy

France had a predominantly agricultural economy, which was little more than at subsistence level. All villages and regions tried to produce their own grain to provide the bread that was the staple of the rural and urban diet. Where possible, peasant farmers would also cultivate a cash crop, like vines to produce **wine**, which could be sold to provide extra income. Other ways in which a peasant's income could be supplemented included the spinning and weaving of cloth.

When agriculture flourished, trade and industry flourished; when harvests were bad, bread prices rocketed and the impact on trade and industry was immediate. A good harvest meant lower bread prices, leaving more income available to spend on other goods; a poor harvest meant high bread prices or shortages, leaving little for the purchase of other goods. High bread prices could quickly lead to contracting demand for goods and hence unemployment amongst urban workers; low bread prices stimulated demand for other goods and increased profits and employment. The importance of the price of bread was recognised; in times of dearth local authorities sometimes introduced price controls to prevent unrest.

The central decades of the eighteenth century were generally ones of relative prosperity in agriculture and hence in industry. Internal trade expanded, though not as much as international trade. Most industry was small scale,

The *taille* was a direct tax on income or land. The *vingtième* was a 5 per cent direct tax levied on income to meet emergency costs such as war. *Capitation* was a poll tax. The *gabelle* was an indirect tax on salt (important because salt was essential as a preservative).

What privileges did the nobility enjoy that the Third Estate did not?

What are the implications of the fact that the bulk of the tax burden fell on the peasantry?

What do the existence and sale of venal offices suggest about the ambitions of the wealthy bourgeoisie?

Wine was France's chief export.

The **guilds** were organisations that comprised master craftsmen, journeymen and apprentices. Each controlled a particular trade, setting standards and regulating that trade. In most towns it was impossible to practise a particular trade without being a member of the guild.

What was the relationship between harvests and the well-being of French industry?

Louis XVI's grandfather Louis XV provided a definition of **absolute** rule in 1766: 'Sovereign power resides in my person alone; the right to make laws belongs to me alone – it is not dependent on or shared with anyone else.'

The right to **imprison** was exercised by using a *lettre de cachet*, an order stamped with the royal seal.

A *lit de justice* was a royal order.

How absolute was royal authority in practice?

controlled by **guilds** and operating in workshops in towns. Master craftsmen ran the workshops employing journeymen (day workers) and apprentices. An important exception was the textile industry. Here merchants avoided guild restrictions by farming work out in rural areas, and they also began to organise workers in factories where they could take advantage of new developments in machinery.

France's main exports were wine and spirits and luxury goods such as silk. Marseilles thrived through its dominance in trade with the eastern Mediterranean, but more important was trade with France's colonies. Chief amongst these were the West Indian colonies with their trade in commodities like sugar. This trade centred on Atlantic ports such as Bordeaux, which, like Marseilles, flourished in the eighteenth century.

Monarchy, government and administration

The monarchy of Louis XVI was **absolute**. The king was theoretically answerable only to God (not to his subjects) for his actions. This was what was meant by divine right and it was symbolised by the anointing of the king in the coronation service. Political power was concentrated in the hands of one man; it was personal and therefore the personality, qualities and weaknesses of the monarch had a decisive impact on political decisions. The king appointed his own ministers and also the 34 *intendants* who were each responsible for a particular region of France. Perhaps the most obvious symbol of the king's absolute power was his right to **imprison** anyone without bringing them to trial.

Although the power of the monarch was theoretically absolute, it was not unlimited. The king felt bound by the customs and laws of the realm and respected the privileges and rights of various bodies and institutions within the kingdom. The kingdom of France had developed over centuries by a process of conquest, inheritance and marriage. As provinces were added, they often retained their own institutions and privileges so that there was no uniform system of government or law for the whole kingdom. For example, some provinces retained their own noble-dominated provincial assemblies (estates) which had various powers. Brittany, for instance, was able to negotiate much of its own tax burden.

Other important institutions were the 13 *parlements*, the most important of which was that of Paris. These were final courts of appeal for their particular region and also had the responsibility of registering royal edicts. Before registration the *parlement* could criticise the edict and ask the king to reconsider. If necessary, in the last resort, the king could force registration by a **lit de justice**. Normally registration was a formality, but *parlements* did protest – for example over aspects of religious policy and tax reform, claiming to represent the interests of the nation against despotism.

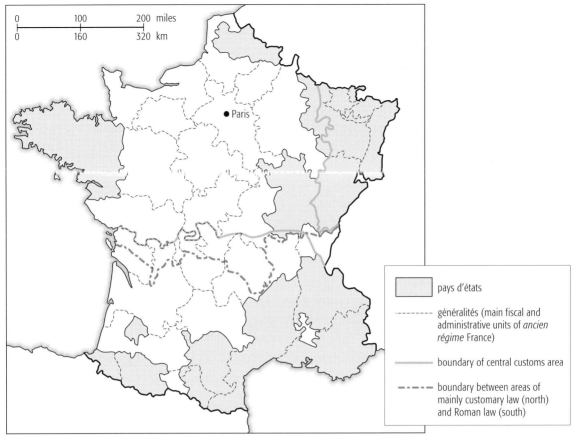

An illustration of some of the administrative chaos of eighteenth-century France. In addition, there were different tax areas, different judicial areas (*parlements*) and other variables.

pays d'états

- - - - - - - généralités (main fiscal and administrative units of *ancien régime* France)

━━━━━━ boundary of central customs area

━ ▪ ━ ▪ ━ ▪ ━ boundary between areas of mainly customary law (north) and Roman law (south)

What happened in the period 1774–89?

A sound grasp of the key events, people and developments in the 1770s and 1780s is necessary to understand the causes and nature of the French Revolution. The pattern of events is complicated.

The starting point for this story is the defeat of France by Britain in the Seven Years' War (1756–63). This was France's second defeat in a major war in less than 25 years. It had three principal effects: it undermined respect for the monarchy by damaging French prestige, its cost left the crown heavily in debt, and it left a crown anxious to reverse its humiliation. This last meant that there was pressure to increase expenditure on the army and navy (especially) and that any international crisis had the potential to turn into a major war with Britain. The pressure to increase expenditure plus the legacy of debt made the crown anxious to maximise its revenues and so to consider reform of the chaotic financial system. However, the damage done to royal prestige

The **Farmers-General** is the name given to those who had the right to collect indirect royal taxes. They were very unpopular and many went to the scaffold during the 1790s.

Parisians paid for six thousand masses when **Louis XV** was ill in 1740, but only three were commissioned during his final days.

Henry IV was king of France between 1589 and 1610 and was credited with ending the French Wars of Religion, bringing unity back to France and re-establishing royal authority.

and the attacks on privilege and vested interests, the results of reform plans, led *parlements* to resist reform decrees and pose as defenders of the liberties of the nation. It did not help that reform was often attempted at times of social and economic hardship and that it inspired the opposition of rival courtiers who sought to discredit and replace reforming ministers.

The last four years of Louis XV's reign saw a determined effort by the crown to trim the powers of the *parlements* (the main institutional obstacle to reform) and to initiate substantial financial reforms. In 1770 royal ministers issued edicts prolonging the wartime extraordinary taxation (the *vingtième*) and ordered that all edicts of the crown should be adhered to, whether registered by the *parlements* or not. The opposition of the Paris *parlement* led to its exile and then abolition, along with several other *parlements*. Meanwhile measures were taken by the *contrôleur général*, Terray, to reduce venality and to renegotiate terms with the **Farmers-General**. However necessary these reforms were, they were deeply unpopular and further reduced the standing of the monarchy. **Louis XV** died a hated man.

Louis XVI succeeded to the throne amidst great hopes of the dawning of a new age, of a new **Henry IV** who would bring prestige, prosperity and unity back to France. Louis, seeking popularity and under great pressure, reversed his predecessor's reforms and restored the Paris *parlement*. However, the

A portrait of Louis XVI. What impression of Louis XVI does this painting give you? How has the artist achieved this?

urgency of the growing financial problems could not be ignored and in 1776 his *contrôleur général*, Turgot, proposed a new package of financial and economic reforms, including stricter accounting procedures, reductions in the number of contracted officials and pressure on the Farmers-General. He also aimed to free up the grain trade and abolish guilds in the hope of increasing food supply and stimulating economic growth. He was opposed by rival ministers such as Maurepas and, of course, the Paris *parlement* refused to register the edicts. Louis XVI, in the face of such opposition, failed to stand by his minister and the reform package collapsed.

As war broke out between Britain and its American colonies in 1776, the financial problems of the French crown remained unresolved. France's decision to support the colonists in their fight for independence in 1778, whilst popular, imposed extra strains on royal finances which in a few years would bring the French monarchy to the point of bankruptcy. But at the time the crown appeared to have found a financial wizard who could provide the revenue necessary to fight Britain without increasing taxation. He was a Swiss Protestant banker called **Jacques Necker**.

Necker raised the necessary cash through loans and some financial reforms. Between 1778 and 1781 he raised 150 million livres in short-term loans whilst also cutting the number of venal offices and ensuring stricter supervision of royal accounts. A stream of credit was secured by the first ever publication of royal accounts in 1781 (the so-called *compte rendu*) which appeared to show a surplus of revenue over expenditure. That Necker succeeded where Turgot and others had failed can be attributed partly to the fact that financial reform was not coupled with more general economic reform and partly to the support of the king and other ministers.

That support was to prove short lived, for Necker's attempts to control the level of war expenditure aroused the opposition of powerful ministers like Vergennes. What is more, the public nature of the *compte rendu* was felt by others to damage the prestige of the monarchy and Necker's ambition to join the inner circle of the king's advisers caused friction because as a Protestant he was debarred. The upshot was that ministerial opponents to Necker persuaded Louis XVI to abandon him in 1781. With him went his reforms.

In the short term, credit continued to flow, but the debts were mounting steadily and interest payments were taking up an increasing proportion of royal expenditure. When Alexandre de Calonne (see page 18) was appointed *contrôleur général* in 1783 he was faced with the task of maintaining the flow of loans to shore up the increasingly weak financial position. In the immediate term he did this by reassuring creditors by prompt payment of interest and high-profile expenditure such as the purchase of new royal palaces, including Saint-Cloud. But in 1784–85 the stream of credit began to dry up. The Paris

Jacques Necker (1732–1804) by Duplessis. Necker was a Genevan banker brought in to manage French finances in 1777. His reputation was based on his apparent ability to keep royal finances healthy during the American War of Independence. Although he was dismissed in 1781, his popularity was such that the king brought him back in September 1788. His second dismissal in July 1789 was instrumental in provoking the Storming of the Bastille. In 1790 he returned to Switzerland.

Alexandre de Calonne (1734–1802), by Vigée-Lebrun. He was an *intendant* before he was appointed *contrôleur général* in 1783. His analysis of the parlous state of royal finances and his plans for a thorough-going reform led to the abortive Assembly of Notables in 1787. Opposition there led to his dismissal. After the revolution in 1789 Calonne left France, eventually to settle in England.

parlement refused to register new loans and the interest rates demanded by financiers began to escalate.

As credit disappeared, Calonne became convinced of the need to come clean about the state of the royal finances and of the necessity of radical and fundamental reform of the financial structure. Calonne blamed Necker's *compte rendu* for creating a false impression of royal finances: there was no surplus. In fact, the annual deficit was over 100 million livres. He proposed a reformed tax structure that would remove the tax privileges of the nobility as well as reforms that would ensure efficient collection and accounting. Whilst Louis XVI was persuaded of the need for reform, the fundamental nature of the proposals required some kind of public endorsement if there was to be any chance of making them stick. Calonne therefore suggested the convening of the Assembly of Notables, a body of hand-picked representatives of the great and the good who might be expected to endorse the reform package.

The Assembly of Notables was gathered in February 1787, but it failed to be the compliant body of yes-men for which Calonne had hoped – too many vested interests were offended by the proposals. The assembly criticised the proposals; they were not convinced, given the *compte rendu* and Calonne's conspicuous expenditure, that they were necessary or that they were practical. Some argued that the assembly did not have the authority to agree to such fundamental reforms. The attacks on Calonne were such that Louis was forced to dismiss him, replacing him with a rival, Brienne. The change of minister failed to make the assembly more amenable and it was dissolved, having declared that only an **Estates-General** could approve new taxation.

The **Estates-General** was an elected assembly which had not met for over 170 years.

None of this public washing of the monarchy's dirty financial linen made the availability of credit any better. Bad harvests in 1786 and a growing economic crisis, partly stimulated by a damaging trade treaty with Britain (the Eden Treaty), caused further problems by reducing tax yields and causing bankruptcies amongst tax officials. Facing imminent bankruptcy, Brienne decided to press ahead with a slightly watered-down version of Calonne's proposals.

The necessary edicts were issued but the Paris *parlement* – posing as the defender of the nation's interests – refused to register them, declaring that only the Estates-General could approve new taxation. This popular move compounded the monarchy's problems and the decision to exile the *parlement* from Paris in August 1787 served only to increase public hostility. But the crown's financial position was now dire and the king was forced to recall the Paris *parlement*, back away from tax reforms and promise the calling of the Estates-General by 1792. There was a possibility that this policy could buy some time, but when the king met the *parlement* in November 1787 in a royal session to register a new five-year loan, he appeared to order registration by a *lit de justice* and protests by the duc d'Orléans led to his exile and the arrest of critics of royal policy. At the very time when the king appeared to be responding to public demand, therefore, he seemed to act in a despotic manner.

What can you infer from this narrative about the abilities and qualities of Louis XVI as a monarch?

The actions of the king stimulated protest. In May 1788 the Paris *parlement*, again as the defender of the nation's interests, issued a declaration of what it believed were the 'fundamental laws' of the kingdom, asserted the need to call an Estates-General and the **right not to be imprisoned without trial**, and claimed that the king could not change the privileges and customs of the people. The monarchy struck back by ordering a drastic reform of the *parlements*, but meanwhile there were riots in provincial capitals across France, notably in Rennes and Grenoble (the 'Day of Tiles'). The Assembly of the Clergy sided with the *parlements*, condemning the reforms and voting only a token *don gratuit*. These events comprise the so-called 'Revolt of the Nobles'.

The assertion of the **right not to be imprisoned without trial** was an attack on the royal power exercised under a *lettre de cachet*.

The significance of the revolt was not that it had widespread popular support (unrest was relatively localised), but that it brought about the final collapse of royal finances. In August 1788 the treasury was empty and the king was forced to bring forward the calling of the Estates-General and to recall Necker. Necker's reputation was enough to steady the nerves of creditors but, apart from recalling the Paris *parlement*, he made it clear that he would do little until the meeting of the Estates-General. The members of the *parlement* re-entered Paris in triumph, hailed as the protectors of the nation's freedoms, whilst the unpopular minister Brienne was burned in effigy.

Until this point there had been relative unity among those opposed to the crown, be they noble or bourgeois, liberal or conservative. However, an opinion

One of the **observers**, the Swiss Mallet du Pan, commented: 'King, despotism and constitution have become only secondary questions. Now it is war between the Third Estate and the other two orders.'

Why did the issue of representation and voting cause such controversy?

There were seven **princes** of royal blood, including the king's brothers, Artois and Provence. Five of the seven petitioned the king in December 1788 not to grant either doubling of the Third Estate or voting by head.

The *cahiers des doléances* form a vast documentary resource about the views of everyone from peasant to lord on the eve of the revolution. They reveal social and economic concerns and many local grievances of the Third Estate as well as comments and suggestions on political and constitutional issues.

The **Reveillon riots** were the result of a rumour that wages were to be cut in a Paris textile workshop. This provoked mass unrest and led to the death of many Parisians as the army sought to reassert control.

expressed by the recalled Paris *parlement* was to transform the situation. This concerned the nature of the proposed Estates-General. The last time the Estates-General had met had been in 1614. Then the representatives of the three orders or estates (clergy, nobility and Third Estate) had met separately and voted collectively. This system meant that the first two privileged orders could always effectively outvote the Third Estate. The Paris *parlement* declared that the 1789 Estates-General should follow the 'forms of 1614'. This outraged the liberal leaders of the Third Estate. What had appeared up to this point a struggle of the nation in defence of its rights against a despotic king was transformed into a struggle between the privileged and unprivileged orders. The claim of the *parlement* to be acting in defence of the nation sounded hollow; it now seemed clear to **observers** that the nobility in their 'revolt' had been acting solely in defence of their privileges and position within the state.

Following the *parlement*'s declaration, a vigorous public debate carried on through pamphlets and in the salons and cafés of Paris ensued. Liberal nobles and bourgeois leaders argued strongly that the representation of the Third Estate should be doubled and voting in the Estates-General should be by head rather than by order. Doubling its representation would give the Third Estate about the same number of representatives as the other two orders combined, whilst voting by head would ensure that the other two orders could not outvote it. Here was an opportunity for the crown to regain the initiative and ally with the Third Estate against the privileged orders, a policy Brienne had advocated in August when he had argued that the Estates-General should be 'truly national in its composition'. The king and Necker hesitated. They referred the issue to an Assembly of Notables, which unsurprisingly rejected the proposals, as did the royal **princes**. Eventually, after long consideration within the royal council, it was decided to double representation for the Third Estate. Nothing was said about voting. This fudge failed to calm the situation and public debate continued as elections for the Estates-General went ahead and each village, town and order drew up lists of grievances – *cahiers des doléances* – for consideration by the Estates-General.

The harvest of the summer of 1788 had been a disaster all across France; many crops were destroyed by heavy hailstorms and food prices were rising rapidly. Hunger and inflation made the other burdens on the unprivileged seem all the more unjust and in need of reform. An example of the impact of economic hardship was the **Reveillon riots** in April 1789. Everywhere the Estates-General was looked to as the body that would solve all problems; it was, as contemporaries saw it, the great hope for France's 'regeneration'.

When the elected representatives of the three orders began to assemble at Versailles in May, the issue of voting had still not been resolved. The crown gave no lead. The Third Estate refused to register their representatives separately from the other two orders until voting in common and by head had been agreed; the other two orders refused to agree to that. This impasse lasted seven weeks. Nothing came from the crown, partly because, perhaps, the king was mourning the death of the dauphin, his eldest son. A change came in June when the Third Estate invited representatives of the other two orders to join them. Whilst not a single noble – even though 46 had supported voting by head – joined the Third Estate, a trickle of clerical deputies (mainly parish clergy) did so. The first crack in the dam had appeared and from then on the situation developed rapidly.

Why do you think that it was parish priests who began to join the Third Estate?

On 17 June the Third Estate issued a final invitation to the other two orders to join them and declared itself to be the National Assembly. The significance of this was that the Third Estate were claiming sovereign power in the state – if it could make the claim stick, a political revolution would have taken place. On 19 June the First Estate, the clergy, voted to join the Third Estate. This finally provoked the king into action. Necker persuaded Louis XVI to summon a Royal Session of all three orders and to offer concessions, but reactionary members of the court persuaded the king to take a less conciliatory line. On 20 June royal troops excluded the Third Estate from its usual meeting place, arousing rumours of a royal military coup. Rather than disperse, the Third Estate assembled in an empty tennis court where, cajoled by new leaders like Mounier and the liberal comte de Mirabeau, they took an oath not to disband until a new constitution for France had been agreed (this was the famous Tennis Court Oath).

Meanwhile preparations went ahead for the Royal Session, and the orders assembled on 23 June. In the session the king outlined planned reforms, but he also allowed the nobility a veto over its future in the Estates-General and instructed the three orders to discuss his proposals separately. These minor concessions were too little, too late. The National Assembly was not recognised. The Third Estate stood firm and even some noble deputies began to join its ranks. On 27 June Louis admitted defeat for the moment, and ordered the rest of the deputies to join the National Assembly.

The fight was not yet over. The king began gathering troops around Paris, arguing they were needed to maintain law and order, although they were deployed to defend strategic bridges and occupied the high ground around Paris. To deputies of the National Assembly and to Parisians the troop movements seemed to presage an attempted coup by the king against the National Assembly and the people of Paris (among whom there was vociferous support for the Third Estate). The rumours seemed confirmed when the popular Necker was dismissed on 11 July and replaced by the conservative Breteuil. Meanwhile food prices had reached a peak and popular unrest simmered. Customs barriers which ringed the city were attacked and grain stores raided.

This painting of the Tennis Court Oath was produced by David, who was later to become a deputy in the National Convention in 1792. What impression is the artist trying to give of this famous event?

The **Palais Royal** was the Paris residence of the liberally minded royal prince the duc d'Orléans. In the 1780s the Palais Royal became a commercial centre and in the late 1780s a base for liberal and revolutionary activity.

The **Bastille** served the dual purpose of royal prison and arms dump. It was a symbol of royal authority and (by this time) despotism, being a prison in which victims of *lettres de cachet* were kept.

As disorder threatened Paris, leading bourgeoisie formed a provisional municipal authority there and hurriedly organised a police force, the *Gardes françaises* or National Guard, to protect property and keep order, and to protect Paris. Whatever the desires of this authority, the situation in Paris was getting out of hand. Popular demagogues, like the passionate Camille Desmoulins, harangued the crowds outside the cafés of the **Palais Royal** and called the citizenry to arms. As a result crowds began raiding gunshops and swordsmiths. On the morning of 14 July the Hôtel des Invalides (the home of war veterans) was raided and the weapons and cannon seized. Short of ammunition, the crowd – accompanied by members of the newly formed National Guard – moved on to the old royal fortress of the **Bastille**. Representatives of the new city authority tried to negotiate entry with the Bastille's governor, but fighting broke out and the fortress was stormed. As the head of the murdered governor was paraded through the streets, the significance of the fortress's fall sank in. Paris was under the control of the supporters of the National Assembly; royal troops within the city had refused to fight.

On receiving the news and being informed by officers that they could not rely on their troops to obey orders, Louis capitulated once more. He had little choice. He told the assembly that the army would be withdrawn from around Paris. Further advice made it clear to the king that even to move away from

Paris would be dangerous as the whole country was on the verge of revolt. Reluctantly, therefore, on 17 July he acceded to the popular demand for the reinstatement of Necker and signalled his acceptance of the revolution by going to Paris. At the Hôtel de Ville he appeared to the public wearing the revolutionary tricolour cockade which sandwiched the white of the Bourbon royal family between the blue and red colours of Paris.

In what ways did the army affect the course of events in July 1789?

The fall of the Bastille had effectively secured the future of the National Assembly, which began work on shaping the principles on which a new constitution was to be framed. In Paris the emergency council was formalised as the Paris Commune. Across France, a relatively bloodless municipal revolution took place as royal authority collapsed. Leaders of the Third Estate organised their own councils and national guards. However, in the countryside law and order broke down completely as news of the revolution, hunger and fears about repression proved a volatile mixture. On the one hand, peasants assumed that their feudal obligations would be abolished; on the other, the presence of bands of armed brigands, and rumours of an aristocratic plot to reverse the revolution and destroy the coming harvest, led to the peasants arming themselves. The result was attacks on chateaux to destroy the legal documents (*terriers*) that recognised the lords' rights over the peasantry. This

The Storming of the Bastille, 14 July 1789, from a contemporary engraving. The crowd was a mixture of artisans, skilled workers and soldiers who had gone over to the people armed with weapons taken from the Hôtel des Invalides. Later in the revolution these kinds of revolutionary activists would be known as *sans-culottes*.

nationwide disorder, the 'Great Fear', was most intense between 20 July and 6 August and forced the National Assembly to react. On the 'Night of 4 August' a seemingly spontaneous surrender of privileges by the nobility and others occurred. In one night it appeared the system of privilege which had determined the nature of French society for hundreds of years was destroyed. The peasants, wrongly as it turned out, assumed that they were no longer bound by their feudal obligations and the Great Fear subsided.

The final stage in this opening phase of the French Revolution came on 26 August 1789, when the National Assembly approved the principles by which the new France would be governed in the Declaration of the Rights of Man and the Citizen. By this time, the *ancien régime* seemed to have been destroyed – the king's authority had been curtailed, an elected assembly had assumed the power to redraw the Constitution of France, and the social system of orders and privilege had been overturned. The declaration was the founding document of the new order.

What were the political and ideological causes of the French Revolution?

Arguably the French Revolution of 1789 had two elements. The first was a political revolution in which the system of absolute monarchy was overturned and replaced by constitutional government answerable to the elected representatives of the people. It was symbolised by the Tennis Court Oath, made secure by the Storming of the Bastille and enshrined in the Declaration of the Rights of Man. Secondly, there was a revolution in the social organisation of France symbolised by the abolition of privilege on the night of 4 August. These two elements are not mutually exclusive. The political aims of the liberals were to some extent also social, including careers being open to talents and opposition to other privileges of nobility. On the other hand, the social grievances of the peasants, such as the desire to get rid of seigneurial rights, implied an Estates-General with legislative power.

The narrative so far may seem to suggest that the French Revolution was a result of the coincidence of two separate crises. At the monarchical level, there was a financial crisis that proved so intractable that a political crisis developed in which the power of the monarchy and then the privileged status of the church and nobility were at stake. Meanwhile, a growing economic crisis reached a peak at the very time the political crisis did the same. At stake on the one hand were the powers of the crown; on the other, the future of a society based on privilege and outdated feudal rights. The opponents of both absolute royal power and privilege looked to the Estates-General that assembled in May 1789 as the guarantor of change and a new and better future.

The political causes of the French Revolution include the influence of new ideas spawned by the Enlightenment, the nature and development of the financial problems of the crown, the failure of attempts at reform, the role of the monarchy and the impact of the American War of Independence.

The Enlightenment

The Enlightenment was an intellectual movement of the middle decades of the eighteenth century rather than a set body of ideas. The term was in use at the time to describe the ideas of a wide range of European thinkers (in France called *philosophes*). These thinkers had in common a belief that by the exercise of reason man was capable of understanding the world. Such understanding would enable him to create a better world. Enlightened thinkers were therefore suspicious and sceptical about features of society, such as aspects of Catholicism and divine right monarchy, that seemed to them to be based on tradition and superstition rather than reason. The Enlightenment concerned itself with almost every branch of knowledge from the physical sciences, through history, religion and education, to government, politics and economics.

What has all this to do with the French Revolution? There is a debate about the impact of the Enlightenment in causing and affecting the course of the French Revolution, but impact it did have. The ideas of *philosophes* like **Voltaire**, **Montesquieu** and **Rousseau** led to a questioning of the existing arrangements in society, politics and religion; whilst the ideas of economic thinkers like François Quesnay helped shape proposals to reform the tax system and the economy more generally.

Rousseau created a new view of the state in his book *The social contract*. Unlike other *philosophes*, he recognised the importance of the emotions as well as of man's capacity for reason. In his view, God gave man reason to know good, conscience to love it and free will to choose it. Rousseau developed the idea of popular sovereignty – the idea that government is legitimate only if it has the express consent of the people and enforces laws that reflect the General Will of the people. The General Will is a difficult concept, but expresses the true will of every citizen, what every citizen would wish if acting in accordance with both what was best for society as a whole and his conscience. Rousseau's ideas were to have an important influence on the course of the revolution, particularly on revolutionary leaders like Robespierre (see page 49).

Enlightened ideas questioned the existing institutions and structures in society, and they suggested some alternatives: religious toleration instead of Catholic intolerance, freedom of speech and the press instead of censorship, free trade and a uniform system of taxation instead of customs' barriers and privileged tax exemption, constitutional monarchy instead of divine right absolutism, and careers open to talents rather than careers reserved for

The breadth of concern of the Enlightenment was reflected in the project of the French *philosophes* Diderot and d'Alembert to draw together all knowledge in one work – the *Encyclopédie*.

Voltaire was the dominant figure in the French Enlightenment and campaigned against intolerance, miscarriages of justice and evidence of what he viewed as political and religious tyranny.

Montesquieu advocated a mixed constitution which entailed a 'separation of powers', that is a system of government where the power of the executive (government) is not held by the same person or group as the power of law making (legislation) or by the same person or group as the power to judge when the law has been broken (judicial power). Montesquieu believed, therefore, that in France the power of the monarch should be limited by a powerful and responsible nobility, and by laws he could not over-ride.

Jean-Jacques **Rousseau** (1712–78) was a Swiss-born *philosophe* who attacked the social and political order of the *ancien régime*. In *The social contract* he argued that the only moral and legitimate government was one based on popular sovereignty and which conformed to the General Will.

On what grounds did *philosophes* criticise existing institutions like the church, the monarchy and the privileged orders?

The **salons** were informal meetings organised by society ladies to discuss the issues of the day.

One failure of **censorship** came with the attempt by the king to prevent the performance of Beaumarchais's play *The marriage of Figaro* in the 1780s, with its attack on aristocratic privilege. It served only to popularise the ideas put forward and stimulate debate about the king's 'tyranny'.

In what ways can the Enlightenment be said to have caused the French Revolution?

privileged orders. However, the *philosophes* were not revolutionaries, nor were they political leaders.

Their audience amongst the educated classes was quite wide (from some artisans upwards). The eighteenth century saw the development of literary societies in many towns and cities across France where intellectual debate could take place amongst the bourgeoisie and liberal-minded nobility and churchmen. In Paris, the *philosophes* were the toast of the **salons**. Writers and journalists spread the ideas and so aristocrats, lowly lawyers and even artisans were exposed to enlightened thinking. Men who would become revolutionary leaders absorbed the ideas destructive of the *ancien régime* – the attacks on the church, on privilege and on the tyranny of unrestrained absolutism. Whether the *philosophes* intended it or not, their ideas provided justification for criticism and for change. The danger of these ideas was recognised and there were attempts to enforce **censorship**, but these often backfired.

The questioning of authority and existing institutions reached down to artisans and workers in the form of scandal-mongering pamphlets and cartoons. The targets of these satires and gossip were the monarchy and the privileged: the king was impotent, the queen promiscuous, the aristocracy perverted. Such criticism did much to undermine respect for the privileged orders and the monarchy.

As serious as this was the failure of the monarchy to adapt to changing circumstances. *Philosophes* were not against monarchy, even absolute monarchy. Voltaire was a correspondent of Frederick II of Prussia and Catherine the Great of Russia. Whereas Frederick II called himself the first servant of his people, Louis XVI was crowned with all the ceremony associated with divine right kingship. Attempts by his ministers to introduce 'enlightened' tax reforms failed partly because the king did not support them with determination.

Enlightened ideas did not cause the French Revolution, but they provided a framework for criticism and a moral justification for change or opposition. *Parlements* could dress up opposition to royal edicts as defence of the nation's interests, and nobility and clergy could similarly resist demands for tax reforms on the grounds that the monarchy should address such demands to an elected assembly.

The financial problems of the crown and the failure of reform

In simple terms, the nature of the financial problems facing the crown can be expressed as follows:

$$\text{costs of war + high ordinary expenditure + poor financial administration + insufficient revenue} = \text{debts}$$

To finance the debt the crown borrowed money but then, of course, had to pay interest, which in turn added to expenditure and thence to the overall debt.

The crown found itself trapped in a spiralling cycle of debt and dependence on credit that made eventual bankruptcy likely unless radical reform was undertaken.

War was very expensive even if you won, and more so if you lost. Between 1740 and 1783 France took part in three **major wars** lasting a total of 20 years. The costs of all three were colossal and cumulative, financed partly out of extraordinary taxation (such as the *vingtième*) and partly by borrowing.

In addition to the high costs of war came expenditure on running the administration and the royal household. The latter was immense. The court at Versailles needed to be maintained with all the glamour that had adorned it since the reign of Louis XIV. Other members of the royal family and their households had to be catered for. Louis XVI's wife Marie-Antoinette (one of whose nicknames was Madame Déficit) and his brother Artois were particularly extravagant. Conspicuous expenditure on building projects like the harbour at Cherbourg, and the purchase of royal palaces like Saint-Cloud, whilst expensive, was deemed necessary to reassure creditors that royal finances were sound. An additional drain on resources was the necessity to dispense royal patronage in the form of pensions, presents, offices and other gifts.

The chaotic nature of financial administration has been indicated above (see pages 13–15). The main points to note include:

- lack of uniformity in the tax system – including the tax privileges of the nobility and clergy, and the variety in incidence of other taxes like the *gabelle* and the *taille* which were calculated differently and in different areas;
- inefficiency and corruption involved in their collection – some taxes were contracted out to the Farmers-General and the right to collect others attached to venal offices, whilst the lack of effective accounting systems made it difficult to measure either income or expenditure accurately.

The inefficiency of the revenue system meant delays and shortfalls in income, making the crown reliant on short-term credit even to pay day-to-day bills. But, of course, the basic problem remained: income was exceeded by expenditure.

The crown and the various *contrôleurs généraux* were not blind to the financial situation but, as we have seen, every attempt at reform failed. There were a number of reasons for this:

1 Financial reforms were sometimes coupled with unpopular economic **reforms**.

2 Reform was sometimes attempted at times of general economic hardship. This factor contributed to the opposition faced by Terray and later Brienne (in 1787–88).

These **major wars** were the War of Austrian Succession, 1740–48; the Seven Years' War, 1756–63; and the American War of Independence, in which France was involved between 1778 and 1783. There were no gains, only losses, in its defeats in the first two wars, and the gains of its victory in 1783 were minimal.

For example, the attempt to link a **reform** package with deregulation of the grain trade by Terray in 1770 and then Turgot led to opposition that contributed to the dismissal of the ministers and the loss of the reform package.

Examples of opposition by **rivals**: Necker's attempts to control war expenditure were opposed by Vergennes; the attempts of Turgot to reduce venality were opposed by officeholders; Calonne's reform package of 1787 was opposed by rivals like Brienne.

Louis XVI failed to maintain his support for the **reforming ministers** Turgot, Necker and Calonne.

3 Reform was opposed by ministerial and court **rivals** and those vested interests who would lose out.

4 The crown failed to support **reforming ministers** when opposition arose.

5 The *parlements*, especially that of Paris, opposed reform measures. The opposition of the *parlements* can be seen in a longer-term context. There had been conflict between crown and *parlement* earlier in the century over religious as well as financial policy. Louis XV attempted to get round the problem by coupling financial reform with reform of *parlements* in 1770, but these reforms were abandoned in 1774 on the accession of Louis XVI. *Parlementaire* opposition became significant again in 1784 and 1785 when the Paris *parlement* refused to register loan decrees and especially in 1787–88 when they opposed Brienne's reform package and later called for an Estates-General and issued their Declaration of the Fundamental Laws of the Kingdom (May 1788). The significance of such opposition lay not only in the damage done to prospects of reform but also in the damage done to the credit-worthiness of the monarchy.

6 The nature of the reform plans themselves. Reform plans were generally aimed at the income side alone and hit at powerful vested interests – by attacking venal offices, attempting more central control of accounts, pressurising the Farmers-General, and attacking the tax privileges of the nobility (Calonne). This, apart from the last, was true of most reform plans, be they Terray's, Turgot's or Necker's. Necker alone, to his cost, tried to link such reforms with control of expenditure.

Which of these reasons do you think are the most important in explaining the failure to enact effective reform?

7 Reform plans were always constrained by the need to maintain a flow of credit to manage existing debt. By the second half of the eighteenth century maintenance of the flow of credit had become a major preoccupation of the *contrôleurs généraux*. Any ministerial crisis, any hint of financial problems could jeopardise that flow or increase the rate of interest demanded. Reform plans – judicious pruning of offices and renegotiation of terms with the Farmers-General – tended, therefore, to be insufficient for the scale of the problem. Expenditure was generally left alone; indeed, Calonne embarked on high expenditure projects to maintain credit. The necessity to maintain credit ever increased. By the mid 1780s over half of royal revenue was being spent on interest payments. By the time root and branch reform was attempted in 1787, it was too late.

The last factor indicates the Catch 22 situation facing the crown in the 1780s. With an annual deficit of over 100 million livres, the crown needed loans, and the need to maintain those loans required financial confidence which was easily threatened when reform was suggested. The debt spiral led eventually to the credit crisis and bankruptcy that brought about the decision to call the Estates-General for 1789 in the summer of 1788. There was more to the political crisis than simply a matter of balancing the books, but the financial crisis facing the monarchy allowed other forces to come into the open. When the Estates-General was called, the whole future of absolute monarchy and the distribution of political power in France was under scrutiny.

The impact of the American War of Independence

In 1776 American colonists rose in revolt against **George III** of England. Against the apparent odds, they were successful and their defeat of a British force in 1778 was enough to persuade Louis XVI to support them. This was not out of conviction that their cause was justified, but out of a hope for revenge against Britain for French defeat in the Seven Years' War (1756–63). The war was ultimately victorious for both the Americans and the French, but its effects on France were to help precipitate the events leading to revolution. There were three main ones:

- the financial impact on the monarchy;
- the economic impact on France;
- the political impact of the American success.

George III was accused of acting as a tyrant by collecting taxes without the consent of the colonists.

The financial impact

Finance could be raised either through extra taxation (*vingtièmes*) or borrowing. The difficulty for the monarchy was that extra taxation was already being levied in order to pay off the debts left by previous wars. That left borrowing. In 1781 the crown issued a set of accounts supposedly showing that the state of royal finances was healthy. This reassured financiers and bankers, who were then willing to lend money to the crown. The problem was that loans had to be repaid and the crown was already having to pay the interest on previous loans. The crown found itself in a circle of debt, having to take out new loans to pay off old ones, with the total debt spiralling ever upwards. By 1786 the annual deficit was running at over 100 million livres and over 50 per cent of royal spending was going directly on interest payments. To avoid bankruptcy urgent financial reform was necessary. It was the attempt to achieve this reform that provoked the political crisis which led to revolution.

The economic impact

Wars are not only expensive, they also disrupt trade. The ports on France's west coast, like Bordeaux, depended on trade with the West Indies and the American colonies. During the war this trade was severely disrupted; for instance, there was a dearth of raw cotton, which affected the textile industry. As many cotton-workers were peasants, their income was adversely affected at a time when prices were rising. The problems were compounded because the end of the war was followed by economic depression.

The political impact

The main factor here is the spread of ideas. The American colonists were fighting for freedom against tyranny. They supported notions of popular sovereignty and constitutional government, and they believed all citizens had basic natural rights. Soldiers who fought in America brought these ideas back across the Atlantic. Frenchmen like the aristocrat Lafayette and visiting Americans like Benjamin Franklin openly discussed these ideas in the Paris salons. Such ideas were, of course, in tune with and influenced by the Enlightenment. Arguably, the success of the Americans in their fight against 'tyranny' gave a little more reality to what had been hitherto issues for intellectual debate rather than action.

On the other hand, victory in the war restored some prestige to the French monarchy. It had secured some measure of revenge for the Seven Years' War. However, the financial impact of the war was to make this restoration of prestige short lived. When trouble brewed in the Netherlands in 1788, France was powerless to act in defence of its interests against Britain and Prussia.

Which of the three impacts do you think was the most important and why?

The role of the monarchy

The accounts given above have drawn attention to some of the weaknesses of the monarchy as an institution and to the crucial role the **personal qualities** of the monarch played in shaping developments. Absolute monarchy was personal monarchy and the abilities, values, company and character of the monarch affected the nature and strength of his rule. The decisions the king made or did not make helped shape events.

In all these areas Louis XVI was lacking. His reign started amidst hopes of a new age, led by a new **Louis XIV**, after the defeats and unpopularity of Louis XV's rule. But Louis XVI's appearance was unprepossessing, in society he was awkward, his pleasures – apart from hunting and eating – were private. He preferred making locks to attending to government business and studying detailed lists of game killed on hunts to discussion with ministers. He was rumoured to be impotent because of the long delay in the arrival of Marie-Antoinette's first child, the parentage of whom was a cause of scandalous speculation.

Marie-Antoinette did not help his cause. She represented the hated Austrian alliance which had brought defeat in 1763 (she was nicknamed, among other more damning descriptions, *l'Autrichienne* – the Austrian bitch), and she did little to redeem herself in the eyes of the French people. Her **activities** were the source of slanderous scandal about her supposed sexual excesses. The

When Louis XVI was crowned the ceremony was performed with all the traditional symbolism of divine right monarchy. He was claiming his birthright as an absolute monarch, answerable to no-one but God. But neither he, nor his predecessor Louis XV, had **personal qualities** equal to the task.

Early portraits of Louis XVI with the sun rising in the background refer to **Louis XIV**, the 'Sun King'. The dawn proved to be false.

Activities that attracted attention were her delight in playing the milkmaid at her model hamlet at Versailles, and her associations with the handsome Swedish comte de Fersen and Louis's extravagant brothers.

Marie-Antoinette, by
Vigée-Lebrun. What
image of the queen does
this portrait suggest?

diamond necklace affair of 1784 is important not because of any truth in the slander, but because the people were willing and indeed keen to believe it. In such ways the reputation of the monarchy was gradually undermined.

More important from a political point of view was Louis's hesitancy and indecisiveness. Even his brother, the comte de Provence, wrote of him: 'The weakness and indecision of the king are beyond description. Imagine balls of oiled ivory that you try to hold together.' His reign was marked by constant changes of direction, or by a lack of direction. He pressed for reform and then retreated from it; he changed ministers whenever the pressure was on (often from a court faction centred on his wife). It was paralysis of effective government at the very top that helped bring about and ensure the success of the revolution of 1789. Indeed, the king can be said to bear major responsibility for bringing things to a head in June 1789. It was the crown's failure in the autumn of 1788 to decide on the issue of voting by head, whilst conceding double representation, that helped focus attention on the role of privilege, whilst the failure to provide any kind of lead when the Estates-General assembled in May helped provoke the crisis in June and the declaration of a National Assembly by the Third Estate. Arguably the king could have won the Third Estate as an ally against the privileged orders by timely concessions, but instead Louis's hesitancy turned it against both the privileged orders and the monarchy.

In the **diamond necklace affair** Marie-Antoinette was accused of contracting venereal disease from the cardinal de Rohan and then spreading it to the rest of the court.

List the ways in which the king could be described as weak.

What were the social and economic causes of the French Revolution?

This section examines the economic and social problems of late eighteenth-century France and how and why they contributed so decisively to the events of 1789.

The bourgeoisie

It is estimated that there were about 2.5 million members of the **bourgeoisie** by 1789, about 10 per cent of the population, compared with only about 750,000 at the end of the seventeenth century.

The **bourgeoisie** was an expanding group in the eighteenth century. Over the eighteenth century the rate of expansion was much faster than that of the population as a whole (*c.*300 per cent as opposed to around 30 per cent). The long-term aspiration of many bourgeois, especially the more wealthy, was to achieve noble status. This could be done by the purchase of certain offices that conferred noble status, or by marriage into a noble family. But these opportunities remained relatively static during the eighteenth century whilst, as the rising numbers of the bourgeoisie testify, the demand rose. What is more, there is evidence that the number of bourgeois entering the ranks of nobility was not vast – for example, fewer than 20 per cent of the 680 new magistrates in the *parlements* between 1774 and 1789 were non-noble.

Enlightened ideas were discussed in the salons, literary societies and cafés of towns and cities across France. Here educated bourgeois intermingled with liberal nobility on terms of relative equality.

Arguably, the bourgeoisie felt an increasing sense of frustration as opportunities for social advancement seemed limited. Such feelings may for some have been compounded by the gradual inflation in prices that eroded the fixed incomes on which many officeholders and lawyers depended. With limited opportunities for advancement and arguably falling resources, that social frustration found expression in support for **enlightened ideas** about careers open to talents and equal rights. Not surprisingly, the bourgeoisie supported the apparently liberal-minded noble protests at the state of affairs as the royal finances deteriorated. Also, they supported the *parlements'* defence of the nation's interests and the demands for an Estates-General; and they turned against the privileged orders when it became clear that these orders, by opposing double representation and voting by head, only sought political influence for themselves. The bourgeois leaders of the Third Estate thereafter wanted not only constitutional limitation on the power of the crown but also abolition of noble privileges. In the enlightened talk of natural rights, equality, popular sovereignty and the irrationality of privilege by birth, the bourgeoisie found justification for their demand for a dominant share of political power.

The **Eden Treaty** hit particular industries very hard as France was flooded with cheap imports – especially cotton goods.

Nor was it simply the professional bourgeoisie that were suffering. From the 1760s economic prosperity began to disappear in many areas, a crisis exacerbated by the **Eden Treaty** with Britain in 1786. Then came the disastrous harvest of 1788 which, by pushing up bread prices, deprived many of the purchasing power to buy manufactured goods. The peasantry and the urban workers suffered most directly from the economic crisis.

The peasantry

In the last quarter of the eighteenth century the growth in rural population was one of the factors increasing pressure on the land, and increasing competition for land led to rises in rents. Meanwhile the general drift of prices was upwards whilst oversupply of labour helped depress **wages**. What is more, in the 1770s and 1780s the standard supplements to farm work – wine production and weaving – were troubled by fluctuations in demand and prices. On top of all this came a large rise in taxation between 1749 and the 1780s. All this was, of course, in addition to the effects of land harvests and the other burdens on peasants such as seigneurial dues (see pages 12–13).

The *cahiers des doléances* drawn up as part of the process of electing an Estates-General reflect the often parochial economic concerns of the peasants. Nevertheless, the Estates-General became a focus for their hopes of redress of some of the burdens from which they suffered – indirect taxes on essentials like salt, the hated *corvée royale* and the seigneurial obligations that hampered their ability to make ends meet.

However, as prices and shortages reached their peak during the ***soudure*** months of June and July, the peasants were to play an important part in determining the course of the revolution. Hunger began to cause sporadic unrest in the countryside as early as January 1789; there were attacks on grain convoys and suspected hoarders. To this was added a kind of spontaneous tax strike as peasants assumed royal taxes, tithes and seigneurial dues would be abolished. Then rumours of the stalemate at Versailles and the resistance of the nobility led to fears of an aristocratic plot to destroy the ripening harvest. The crisis of July in Paris created panic in the countryside and the presence of roaming bands of brigands only reinforced suspicions. In the three weeks after the Storming of the Bastille order broke down in the countryside, fear of brigands being coupled with a desire to destroy the legal evidence (*terriers*) of peasants' seigneurial obligations. During the Great Fear of July and early August chateaux were attacked and sometimes burnt along with the *terriers*.

To the representatives in the National Assembly the anarchy in the countryside appeared to put property of all kinds at risk. The assembly, keen to restore order but unwilling to sanction use of the royal army in case it was turned against them, decided on drastic action. The result was the night of 4 August (see page 24). Along with seigneurial dues went all other noble privileges and those of provinces, towns and the church. Venality of office followed. By the morning of 5 August it seemed the whole social system of the *ancien régime* had been swept away. It was enough to end the Great Fear; the peasants, it

Was the bourgeoisie rising or falling in the eighteenth century?

Wages rose at only one third the rate of prices.

The term *soudure* was used to describe the dangerous months (May–August) between the exhaustion of the previous year's grain and the new harvest. The term refers to the idea of 'making ends meet'.

appeared, had got what they wanted – indeed, they had got more. The abolitions of that night went far beyond the demands of the *cahiers*.

The towns

Bad harvests did not, of course, affect only the peasantry. Increases in food prices directly affected the urban poor and the economy generally. For urban workers the proportion of income spent on bread went up from about 50 per cent in the summer of 1788 to around 80 per cent the following year. There was then much less to spend on manufactured goods such as textiles. The slump in demand led to cuts in production and hence to unemployment or wage cuts. Towns, like the countryside, were therefore threatened with unrest at the very time the Estates-General met. When royal authority collapsed in July 1789, towns – concerned at the potential unrest – mirrored Paris in setting up their own councils and citizens' militia to keep order and protect property. This municipal revolution, along with the Great Fear, serves as a corrective to the view that the revolution was a purely Parisian affair.

Paris in 1789 was by far the largest city in France, with a population of around 650,000. It was also the capital and the centre of fashionable society and the luxury trades.

However, it was in Paris that the central drama of the revolution was played out and it was the people of **Paris** who were to have a crucial part to play, not only in the events of 1789 but in the general course of the revolution after 1789. The bulk of the population were workers and artisans whose livelihoods were based around the relatively small workshops (typically employing 15–20 men) of various trades (cabinetmakers, silversmiths, tailors and so on). Such trades were hit hard by the economic difficulties of the 1780s. Tension in Paris rose as the number of very poor people swelled through unemployment and as wage cuts and bread prices escalated while the dreaded *soudure* approached. This tension was fuelled by the vigorous political agitation surrounding the calling and meeting of the Estates-General in the winter and spring of 1788–89. The Reveillon riots of April were an indication of the Paris powder-keg which threatened mass disorder. The riots, although essentially economic in motivation, did have a political element; the crowds adopted some of the slogans bandied about by agitators.

Some of the more extreme leaders of the 'patriot' party who supported the claims of the Third Estate began to see the potential of employing the people of Paris to further their cause. The combination of unrest caused by hunger, political stalemate at Versailles, the concentration of royal forces around Paris and the passionate oratory of demagogues like Camille Desmoulins provided the combustible material which exploded between 12 and 14 July. The irony was that the Storming of the Bastille and the king's acceptance in Paris of the 'revolution' on 17 July did little materially for the people of Paris. Hunger remained and economic forces would ensure that the people of Paris would intervene decisively to affect the course of the revolution again in the future.

Conclusion

In 1789, two crises came together: a political and constitutional crisis brought about by the parlous financial situation of the crown and a social and economic crisis brought about by long-term developments in the economy and the severe crisis resulting from the disastrous harvest of 1788. The decision to call the Estates-General not only focused attention on questions of privilege and representation and invited all the people to air their grievances – be they economic, social or political – but also aroused hopes of a better future and a solution to all problems. When the fate of this assembly (then the National Assembly) seemed threatened by counter-revolution in mid July 1789, the people were ready to rise in its defence. The Storming of the Bastille secured its future and ensured the overthrow of absolute monarchy and social privilege. It marked the dawning of a new age.

Summary questions

1 Explain the *two* main effects of the American War of Independence on France.

2 Compare the role of the Third Estate, the nobility and the clergy in political events from the spring of 1788 to the summer of 1789.

2 The course of the French Revolution, 1789–95

Focus questions

◆ What were the main features of the French Revolution of 1789?

◆ Why did the French Revolution become more radical up to 1794?
 (a) How did the revolution develop between 1789 and 1792?
 (b) Why did a reign of Terror develop?

◆ What was the role of the Jacobins, Paris and the *sans-culottes*?

◆ What was the impact of war, economic crisis and religious division on the course of the revolution?

Significant dates

1789 **14 July** *Journée*: Storming of the Bastille.
 4–11 August August Decrees abolish privilege in France.
 26 August Declaration of the Rights of Man and the Citizen sets out the principles on which the new France will be governed.
 5–6 October *Journée*: women of Paris and the National Guard bring the royal family from Versailles to Paris.

1790 **12 July** National Assembly passes the Civil Constitution of the Clergy, which reorganises the Catholic church.
 14 July La Fête de la Fédération, a celebration with representatives from across France of the anniversary of the Storming of the Bastille.
 27 November National Assembly requires all clergy to take an oath of loyalty to the Constitution.

1791 **20 June** Flight to Varennes: the king's attempt to flee from Paris fails.
 17 July Massacre of the Champs de Mars: National Guard opens fire on a crowd signing a petition for a republic.
 27 August Declaration of Pillnitz; Austria and Prussia seem to threaten to intervene in France.
 13 September King agrees to the new Constitution.
 1 October New Legislative Assembly opens.
 November–December King vetoes decrees against *émigrés* and refractory priests.

1792 **20 April** France declares war on Austria.
 20 June *Journée*: crowds invade the Tuileries and force the king to wear the *bonnet rouge* and toast the nation.

10 August *Journée*: crowds attack the Tuileries and force the assembly to suspend the king. The king is overthrown.
2–6 September September Massacres: *sans-culottes* kill over 1,000 prisoners suspected of counter-revolution (the 'First Terror').
20 September Battle of Valmy: citizen volunteers and regular troops beat the Prussian invaders.
21 September New National Convention declares a republic.
19 November Edict of Fraternity: Convention declares help for all oppressed peoples.
December Trial of the king.

1793 **21 January** King is guillotined after a vote in the Convention.
February France declares war on Britain and Holland.
March French defeat at Neerwinden; levy of troops provokes revolt in the Vendée.
31 May–2 June *Journée*: crowds force Convention to expel Girondins.
23 August *Levée en masse*: Convention decrees an early version of total war.
5 September *Journée*: crowd forces the Convention to pass a series of emergency measures, including the General Maximum on prices and wide powers for dealing with suspects (the 'Terror' begins).
4 December Law of 14 Frimaire asserts central control over the Terror.

1794 **24 March** Execution of the Hébertists.
5 April Execution of the Dantonists.
7 May Cult of the Supreme Being is declared.
10 June Law of 22 Prairial passed to allow more rapid revolutionary justice. The 'Great Terror' begins.
26 June French victory at Fleurus over the Austrians.
27 July *Journée of 9 Thermidor*: Robespierre is overthrown and executed the following day.
12 November Paris Jacobin Club is closed down.

1795 **22 August** Convention agrees a new moderate Constitution (the Constitution of the Year III).

Overview

From the Storming of the Bastille to the institution of the revolution's third Constitution in 1795 represents a period of constant crisis in France. Between 1789 and 1794 the revolution became ever more extreme as constitutional monarchy gave way to a republic, which then experienced the excesses of the 'Reign of Terror' in 1793–94 as the government sought to deal with the combined threats of internal revolt, counter-revolution and foreign invasion. The overthrow of Robespierre, the principal figure of the Terror, in July 1794 saw a return to a more moderate approach. The history of this period is complex, and the key issue is the causes of the political instability that rocked France.

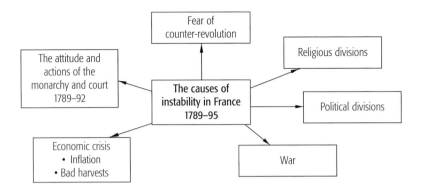

The summary diagram above highlights some of the main causes. However, our starting point is the nature of the revolution that occurred in the summer of 1789.

What were the main features of the French Revolution of 1789?

What were French people demanding in 1789?

In the Third Estate, every village, urban guild and corporation was entitled to draw up a ***cahier de doléances***; these lists were then reduced to a single *cahier* for the Third Estate in each of the 234 electoral constituencies. Hereditary nobles and the clergy similarly produced lists for their order in each constituency.

The **concerns** include the high price of salt, the burdens imposed by seigneurial rights (everything from hunting rights to dovecotes), taxes, forced labour on the roads, tithes, the threat posed by spinning machines to domestic industry and general poverty.

As part of the process of electing the Estates-General in 1789, the people of France were invited to draw up their grievances in ***cahiers de doléances***. Together these *cahiers* comprise a remarkable snapshot of French public opinion on the eve of the revolution. No co-ordinated attempt was made by central government to influence the drawing up of the *cahiers*, although there is evidence that 'patriot' activists did provide model *cahiers*. At the village level, however, the concerns of the peasantry come through. At the constituency level, the *cahiers* of the Third Estate more closely reflect the interests of the bourgeoisie, with the popular (and parochial) demands made by the peasantry often edited out.

The *cahiers* of rural communities reveal a host of socio-economic demands which reflect the day-to-day **concerns** of peasants. They tend not to concern themselves with broader political issues and instead express loyalty and the hope that Louis XVI will improve their lot. The *cahiers* of urban workers reveal a similar concern with socio-economic issues. The cobblers of Pontoise, for example, complain at indirect taxes like the *gabelle*, problems of trade and grain supply, militia duty and billeting, and the destruction caused by pigeons and other game.

There is a good deal of similarity between the general *cahiers* of the Third Estate drawn up at constituency level and those of the nobility. The majority of *cahiers* for both orders included demands for the abolition of *lettres de cachet*, the establishment of a constitution, Estates-General control of taxation, freedom of the press and, surprisingly perhaps, the abolition of tax privileges. Nevertheless, there were significant differences. For instance, the majority of Third Estate *cahiers* demanded abolition of seigneurial rights and greater economic freedom.

Overall, we can conclude that the middle and upper classes were agreed on the need for some kind of constitutional regime, if not on its exact form and the role of the Third Estate within it. The issue of seigneurial rights divided the Third Estate from the nobility, whilst the main concern of the peasantry was that the burdens upon them should be eased. The events of June and July 1789 brought out both the desire for a constitutional regime and the determination of the Third Estate to ensure that they had a leading role in that Constitution. That had been clear from the events of the previous autumn, from the moment when the *parlement* of Paris declared in favour of the 'forms of 1614' (see page 20). From that point onwards Third Estate leaders and some liberal nobles campaigned for double representation of the Third Estate and voting by head. The former was conceded by the king in December, but the latter – which would have given effective power to the Third Estate – was not. The reluctance to grant voting by head brought about the June/July crisis. The events of August also ensured that both the political power and the privileges enjoyed by the first two orders, including seigneurial rights, were overturned.

On what issues did the Third Estate agree with the nobility and on what did they disagree?

What were the main concerns of the peasantry?

The August Decrees and the Declaration of the Rights of Man and the Citizen

The key features of the revolution of 1789 are contained in the August Decrees passed by the National Assembly (4–11 August) and the Declaration of the Rights of Man and the Citizen (26 August). Together they represent the overthrow of the *ancien régime*'s social and political system and its replacement with a system based on equal rights, property and limited government.

July and early August saw the breakdown of order. The setting up of a bourgeois authority and the National Guard in Paris was mirrored by similar events in municipalities across France. In the countryside the Great Fear – a compound of rumour, fear of aristocratic reaction, brigands and desire to overthrow feudalism – spread rapidly. Partly in response to this, the remarkable session of 4 August took place. That night saw the National Assembly abolish feudalism alongside church, noble, corporate and provincial privileges. Serfdom, peasant dues to their lord, church tithes and privileges, noble tax and judicial privileges, venal office, guild privileges, provincial tax and other privileges were all given up. The principles of equality and meritocracy were asserted in what appeared to be a spontaneous outburst of patriotic or revolutionary enthusiasm. Over the next week a series of decrees was passed formalising the decisions.

Superficially, it might seem that the peasantry got all that they wanted. However, there was a sting in the tail. Landlords were to be compensated for the loss of all those dues that the assembly viewed as property rights. The peasants would have to pay landlords (many of whom were bourgeois rather than noble). This concern of the assembly to compensate landlords for loss of seigneurial dues and venal officeholders for loss of office reflects a common concern amongst the bourgeoisie (and nobility) about property. Defence of property underpins these decrees, as it did the setting up of the National Guard. The egalitarianism of 1789 reflects the concerns of the educated and the propertied; it did not imply economic equality.

The Declaration of the Rights of Man and the Citizen of 26 August 1789 was about the **principles** upon which the new France was to be established. It set out 'the natural, inalienable and sacred rights of man'. It asserted, among other things, that:

The declaration was a mixture of general and specific **principles** that reflected the liberal and enlightened thinking typical of the *philosophes* and was presaged in the American Declaration of Independence of 4 July 1776.

- men are born free and remain free and equal in their rights;
- the purpose of government is the maintenance of these rights, which include 'liberty, property, security and resistance to oppression';
- all government power is derived from the nation, the people (popular sovereignty);
- the law, which is there to protect the equal freedom of all, is the expression of 'the general will' given voice by an elected assembly;
- all are equal before the law;
- careers and offices should be open to talent (meritocracy);
- no-one can be arrested without legal cause;
- punishment for wrongdoing must fit the crime;
- there should be freedom of speech, of the press and of conscience;
- taxation necessary to finance government should be borne equally by all citizens in proportion to their means;
- taxation should be agreed by an elected assembly;
- members of the government should be answerable for their actions;
- the powers of the executive, judiciary and legislature should be separate to ensure constitutional rule;
- the right to property is inviolable.

In what ways did the Declaration of the Rights of Man and the Citizen contrast with the principles of the *ancien régime*?

With which principles in the declaration would you agree and why?

To a modern person, living in a liberal democracy, little appears contentious in all this. At the time, this statement of principles was revolutionary and represented a fundamental breach with the past. Absolute monarchy was gone and privilege was gone. Government power now came not from God but from the people, and government power could not infringe the natural and equal rights of citizens.

The position of the king and the October Days

The declaration did not mean the end of monarchy. No-one in the assembly saw an alternative to the monarch as the head of government, but there was debate over the exact extent of his powers, a debate coloured by the attitude of the king and the fears of the revolutionaries. The crucial issue was the extent of the king's powers. In particular, should the king have the power of veto over legislation passed by the elected assembly?

For the king, the answer was 'yes', for without that he would be but a puppet king, there merely to do the bidding of the assembly. For a group of representatives in the assembly that became known as *monarchiens*, the answer was also 'yes'. However, there was a more powerful lobby in the assembly, led by Abbé Sieyès, which distrusted the king. They had feared giving the king authority to use the army to crush the violence engendered during the Great Fear, and now feared the king would use any veto to reverse and frustrate the revolution.

In the event, the assembly voted to give the king a suspensive veto – effectively the power to prevent laws passing for up to four years. This was included in the Constitutional Articles that set out the relationship between the elected assembly, the monarchy and the judiciary. The sovereignty of the nation was re-emphasised, the position of the French monarchy as the head of the executive was agreed and the institution of a permanent elected National Assembly as the legislature was laid down. There would also be an independent judiciary. The king appointed ministers and ran the executive but had no power to initiate legislation, and his ministers were to be responsible for their actions. The National Assembly was to be elected every two years and was to consist of a single **chamber**. It had sole legislative power and the power to grant taxation.

These articles, the August Decrees and the Declaration of the Rights of Man were given to the king for his assent. He hesitated, voiced criticisms and would not agree. It was this reluctance that helped provoke the second Parisian *journée* of 1789 and another turning point in the course of the revolution.

Although the 1789 harvest had been good, a drought in September left the watermills powerless, bread prices remained high and bread was in short supply. This was compounded by unemployment in the luxury trades on which so many Parisian workers depended. The economic unrest that underlay the events of July, therefore, continued to simmer in Paris. Meanwhile, populist politicians and journalists in Paris kept the people aware of events at Versailles, and the king's continued reluctance to agree to the August Decrees and the Declaration of the Rights of Man caused anger. However, the immediate stimulus to the events of 5 and 6 October was the reported actions of the officers of the Flanders regiment newly arrived at Versailles. The arrival of

The *monarchien* members, who included Mounier, believed the king should have the power of veto as the only means likely to secure his full acceptance of the revolution, a revolution they wanted to stop where it was in the summer of 1789.

How far do the proposals in the Constitutional Articles reflect the principle of the Separation of Powers advocated by Montesquieu (see page 25)?

It was feared that a second **chamber** would allow a return of noble privilege and power.

In this context, *journée* is a term that refers to a revolutionary 'day' when the people of Paris rose up in protest, often with decisive effect, as on 14 July 1789 and 10 August 1792.

An anonymous sketch of the march of the women to Versailles in October 1789.

In the summer of 1789 revolutionaries adopted the **Tricolour** symbol of red, white and blue. Red and blue were the colours of Paris (and so for the people) whilst white was the colour of the royal family. It quickly became a powerful symbol of the revolution.

military forces aroused fears that the king would use force, as he had appeared to threaten in July, but the event that sparked anger and action was the trampling of the revolutionary **Tricolour** cockade by drunken officers at dinner and the toasting of the white Bourbon colours. The mixture of economic despair, political distrust, anger and fear resulted in a motley crowd of women and men marching to Versailles on 5 October to demand bread, the Rights of Man and the king's presence in Paris. The crowd was followed by 20,000 National Guards. On 6 October the crowd invaded Versailles and stormed the royal chambers. Marie-Antoinette barely escaped capture, even murder, by the crowd and her fear was so great that her hair turned white. When the crowd demanded that 'the baker, the baker's wife and the baker's boy' return with them to Paris, the king was forced to agree. The next day the royal family took up residence in the Tuileries palace. The National Assembly followed in their wake.

The significance of these events was momentous. The immediate consequence was that the king was forced to accept the August Decrees, the Declaration of the Rights of Man and the Constitutional Articles. But the king had not agreed freely – and he did not feel bound by such forced acceptance. He would co-operate, do what was constitutionally required of him, but would not embrace the spirit of the revolution. The king and the National Assembly were now in the centre of Paris and subject to popular pressure, scrutiny and intimidation as never before. However, the consequences of this fact were not to be fully felt for over a year. This was in part because food prices stabilised and the economy began to recover. For the moment, it appeared, the revolution was back on course and the National Assembly could continue its work of drawing up the details of the new Constitution and government of France.

Why can the October Days be seen as a turning point in the course of the revolution?

Why did the French Revolution become more radical up to 1794?
(a) How did the revolution develop between 1789 and 1792?
The reforms of the National Assembly (the Constituent Assembly)

It took two years for agreement to be reached on all the details of the new Constitution. In September 1791 it finally came into force, but was to last less than a year. Part of the reason it failed was that some of the decisions taken about it broke the revolutionary consensus of the summer of 1789. The issue of the veto had begun to divide members of the assembly and the king was always a reluctant party to the notion of constitutional monarchy. However, for a while after October 1789 it appeared that a period of harmony and progress had begun, perhaps best symbolised by a celebration of the anniversary of the Storming of the Bastille in the Fête de la Fédération on 14 July 1790.

Reforms covered government, the law, finances, the economy and the church. The principles of the declaration were applied in producing a system that aimed to be uniform across France and its people, decentralised (election from below rather than appointment from the top downwards) and humanitarian.

Active and passive citizens

The issue of citizenship was to become divisive. Whilst all Frenchmen were to be equal citizens, when it came to politics and eligibility for office some were more equal than others. It was decided to distinguish between 'active' and 'passive' citizens for the purposes of the right to vote. To be an active citizen, with the right to vote in the primary stage of local and national elections, a Frenchman had to pay the equivalent of three days' labour in taxes. This effectively excluded the poorest 40 per cent of citizens from the electoral process. To be eligible to vote in the second stage of elections and to hold public office, a further hurdle had to be passed – payment of the equivalent of ten days' labour in taxes. To be eligible to be elected to the National Assembly (known as the Legislative Assembly from October 1791), the equivalent of a *marc d'argent* (50 days' labour) in taxes had to be paid.

The combination of indirect elections and a wealth qualification effectively ensured middle-class domination of government at both local and national level. Local bourgeois property owners, small merchants and artisans tended to dominate local government. This in itself was a revolution as these social groups had not played a direct role in government before. However, the arrangement was divisive because it excluded the less wealthy elements of society from involvement in politics. The abolition of the distinction between active and passive citizens became a key demand of the *sans-culottes* and popular clubs in Paris.

Why do you think the assembly decided on the distinction between active and passive citizens?

Reform of local government

France was divided into 83 *départements*, further subdivided into districts and thence into communes. These administrative levels were run by elected councils. Local councils were given responsibility for assessing and collecting direct taxes; maintenance of law and order; carrying out public works; control of the National Guard; upkeep of churches; registration of births, marriages and deaths; grain requisition and other matters. Efficiency and effectiveness varied widely. Rural communes often struggled to find sufficient literate people.

Finance and church lands

Revolution had not resolved the poor state of government finances. Indeed, it had made matters worse, for many saw the revolution as meaning they no longer needed to pay taxes. While a new tax system was worked out, it was decided to continue with the existing system, but this was unacceptable to people locally. In the spring of 1790 the hated *gabelle* was abolished, followed by a number of other indirect **taxes** in succeeding months. Such popular moves hardly helped balance the books.

Direct **taxes**, like today's income tax, are paid directly by the citizen to the state. The main direct tax proposed before and during the revolution was on land. The more land you owned, the more tax you paid. Indirect taxes are taxes on goods or services, like the present system of VAT. These push up the price of goods.

That is partly why the assembly turned to other sources of income – their target was the Catholic church and its immense landed wealth. In November 1789 the assembly voted to place church property at 'the disposal of the nation'. The state took over the property and also took on responsibility for paying the clergy. The state then sold the lands and issued paper bonds, which from April 1790 became a paper currency, the *assignat*, based on the security of the former church property. When the issue of *assignats* went beyond the value of the lands on which they were based, inflation inevitably developed. The solution to the financial problems became the source of further financial and economic difficulty.

The **church lands** became known as *biens nationaux*.

It was hoped that the clergy, if dependent on the state for their income, would be loyal to the revolution, and also that the purchasers of the **church lands** would have a personal stake in the revolution. Those who bought them were a mixture of bourgeoisie and wealthier peasants. The poorer peasantry reaped no benefit – a factor that helped turn some peasantry away from the revolution, especially in areas such as the west of France where Catholicism was strong.

The new tax system was introduced in 1791, based around a direct tax on land (similar to that proposed by Calonne in 1787). In addition, there was a property tax and customs duties. The system fulfilled the principle of fairness, as liability depended on wealth and was uniformly applied across France.

Economic reforms

In economic matters the principle of laissez-faire was applied – that trade and industry should be free from government interference. This approach meant free trade, no internal tariffs and no price controls, even in essentials like grain. However sound this was economically, it was to arouse objections from the poor, especially in times of dearth. Economic policy was to become a source of division in the crisis years from 1792 onwards, when peasants and workers demanded price controls.

Further economic reforms to facilitate trade and industry included the introduction of a uniform system of weights and measures (the metric system) across the whole of France. More contentious was the abolition of guilds and prohibition of trades unions (the latter under the Le Chapelier Law) in 1791.

Which groups would benefit most from the economic changes and why?

Law and justice

The assembly aimed to produce a uniform system of law across France; although some measures (such as the abolition of *lettres de cachet*) were taken to rationalise the different laws operating across France and remove the worst abuses, a uniform French legal code was to be the achievement of Napoleon. However, much was done to rationalise the system. All the old law courts (including *parlements*) were abolished and a new system based on the *départements* was introduced. At the lowest level, justices of the peace sought to resolve disputes in minor civil cases. More serious cases went to courts at district level. Criminal cases were tried at *département* level in front of a 12-man jury. Above this was the Court of Appeal, whose judges were elected by the *département* assemblies. These reforms made the French judicial system accessible, fair and relatively cheap.

In order to make the penal system more **humane**, torture and mutilation were abolished and the number of capital crimes was reduced.

The guillotine, intended to be a uniform and **humane** method of execution but for so many the most potent symbol of the violent excesses of the revolution during the Terror, was actually introduced during these years.

The religious question

The future of the Catholic church in France was to prove one of the most divisive issues of the constitutional monarchy. Perhaps more than any other issue, it was to break the revolutionary consensus that had emerged in 1789. Although members of the clergy had played a crucial role in June 1789 by joining the self-proclaimed National Assembly, the **church** lost out in the August Decrees and Declaration of the Rights of Man. The pope was threatened with loss of influence over the French Catholic church when the state took over responsibility for paying the clergy, and seemed likely to lose control over the papal territory of Avignon (in southern France) as patriots there sought its annexation to France.

In July 1790 the assembly passed the Civil Constitution of the Clergy. This reorganisation was necessary after the changes of the previous months, but it was also seen as a chance to reform the worst abuses within the church. Much of it was acceptable to most of the clergy. Salary scales for clergy were laid

Among other things, the **church** lost tithes, its feudal dues as a landlord and its status as state religion; it also had to accept freedom of speech and conscience. It lost its lands to the state and in 1790 most religious orders of monks and nuns were closed down.

down, residence in one's parish or diocese was required, and parishes and dioceses were reorganised to mirror the reforms in local government. For instance, there would be 83 bishops (1 per *département*).

However, the arrangements for the selection of clergy were contentious. All churchmen were to be elected by the people. Bishops would be chosen by the *département* assemblies and parish priests by district assemblies. There was to be no role for the pope. Very quickly attitudes to the Civil Constitution became a litmus test of attitudes to the revolution. '**Patriots**' fully supported the Civil Constitution, whilst conservatives viewed it with alarm, seeing it as an attack on the Catholic faith. The debate was carried out in the press with ever greater virulence, helping to polarise opinion.

'**Patriot**' was a term used to refer to supporters of the revolution. To be a good patriot required obedience and enthusiasm for the revolution and the changes it brought. By implication, critics and opponents of these changes were 'traitors'.

For what reasons did decisions about the Catholic church begin to cause divisions in France?

Louis XVI had reluctantly accepted the Civil Constitution in August 1790, but the pope, Pius VI, had yet to give a clear indication of his opinion. Many clergy co-operated with the new reforms pending a decision from the pope, but others refused. This helped provoke the crisis that led to the assembly's decision in November 1790 to require all clergy to swear an oath of loyalty to the nation, the king and the law and to uphold the Civil Constitution. Effectively, the clergy – and by implication all Catholics in France – were being asked to declare publicly for or against the revolution. The issue split the church and the nation. Nationally about half the clergy refused to take the oath, but the level of refusal varied considerably. It was very low in anti-clerical Paris, but very high in the west – in Brittany and the Vendée, for instance. Patriots called for non-juring or refractory priests (those who refused the oath) to be lynched and began to equate Catholicism for the first time with potential counter-revolution. On the other hand, those opposed to the revolution now had the chance of winning some popular support.

In April 1791 the pope finally made public his opposition to the Civil Constitution and the oath. It was now legitimate for 'good Catholics' to oppose the revolution. One of those was the king. The religious issue finally persuaded him to try to escape the clutches of the revolutionaries in Paris and seek to rally support away from the capital.

The Flight to Varennes and its consequences

Louis XVI had begun planning some kind of escape from Paris as early as October 1790, but it was probably only after the enforced oath on the clergy that he decided he could not work with the proposed Constitution. Using Marie-Antoinette's confidant, the Swedish comte de Fersen, as an intermediary, arrangements were made for escape. The plan was to leave Paris and head for Montmédy near the French frontier with Austrian territory, in an area where the army was under the command of a royalist sympathiser. There Louis probably hoped to rally support and negotiate a moderate settlement with the revolutionaries in Paris, although his brother the **comte de Provence** claimed his intention was to leave France altogether and return at the head of Austrian armies. An escape towards Montmédy allowed both possibilities. The final decision and timing of the attempted flight was provoked by the Paris mob at Easter 1791. On 17 April Louis and his family had been prevented from leaving the Tuileries for the palace of Saint-Cloud, where he hoped to attend a mass carried out by a refractory priest. The date for escape was set for 20 June.

Whilst the religious issue more than anything else had finally made Louis accept his wife's advice to try to leave Paris, the decision was taken in view of longer-term dissatisfaction with the course of events since July 1789. Since October 1789 Louis had been a virtual prisoner in Paris. He had become increasingly frustrated about his lack of influence over the Constitution and lack of effective control over government. He was also concerned about increasingly radical ideas emerging from the Jacobin Club (see page 68) as the final touches were being made to the constitutional arrangements. The last also had a bearing on the timing of the escape – he wanted to leave Paris before he was asked to approve the new Constitution.

Whatever might have happened had the escape succeeded, the point is it failed. Disguised as a Russian aristocratic family – hardly inconspicuous – and using a fake passport, Louis and his family did successfully get out of Paris. Slow progress on the roads meant the detailed planning, dependent on precise timings, began to unravel. Planned escorts on the route dispersed, believing that the escape had been postponed or failed. Identified by a diligent post-master, the royal party was arrested at Varennes. Louis was brought back to the Tuileries through the condemning silence of the Parisian crowds.

The failure of the escape proved a major turning point. To radicals it proved that the king could not be trusted and that the revolution would enjoy no stability while he was on the throne. For the first time, the idea of a republic began to gather some popular support. Such a prospect horrified moderates in the National Assembly because they associated it with mob rule, anarchy and attacks on property. To such men, whatever the difficulties, a constitutional monarchy was the only option – they had to make it work and, in the short term, they held the whip hand. They controlled the assembly and the forces of law and order – the Parisian National Guard under Lafayette. The use of force was to win the assembly the breathing space it needed to get the Constitution finalised and approved. The problem in the longer term was that the successful operation of the Constitution depended on a discredited king who had made plain his opposition to the whole project.

The divisions that the king's attempted flight opened up were violently demonstrated by the Champs de Mars massacre of 17 July 1791. In early July

The **comte de Provence** (1755–1824) was one of the brothers of Louis XVI (the other was the comte d'Artois). In 1814 he was to become Louis XVIII after the defeat of Napoleon. Provence was critical of the revolution and left France in June 1791 at the time of the Flight to Varennes. He was to organise an army of royalist exiles to fight the republic, and proclaimed himself Louis XVIII after the death of Louis XVI's son in 1795.

What evidence is there in this and previous sections that revolutionaries had reason to distrust the king?

What impact did the attitude and actions of the king have on the course of events between 1789 and 1791?

the radical and popular Cordeliers Club (see page 69) supported a petition asking the assembly to remove the king from power. The petition was to be signed in public on 17 July, but the demonstration by a 50,000-strong crowd (mainly of the poorer elements of Parisian society) turned violent when the crowd lynched two suspected government spies. Lafayette used the violence as an excuse to disperse the crowd. The National Guard opened fire on the crowd and some 50 were killed. Subsequently, Lafayette imposed martial law and attempted to round up **radical leaders** and all radical activity was stifled. This was the first time that different elements of the revolutionary movement had come to blows. For the moment the moderates had won – it would not be until the following year that the radical popular movement would attempt to impose its will again.

Meanwhile, the Jacobin Club split. A smaller radical element, led by Robespierre, supported the Cordeliers' call for the deposition of the king, but the majority of moderate members left to form a new society, the Feuillants. This secession from the main Jacobin Club won only muted support amongst provincial Jacobin clubs – only 72 out of 900 followed the Feuillant lead and most of those returned to their association with the Parisian Jacobin Club later. Others sent petitions demanding the king be put on trial. News of Varennes led local authorities to put National Guards on alert and in many places there was renewed persecution of refractory priests; membership of Jacobin clubs soared. The sense of crisis was deepened by the widespread fear of a possible **Austrian invasion**. In this atmosphere members of the moderate Feuillant group sought an accommodation with the king over the Constitution. However, attempts to amend the Constitution were thwarted in the assembly. The king finally agreed to it in September 1791. The most immediate impact was the dissolution of the National Assembly and the election of the new Legislative Assembly.

The new Legislative Assembly: priests, *émigrés* and war

Only active citizens could vote in the elections for the new assembly and only about a quarter of them did so. The membership of the assembly was totally new because the previous assembly had passed the **Self-Denying Ordinance**. However, it did not appear at first that the new assembly would be radical in its approach. At the start 264 deputies were members of the Feuillant Club, 136 were members of the Jacobin Club and about 350 belonged to neither. It was an almost exclusively bourgeois body.

Two issues dominated the business of the assembly in autumn 1791, and attitudes to both became another test of revolutionary zeal and, crucially, of the trustworthiness of the king. These issues were refractory priests and *émigrés* (see page 86). Refractory priests were condemned by some as unpatriotic and

Most of the **radical leaders**, however – like Danton, Hébert and Marat – went into hiding.

Fear of **Austrian invasion** was heightened by the Declaration of Pillnitz in August, in which the rulers of Austria and Prussia appeared to threaten military action to restore the liberty of the French royal family.

What does the fact that only a quarter of active citizens voted in the elections for the Legislative Assembly tell you?

The **Self-Denying Ordinance** prevented existing deputies from standing for election to the new assembly. This decision had been engineered by Robespierre earlier in 1791 to prevent his opponents from dominating the new assembly.

it was proposed that they be declared suspects. Meanwhile, the number of people leaving France escalated in the wake of Varennes – over four thousand army officers had left to join *émigré* forces in Coblenz and other centres by the end of 1791. It was proposed that *émigrés* be given an ultimatum – return by January 1792 or face confiscation of all property and condemnation as traitors.

The **instigators** of these proposals were gathered around Brissot. Brissot did not trust the king and wanted a republic after Varennes. He found support amongst about 130 deputies but also needed to win the support of many neutrals. He played on doubts about the trustworthiness of the king and the court and fears of counter-revolution: *émigré* forces gathering on the frontiers of France, Austria and Prussia had made plain their hostility in the **Declaration of Pillnitz**; the refractory clergy represented a potential fifth column within France; and members of the court (a so-called 'Austrian Committee') were plotting against the revolution. When the king refused to sanction the decrees against refractory priests and *émigrés* in November he played into Brissot's hands, seemingly confirming the fears of patriots about the king's lack of commitment to the revolution and sympathy for counter-revolutionary forces. What was needed, Brissot argued, was war against the *émigrés* and their foreign protectors. War would arouse enthusiasm for the revolution and show its resilience; it would expose counter-revolutionary elements in France; and it would be successful because the French would be bringing liberty to the subject peoples of tyrant kings. What is more, the international situation was promising because Britain would remain aloof, and Russia was preoccupied with Poland.

Meanwhile, Louis XVI was being persuaded of the case for war by Marie-Antoinette and other courtiers. From the court's perspective, war would be a good thing because the French army would be defeated and Louis XVI would be restored to his full powers by the intervention of Austria and Prussia. There was a strong case for believing this to be true because of the chaotic state of the French army in the wake of the exodus of officers. What is more, the court could pass on French military plans to Austria. Others advocated war too, such as the marquis de Lafayette, who hoped that war would enhance his position in France (he was a general) and revive aristocratic leadership of France whilst silencing both royalist and republican extremists.

Interestingly, **Maximilien de Robespierre**, speaking in the Jacobin Club, was a lone voice against the clamour for war. He believed war would play into the hands of the court and ambitious generals like Lafayette. There were enemies enough at home without tackling those abroad. War would be a disaster for the revolution and for France. His protests, however, fell on increasingly deaf ears and his patriotism was questioned.

The **instigators** are sometimes referred to as Brissotins or Girondins (many were deputies from the Gironde region).

In the **Declaration of Pillnitz**, August 1791, Leopold II of Austria and Frederick William II of Prussia seemed to threaten intervention in France on behalf of Louis XVI.

Maximilien de Robespierre (1758–94), nicknamed 'The Incorruptible', was elected to the Estates-General in 1789. He joined the Jacobin Club in Paris and became known for his radical and democratic views. He supported the overthrow of the monarchy in August 1792 and was elected by Paris to the National Convention, where he attacked the Girondins and urged the execution of the king. He became a leading figure of the Terror after he joined the Committee of Public Safety in July 1793. Influenced by the works of Rousseau, he hoped to create a Republic of Virtue and sought to purge France of all critics. His many enemies eventually co-operated in securing his arrest and execution by guillotine on 28 July 1794.

Why did both the assembly and the court want war?

A sketch of the Jacobin leader Maximilien de Robespierre in 1793 by the revolutionary artist David. It was made as Marie-Antoinette was taken away to the guillotine. What impression do you get of Robespierre from this picture?

'**Aristocrat**' came to be used as a catch-all term of abuse for anyone not committed to the revolution.

Paris was divided into 48 **sections** for administrative purposes, each with its own assembly.

The ***bonnet rouge*** was the red cap of liberty. It was a symbol taken from Rome – the red hat was worn by freed slaves.

From December Louis began to play a double game. At the request of the assembly he sent a demand to the ruler of Trier to drive out the *émigrés* from his territory, but at the same time made clear in correspondence that he hoped the demand would be ignored. In early 1792 the king appointed a Girondin ministry committed to war. News of the alliance of Austria and Prussia in February 1792 was enough to persuade the doubters in the assembly, and in April 1792 war was declared in the name of the French nation in defence of liberty against the king of Hungary and Bohemia (Austria). Brissot's claims about the war would now be put to the test.

War and the overthrow of the monarchy

The war did not prove the victorious parade Brissot had predicted; quite the reverse. The shambolic French army was in no fit state to wage war and retreated headlong. Discipline was so poor that General Dillon was murdered by his own troops after an unsuccessful skirmish with Austrian forces at the end of April, and in May Lafayette was so concerned about the state of the army that he urged the assembly to open peace negotiations.

The poor performance of French forces was blamed on treason and traitors within France – refractory priests, **aristocrats** and, not least, the court. In May Brissot and other Girondins accused the 'Austrian Committee' of betraying France. Meanwhile, the assembly passed decrees for the deportation of refractory priests, the disbandment of the king's guard and the calling of provincial National Guards (known as *fédérés*) to help defend Paris.

The king then vetoed the decrees and dismissed his Girondin ministers, which seemed to confirm suspicions about his trustworthiness. The situation in Paris was volatile. There was a sense of crisis because of the failure of the war effort, and also the return of economic problems – unemployment and inflation. The crisis, plus the suspicions of royal treason, proved an inflammable mixture that radical politicians and popular clubs were able to exploit. The call for a republic and for the decrees passed by the assembly in early June became ever more insistent and culminated in another revolutionary *journée* on 20 June. In part this was a response to an attempt by the moderate marquis de Lafayette to gain control of events by calling for the abolition of political clubs and accusing the Jacobins of running a state within the state. Lafayette's denunciation of the Jacobins was taken to presage a military coup. In response the leaders of the Paris **sections** called for a demonstration. Crowds invaded the Tuileries and forced the king to don the ***bonnet rouge*** and drink the health of the nation. But the crowd then dispersed. There was no overthrow of the monarchy at this point but, although the king refused to recall his Girondin ministers and maintained his vetoes, the assembly went ahead with the establishment of a camp for 20,000 *fédérés* who were marching to Paris. Amongst them was a detachment from Marseilles who marched singing a revolutionary song that became known as the Marseillaise and was adopted as the French national anthem in the nineteenth century. These National Guards from the provinces tended to be radical and republican.

At the beginning of July the assembly declared an emergency – *la patrie en danger* – which meant its decrees no longer needed the king's sanction. Events developed increasingly rapidly. By the beginning of August *fédérés* had arrived from across France, the assemblies of the 48 Paris sections were in permanent session, petitions demanding the overthrow of the monarchy had been made to the assembly, the Girondin leaders had blotted their republican reputation by trying to negotiate a deal with the king, and passive citizens had been admitted to the National Guard and to some Paris section assemblies. As far as the radicals and their *sans-culotte* supporters (see page 70) were concerned, the only solution for France and the revolution was the overthrow of the king and the establishment of a democratic republic.

Meanwhile the Prussian army advanced into France. Its commander, the duke of Brunswick, issued his demands (the Brunswick Manifesto) threatening death to all who opposed his advance or who harmed the royal family. News of this manifesto effectively sealed the king's fate. For the revolutionaries the message was clear: the king was their enemy and their only chance of survival was to overthrow him and to fight in defence of the revolution. Petitions demanding the overthrow of the king flooded in to the assembly, but it was reluctant to take the decision. Another revolutionary *journée* persuaded it. On 9 August *sans-culottes* overthrew the municipal authority of Paris and a revolutionary commune was set up in the Hôtel de Ville which planned and organised the *journée* of the following day. On 10 August a crowd of National Guards (including passive citizens) and *fédérés* attacked the Tuileries, slaughtering the Swiss guards and suffering around three hundred casualties themselves. The king sought refuge in the assembly but, overawed by the crowd, it decreed his overthrow. Under the intimidating gaze of the crowd, the assembly recognised the revolutionary commune and went on to decree that there should be elections (on the basis of universal manhood suffrage) for a new National Convention. In the interim a Provisional Executive Council of six ministers was set up.

The experiment in constitutional monarchy had failed and the movement from absolute monarchy to democratic republic was almost complete. Constitutional monarchy had failed for a number of reasons, including the attitude and actions of the monarchy, the breakdown in the revolutionary consensus, the religious issue, the *émigré* threat, war and economic crisis. The attitude and actions of the king were crucial because his obvious reluctance to accept the decision of July 1789 bred suspicion and distrust of him. The attempt to

In what ways did the war affect the course of events in France?

escape from Paris in June 1791 and his vetoing of decrees against *émigrés* and refractory priests deepened distrust and hardened the attitudes of revolutionaries, whilst giving heart to those opposed to the revolution. It is at least arguable that if Louis XVI had genuinely and fully embraced the revolution of 1789 he could have survived as a constitutional monarch. However, he did not. His actions and those of his wife and brothers lent credibility to the arguments of those who wished for a republic.

The king's ambivalence certainly contributed to the breakdown in the revolutionary consensus. Whilst divisions had been there from the start, the Flight to Varennes deepened divisions and lent weight to the arguments of radicals that a republican solution was the only way forward. Meanwhile, religious division split the country and aroused fears of counter-revolution, fears compounded by the noisy sabre rattling of *émigrés* outside French frontiers. Inflation, hunger and renewed economic crisis added to the sense of insecurity. In this atmosphere war came to be seen as a way of resolving all problems. It did, but not in the way that its advocates at court or in the Legislative Assembly envisaged. The war in the summer of 1792 brought not the victorious vindication of revolutionary ideas and national unity that its supporters had envisaged, but instead defeat and crisis. Whilst the royalist advocates of war were correct in predicting defeat, this did not bring about the restoration of royal power, but its final overthrow.

(b) Why did a reign of Terror develop?

The 'First Terror': the September Massacres

Georges Danton (1759–94) was a lawyer who became associated with the radical politics of the Parisian *sans-culottes*, prominent in the Cordeliers Club. A charismatic figure able to rouse the crowd in defence of Paris in the summer of 1792, and a supporter initially of the Terror, he was to become disillusioned with the excesses of republican government and began calling for its moderation (especially of dechristianisation) in the winter of 1793. He alienated Robespierre in spring 1794 and was guillotined on 5 April.

The overthrow of the monarchy and the decision to hold elections for a new democratically elected assembly undermined the authority of the Legislative Assembly. After 10 August, many members of the assembly, especially those most closely associated with the constitutional monarchy, stayed away or went into hiding. The three hundred or so members who remained appointed the Provisional Executive Council, which included the popular leader **Georges Danton** as minister for justice. This was designed to appease the *sans-culottes*. However, the Paris Commune provided a rival focus of authority and tended to dominate affairs over the next six weeks. Under its pressure the assembly voted to deport refractory priests and, in an attempt to win over the peasantry, abolished feudal dues without compensation and ordered that the lands of *émigrés* be sold off in small lots. What to do about the king, who remained suspended from his functions, was left to the new Convention.

The political crisis did not disappear with the overthrow of the king. Indeed the advance of the Prussian forces deepened it. Fear of counter-revolution and military defeat resulted in desperate measures. On 11 August the assembly

This picture, by Béricourt, shows the burial of bodies following the September Massacres.

granted powers to local authorities to enforce general security, in particular to arrest 'suspects'. It later sanctioned the searching of suspects' homes. In Paris this very quickly led to the prisons becoming full to bursting with refractory priests, monks, nuns and aristocrats. The commune prohibited the publication of royalist journals and public religious ceremonies.

Meanwhile, the news from the front was dire. On 17 August the disillusioned **marquis de Lafayette** had emigrated. The key fortress of Longwy fell on 23 August and on 1 September Verdun surrendered too, leaving the road to Paris wide open. In these desperate circumstances, Danton made an impassioned plea for volunteers to go to the front and thousands responded. As volunteers marched away, the fearful panic in Paris reached new heights and sparked off one of the most horrific episodes of the revolution. In the last days of August the fear of counter-revolution was strong and became focused on the suspects in prison. Supposing they broke out whilst the men were away fighting? Was there a conspiracy to take over the city of Paris and hand it over to the Prussians? **Jean-Paul Marat**, the self-proclaimed 'friend of the people' and member of the commune, called for the conspirators to be killed. On 2 September armed bands of *sans-culottes* began visiting the prisons and in a mockery of justice 'tried' inmates. Over five days more than a thousand men and women were executed, although rather more were released. The men who undertook this task were paid for their work. Nothing was done by the commune to prevent the massacres; Robespierre and other Jacobin leaders even tried to have the Girondin leaders arrested and imprisoned because of their last-ditch attempts to secure a deal with the king in late July.

The **marquis de Lafayette** (1757–1834) was a wealthy liberal aristocrat who had found fame in the American War of Independence. His liberal and military prowess resulted in his becoming the first commander of the Parisian National Guard in 1789. His popularity waned after his involvement in the massacre of the Champs de Mars. He became an army commander in 1792. Worried at the course of the revolution and having failed to save the king, he defected to the enemy.

Jean-Paul Marat (1744–93) held radical views about the course of the revolution, advocating democracy and being instrumental in the September Massacres. His involvement in these, along with violent outbursts and radical journalism (through his paper *L'Ami du peuple*), made him a prime target for the Girondins. They attempted, unsuccessfully, to have him condemned by the Revolutionary Tribunal in April 1793. However, a Girondin sympathiser, Charlotte Corday, murdered him in July 1793 whilst he was bathing, making him a revolutionary martyr.

The September Massacres had a profound impact both in France and abroad. They were the foundation of the intense hostility between the Girondins and the Parisian Jacobin leaders. That meant that the new Convention, which was being elected at the time of the massacres, was deeply divided from the start. Moderate opinion everywhere was shocked by the scale of the murders, and royalists and foreigners tended to regard Jacobins and *sans-culottes* as little more than bloodthirsty savages, *buveurs de sang* (drinkers of blood). On the other hand, many Parisians saw the massacres as justified and necessary.

The National Convention: Montagnards *v.* Girondins

Elections were held at the end of August and start of September. In Paris, especially, they took place against a background of fear and crisis. Not surprisingly, perhaps, all 24 **members** for Paris were Jacobins, republicans and supporters of the commune. Outside the capital about two hundred Girondins were elected, although the majority of deputies were uncommitted. The uncommitted members became known as the 'Plain' because of where they sat in the assembly; whilst the Parisian Jacobins and their supporters sat on the tiered seats to the left of the president and became known as the 'Mountain' (the latter deputies will be referred to as **Montagnards**).

On the day that the Convention assembled, 20 September 1792, the mixture of regular and volunteer forces of the French army defeated the Prussians at the Battle of Valmy. It was a decisive battle because from this point on the Prussians were on the retreat, and it also seemed to vindicate the revolution. An untrained, volunteer army fighting in defence of its beliefs had defeated the best army in Europe, and Paris and the revolution were saved – at least from imminent defeat.

On 21 September the new assembly took the decision that the Legislative Assembly had been reluctant to take by declaring a republic. This act of relative unity in the Convention soon gave way to friction between the Girondins and the Mountain, characterised by bitter personal attacks. At one level the mutual antipathy seems hard to understand because they shared a number of important beliefs: both were republican, anti-clerical, anti-privilege and liberal in outlook and both were determined to win the war. However, the Girondins, whose support came mainly from the provinces, feared the domination of Paris and the influence of the *sans-culottes*. The Mountain's power base was Paris and drew support from popular clubs, the *sans-culottes* and the Paris sections. In general, the Montagnards were prepared to be more militant and were more willing to adopt extreme measures to secure their ends. Whilst the Girondins supported the decentralised spirit of the period after 1789, where local affairs were controlled locally (federalism), the Mountain saw

The **members** included Robespierre, Marat, Hébert and Danton.

The **Montagnards**, sitting on the left of the assembly, were the most radical grouping in the Convention. Since this time the political term 'left wing' has been applied to radicals, while 'right wing' has been applied to conservative or reactionary politicians.

Paris as the centre of the revolution and tended towards a more centralised approach. The Girondins were deeply suspicious of the Mountain because of the association of many Montagnard deputies with the horrific events of summer 1792 and the attempt to put Girondin leaders on trial. Meanwhile, the Mountain viewed the Girondin leaders with suspicion because of their attempted deal with the monarchy in July 1792.

At first Girondins dominated the Convention. They benefited to some degree from the successful prosecution of the war. In October and November French armies rolled back their enemies, occupying the Rhine, Nice, Savoy and – after the Girondin General Dumouriez's major victory at Jemappes – the Austrian Netherlands (Belgium). The euphoria resulting from these victories led to two important developments. First, on 19 November the Convention passed the **Edict of Fraternity**. Secondly, deputies began to speak in terms of expanding France to its 'natural frontiers' of the Rhine, the Alps and the Pyrenees, a process that began with the annexation of Savoy (November).

The politics of the Convention was dominated by the struggle between Girondins and Montagnards. Girondins mounted public attacks on Robespierre, Danton and Marat; whilst Brissot and other Girondins were expelled from the Jacobin Club in Paris. The crucial political issue was the fate of the king: in a very real sense unfinished business left over from the declaration of a republic. The difficulty was how to deal with the king in a way that looked legitimate. The obvious route was to try him for treason. But could a king commit treason? In which court could he be tried? What if he were found innocent of the charges? If he were found guilty, what punishment should be given? The Montagnards pressed for his trial, whilst Girondins unsuccessfully argued against this. One reason for this was the discovery in the Tuileries of an iron chest containing royal and other correspondence. There was little that was directly incriminating, but it helped reinforce the idea that the king had negotiated secretly with the revolution's enemies. It was decided that the Convention should act as a court and the king's trial began on 10 December. Whatever the evidence for or against, it was impossible not to find him guilty, so the crucial issue was what the punishment should be. Popular opinion in Paris was for death, but the Girondins tried to win support for a national referendum on his fate. This failed and only served to reinforce Montagnard and *sans-culotte* suspicion of the Girondins' motives. Meanwhile Girondins tended to brand all Parisians and Montagnards as ***Septembriseurs***. The vote to find the king guilty was unanimous, but the public and open vote on the death penalty split the Convention, although the majority was in favour of execution. A second vote for a reprieve was also defeated and the king was publicly executed by guillotine on 21 January 1793.

On what issues did the Girondins and Montagnards agree and disagree?

The **Edict of Fraternity** offered French aid to all subject peoples wishing to secure their liberty; the French Revolution was now for export.

The *Septembriseurs* were those who carried out the September Massacres.

What alternatives were there to putting the king on trial and executing him?

Why do you think alternative solutions to the problem of what to do with the king were rejected?

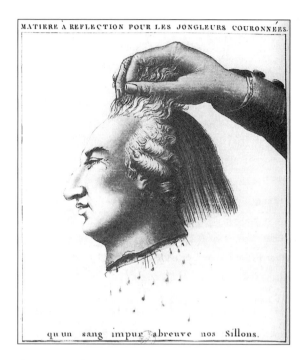

MATIERE À REFLECTION POUR LES JONGLEURS COURONNÉES.

qu un sang impur abreuve nos Sillons.

A poster printed after Louis XVI's execution in January 1793. The heading reads 'Matter for reflection for the crowned jugglers (other monarchs)'. At the base is written 'so impure blood doesn't soil our land'. What point does this poster make?

The trial of the king and the debates surrounding it reflected a shift in the balance of power in the Convention. The Girondins who had urged a referendum had been defeated; the Montagnards had won. However, it was not until July 1793 that the Montagnards fully established their control over the Convention.

War, rebellion and Montagnard triumph, February–June 1793

French victories in the Netherlands, along the Rhine, in Switzerland and northern Italy alarmed the Great Powers, perhaps more than the execution of Louis XVI. Britain, for instance, was extremely concerned that France might control the whole Channel coast. To let that happen would go against the basis of British foreign policy towards the continent since the sixteenth century. The French believed that victories would continue and that Britain would either succumb to its own revolution or be easily defeated. The Convention declared war on Britain and Holland in February 1793 and on Spain in March. As a result of these actions a powerful coalition of states was now at war with France.

The French army, under General Dumouriez, was decisively defeated by an Austrian army at Neerwinden in March. The general, closely associated with the Girondins and concerned about the course of the revolution, then decided to march on Paris with his army. When it refused to obey, he, like Lafayette before him, defected to the Austrians. The French forces now found themselves on the defensive, pushed out of Belgium and back from the Rhine.

Whatever the effect on the military effort, Dumouriez's desertion served to discredit the Girondins still further in Paris and in the Convention.

Moreover, popular counter-revolution had broken out in the Vendée in the west of France as a result of the decision in February to raise 300,000 troops for the war effort. The levy of soldiers was the final straw in growing discontent amongst a peasant rural population which was relatively highly taxed, had resented the Civil Constitution of the Clergy and had failed to benefit from the sale of church lands. The peasantry looked to local, largely royalist nobility for leadership. In this way popular revolt became bound up in counter-revolution. The anger and resentment of the peasantry was taken out on local officials, National Guards and constitutional priests, many of whom were murdered. Whilst essentially local in character, the revolt was so serious that 30,000 troops were sent to deal with it.

The effects of defeat in war and internal rebellion were compounded by increasing economic problems. To pay for the war more *assignats* had been printed; their value dropped, resulting in rapid price inflation. Bread was scarce as farmers were unwilling to sell grain for increasingly worthless paper money. The result was popular unrest and demands for price controls and supplies from the *sans-culottes*.

> Identify the main elements of the crisis facing the government in the spring of 1793.

In an effort to control the growing crisis, the Convention, increasingly influenced by the Mountain, passed a series of measures between March and May. It set up the **Revolutionary Tribunal** in Paris to try those suspected of counter-revolution. It sent deputies from the Convention, who were known as representatives-on-mission, to the provinces and the army with wide powers to oversee conscription and keep a watch on generals. It sanctioned the setting up in each commune of a *comité de surveillance* (watch committee) to keep an eye on foreigners and suspects, and sanctioned summary trial and execution of rebels and *émigrés*, should they return to France.

> The **Revolutionary Tribunal** was an attempt to avoid the possibility of a repeat of the September Massacres.

In April the Convention set up the Committee of Public Safety to oversee and speed up the work of government during this crisis. This was a committee drawn from the Convention and responsible to it. It was not initially dominated by Montagnards – there were only two among the nine members. Finally, to appease the *sans-culottes*, in May the Convention imposed price controls on grain (known as the Maximum). Significantly, this last measure was opposed by the Girondins, who also attempted to pass several measures to limit the power of the commune and to bring provincial National Guards to Paris to protect the Convention. They thereby increased the hostility of the *sans-culottes* towards them.

> Why were so many of the deputies of the National Convention opposed to price controls? (Think about their social status and what that implies about their economic views.)

The Girondins compounded this hostility and that of Montagnard leaders by refusing to stop their attacks on the *sans-culottes*, whom they regarded as being nothing but bloodthirsty savages. They had even put the popular hero

Marat on trial before the Revolutionary Tribunal. His acquittal marked a further decline in the fortunes of the Girondins. As a result Robespierre sided with the *sans-culottes*, urging them to rise up against the Girondin deputies. Paris was in a state of insurrection from 31 May. News of the overthrow of the Jacobin administration in Lyons was the final spur to action and, on 2 June 1793, 80,000 Parisian National Guards surrounded the Convention and demanded the expulsion of the Girondins and a Maximum on prices of all essential goods. The Convention agreed to the expulsion and arrest of 29 Girondin deputies. From this point on for more than a year, the Convention was dominated by the Montagnard minority, the deputies of the Plain seeing the alternative as the overthrow of the republic.

The Development of the Terror, July–September 1793

This period of the French Revolution is complicated. Perhaps it is best seen as a period of emergency government (Terror) when the future of the revolution was beset with immense problems caused by war, rebellion and civil war, economic crisis and – at the centre – a struggle for influence and power amongst different groups. In one sense the Terror was very successful as the revolution

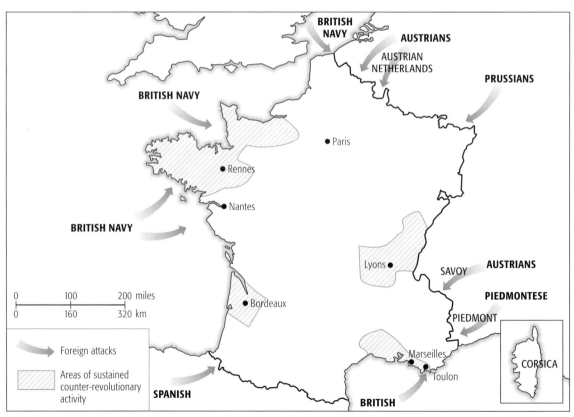

The revolution assailed on all sides, 1793.

survived, foreign enemies were defeated, counter-revolution and other internal threats were suppressed, even the *sans-culottes* were tamed and a degree of economic stability returned. However, this period also witnessed the most horrific destruction, massacres and murders, thousands guillotined as a result of summary justice under the Revolutionary Tribunal, mass destruction of churches, blood letting amongst the leading members of the republic and the bizarre attempt to set up a kind of revolutionary religion in the 'Cult of the Supreme Being'. Although there was no leader as such, the dominant personality in all this came to be Robespierre.

Between June and September the Committee of Public Safety (CPS), the central institution of the Terror, was reorganised. Membership was increased from 9 to 12 and it came to be dominated by Montagnards. There was no one leader and decisions were taken collectively. Although the membership had to be re-elected by the Convention once a month, it remained relatively stable after September 1793. Barère was its spokesman in the Convention. **Lazare Carnot**'s talents were directed to the war effort. Robespierre, important for his influence in the Parisian Jacobin Club and with the *sans-culottes*, joined the CPS at the end of July. Other members included Robespierre's allies Saint-Just and Couthon, and Collot d'Herbois and Billaud-Varenne who were close to the *sans-culottes*.

The remit of the CPS was the conduct of the war outside and inside France and the maintenance of supplies to the army and the civilian population. It had a sister committee, that of General Security (CGS), which was responsible for the pursuit of counter-revolutionaries, the treatment of suspects and other matters of internal security. A dominant figure here was the Jacobin Fouché. One problem that became increasingly apparent was that there was no clear dividing line delimiting where the authority of the CPS ended and that of the CGS began.

Whilst these two committees became the most important institutions of the Terror, there were three other groups that had a vital role. These were the local watch committees, representatives-on-mission and the revolutionary armies (of which the Parisian was the most important). For much of the period until the end of 1793, there was no clear structure of control or direction over these various bodies. Only in December 1793 was a serious attempt made to clarify the relationship between the various bodies and assert the primacy of the CPS. This is partly why some historians refer to the period between July and December as the 'anarchic Terror'.

The Federal Revolt

One immediate result of the purge of the Girondins on 2 June was a widespread protest from the provinces, which resented the domination of Paris,

Lazare Carnot (1753–1823) was a Jacobin with military expertise. He was a representative-on-mission between August 1792 and August 1793, when he was elected to the CPS. He was nicknamed the 'Organiser of Victory' for his efforts in 1793 and for the organisation of the *levée en masse* in particular. His reputation meant he did not fall with Robespierre and he was chosen as a director under the terms of the new Constitution in 1795. He also briefly served Napoleon as war minister after 1799, before retiring into private life.

its commune, the Jacobin clubs and the *sans-culottes* over the Convention. Serious anti-Jacobin movements broke out in eight *départements* and in the major cities of Lyons, Marseilles and Bordeaux. This resistance to the authority of the Paris-dominated Convention was referred to as 'federalism' or the Federal Revolt. It is important to distinguish it from counter-revolutionary unrest in the Vendée. It was not anti-revolutionary or anti-republican; it was anti-Jacobin and anti-Parisian control. It represented a considerable threat to the government, especially in the context of the other problems facing it. And, occasionally, as in the case of **Toulon**, resistance to the Jacobins led to collusion with royalists and foreign enemies. Fortunately, the Federal Revolt was not co-ordinated and in the end government forces were able to deal with protests one by one during autumn 1793.

Toulon was occupied by the British.

War

The war had continued to go badly and suspicion continued to fall on generals. (Custine was guillotined in the summer on suspicion of intriguing with the enemy.) Foreign armies were advancing within France. The scale of the military problems led to emergency measures that were to transform the nature of warfare. In August, Carnot ordered the *levée en masse*, an attempt to harness all the resources of the state for war. Mass conscription was introduced, with all young men between 18 and 25 called to the colours, whilst older and married men were to help with supplies and women and children were to help with making uniforms and other materials. Even old men were to be wheeled into the town squares to exhort the young to fight. This massive effort led to the growth of the French army to over 500,000 men, eventually to nearly a million.

The Terror: September–December 1793

Whilst the two committees began to take decisive action to deal with war, Federal Revolt and counter-revolution, the economic problems of the poor remained. The Convention – with its bias, even amongst Jacobin deputies, towards economic liberalism – was unwilling to take much action beyond the Maximum introduced in May. But all through the summer there were calls from *sans-culotte* leaders like Hébert for general price controls, death for hoarders and vigorous prosecution of all potential counter-revolutionary activity. This contributed to the insurrection of the *sans-culottes* and the Paris sections on 5 September 1793. They invaded the Convention and demanded recognition of their grievances. Faced with this intimidation and urged on by the Jacobin leaders, the Convention agreed to the *sans-culotte* programme and voted two Jacobins who were popular with them, Billaud-Varenne and Collot d'Herbois, on to the CPS. At the end of the month the

Convention passed the Law of the General Maximum, which limited prices of grain and other essentials to one third above the 1790 price and wages to one half above the 1790 figure. Prices would be enforced, hoarders rooted out and food supplies secured by using the *sans-culotte* revolutionary army raised in Paris.

The device of the revolutionary army was copied in the provinces too, although without official Convention sanction. In practice the revolutionary armies were used not only to secure food supplies for the cities and the army, but also to help to suppress royalist unrest in Brittany and the Federal Revolt in Lyons, and to enforce 'dechristianisation' (see page 62) in the countryside. The Convention only ever accepted the institution of the Parisian army reluctantly and viewed these *sans-culotte* forces with suspicion.

Anyone the revolutionary armies suspected of hoarding and those who were unwilling to sell their grain under the terms of the General Maximum could be arrested as a suspect under the terms of the **Law of Suspects** passed by the Convention on 17 September. Fear did much to ensure compliance, and certainly the revolutionary armies appeared to be successful in securing food supplies, even if this meant ensuring the hostility of the peasantry to Jacobin rule.

The terms of the **Law of Suspects** were so widely drawn that almost anyone not expressing enthusiastic support for the republic could be placed under suspicion.

How did the Convention deal with the economic grievances of the *sans-culottes*?

Popular pressure in Paris had demanded economic controls; it also demanded vigorous action against suspects and counter-revolutionaries. In particular there was pressure to put Marie-Antoinette and the Girondin leaders on trial. Despite Robespierre's efforts to prevent them, during October a series of show trials in the Revolutionary Tribunal led to the executions of Marie-Antoinette and 20 leading Girondins, followed in November and December by others. In the last three months of 1793 about 180 victims were guillotined (this compares with the 66 before September 1793). This blood letting was in part due to the continued emergency facing France, which justified the formal suspension in October of the proposed democratic Constitution. The crisis required emergency measures and democracy would have to wait for better times. The government would be 'revolutionary until the peace'.

Whilst the Revolutionary Tribunal in Paris gave the semblance of formal procedure and central control, elsewhere it was more difficult to control the situation. Local watch committees, the revolutionary armies and individual representatives-on-mission interpreted the law and their own brief according to their particular prejudices and circumstances. The measures adopted in areas of Federal Revolt and the Vendée rising were the most extreme. While counter-revolution and Federal Revolt were in the main crushed by regular military forces, the victory was often accompanied by extreme violence and the aftermath saw further excessive bloodshed and destruction.

Suspects were rounded up by the hundred. The **vengeance** was too much for the guillotine in the city square to cope with, so the expedient of blasting the victims away by the use of cannon was employed. These *mitraillades* and other executions accounted for approaching two thousand deaths.

General Westermann reported, 'the Vendée is no more. It has died beneath our sabres, together with its women and children. I have crushed the children under my horses' hooves, massacred the women – they, at least, will not give birth to any more brigands'.

Can you explain the excesses of the Terror in areas of revolt?

At Lyons a combination of regular forces and the Parisian revolutionary army had defeated the rebels in October. Whilst the initial representative-on-mission had urged moderate punishment, his replacements Collot d'Herbois and Fouché, at the behest of the Convention, sought to make an example of France's second city. It was to be totally destroyed and renamed Ville Affranchie (freed town). Indeed, much of the town was systematically torched, but even more extreme was the **vengeance** exacted on the populace.

Even worse occurred in **the Vendée**. The crushing of the revolt had been bloody enough. No quarter was shown by the army which literally destroyed everything in its path. The revolt in the Vendée had also resulted in the arrest and imprisonment in Nantes of hundreds of suspects, many of them priests and nuns. In Nantes, Carrier, the representative-on-mission, was responsible for the execution of around two thousand suspects by tying them up naked in sealed barges which were then towed into the Loire estuary where they were holed and sunk. A gruesome feature of these *noyades* was the use of so-called 'underwater marriages', in which a priest and a nun would be tied together.

These excesses were the most extreme. Areas of counter-revolution and revolt suffered dearly for their opposition to the Jacobins. It is difficult to know just how many died as a result of the Terror outside Paris. Whilst some areas suffered acutely others remained relatively untouched. Certainly the scale of the slaughter was highest in the Vendée, where victims were numbered in thousands. One historian has put the total as high as 50,000–60,000 for the whole period of the Terror.

Religious Terror: dechristianisation

Particularly since the Civil Constitution and the division it caused, the Catholic church had been linked with real or potential counter-revolution. What is more, religion was associated with the *ancien régime* and superstitious practices. For many it had no place in a rational secular republic. It is not surprising that the crisis of 1793 should be accompanied by a renewed and more virulent attack on religion. Its sources can be found partly in the initiatives of individual representatives-on-mission and partly in the Convention itself. On 5 October 1793 the Convention adopted the new Republican Calendar which abolished religious holidays and Sundays. Months were now named after seasonal features, and seven-day weeks were replaced by ten-day *décades*. The yearly calendar was dated from the creation of the republic (22 September 1792), rather than from the birth of Christ. The Convention thereby symbolically divorced the state from the church. (See appendix, page 203.)

Before this, however, Fouché, as representative-on-mission in Nevers, had started a more thorough attack on religion, which was taken up by the Paris Commune. He, an ex-priest, believed that Catholicism was incompatible with the revolution, required priests to marry or adopt orphans, removed all signs of religion from cemeteries (replacing them with the slogan 'death is an eternal sleep') and banned public exercise of religion. The Paris Commune went further and sanctioned the destruction of religious and royal statues, changed street names with religious connotations, banned clerical dress, encouraged clergy to give up their vocation and closed churches. Notre-Dame was turned into the Temple of Reason. The Convention seemed to encourage dechristianisation by authorising the deportation of any priest denounced by six citizens. Amongst the keenest advocates of dechristianisation were the *sans culotte* revolutionary armies whose passage through the countryside was marked by the vandalisation and closure of churches.

What were the main features of dechristianisation?

However popular it was amongst the *sans-culottes*, dechristianisation alienated much of the population – especially in rural areas. Robespierre, never an advocate of the policy, was amongst the first to recognise the detrimental effect it was having. He attempted to get the Convention to order a halt. Although he eventually persuaded it to reaffirm the principle of religious toleration in its decree on the 'liberty of cults' (6 December). This had little practical effect and dechristianisation was to continue into 1794.

Robespierre and the Great Terror

Dechristianisation was another example of how the Terror seemed outside the control of either the great committees (CPS and CGS) or the Convention and led to support for moves to give the CPS more power. The Law of 14 Frimaire (4 December 1793) attempted to assert central control by 'constituting revolutionary government'. By this decree government power over internal administration and police was placed in the CPS (which remained answerable to the Convention). The authority of the CGS over revolutionary tribunals was also made clear. Representatives-on-mission lost their independence and all unofficial bodies, including local revolutionary armies, were abolished. A highly centralised system was adopted, although it took some months to establish the authority of the CPS fully.

By this time the problems which had beset the revolution in the summer of 1793 were receding. The Federal Revolt and the Vendée rising had been crushed by the end of the year. Meanwhile, the energetic administration of Carnot had helped turn the tide against France's foreign enemies. In the north, the Austrians were pushed out of France after the Battle of Wattignies (October), and in the east out of Alsace in December; in the south the Spanish were pushed out of Roussillon and the British out of Toulon. Meanwhile, the economy had recovered, partly because of the controls on prices and partly because of the forced loan on the rich (September 1793). As a result the *assignat* had doubled in value from its low point in August.

Why did some begin to call for an end to the Terror at the end of 1793?

A sketch of Danton on his way to the guillotine, 1794, by J.-B. Wille. What impression do you form of his character from this?

Jacques Hébert was born in 1755 and guillotined in March 1794. He was the publisher of the radical newspaper *Le Père Duchesne* and a member of the Cordeliers Club. He was one of the prominent leaders of the *sans-culottes* and helped co-ordinate the *journée* of 5 September 1793. He and his followers supported dechristianisation and clashed with the Dantonists over the course of the revolution in the winter of 1793/94. His extremism eventually earned him the enmity of Robespierre and he was arrested and executed in March 1794.

The purging of the **Hébertists** proved to be the end of the *sans-culottes* as a political force, and also the end of the influence of the Paris Commune – its leader lost his head in April and thereafter its personnel were purged.

In this atmosphere of recovery some, amongst whom Danton was prominent, began to argue first for an end to the anarchic Terror of the autumn, and then for a moderation of revolutionary government overall. Those who advocated such measures were referred to as 'Indulgents'. They were opposed by the *sans-culotte* leaders like Hébert and the Paris Commune. **Jacques Hébert** and his followers found themselves under attack, and some leaders – like the head of the revolutionary army, Ronsin – were arrested. However, at this point the Hébertists were still too influential to be cowed. Robespierre and others on the CPS found themselves caught between the Indulgents on the one hand and the Hébertists on the other. Mutual denunciations raised the political temperature in the capital and unrest once more threatened. But this time the response of the *sans-culottes* in Paris was muted, which encouraged the CPS to take action. In March 1794 **Hébertist** leaders were denounced and arrested, accused of fomenting insurrection, tried by the Revolutionary Tribunal and guillotined. That everything went so smoothly was in part due to a timely intervention to steady the price of bread in Paris. The revolutionary army was dissolved at the end of March.

The end of the Hébertists was not to be the triumph of the Indulgents or the end of the Terror. This was because of Robespierre, who had by 1794 developed a vision – drawn to some degree from his reading of Rousseau – of a Republic of Virtue, which if it was to be achieved required the purging of all corrupting elements. Amongst these he counted Danton and the Indulgents who had been implicated in a financial scandal. They were denounced in the Convention as 'partisans of royalism', arrested, put on trial and executed on 5 April.

This marked not the end of the Terror but the start of a more intensive phase. All provincial revolutionary tribunals were closed down and prisoners were now transferred to Paris. The resultant swelling numbers in the prisons led to a measure to speed up the work of the Revolutionary Tribunal. Henceforward, under the Law of 22 Prairial (10 June 1794) trials would be limited to deciding only on liberty or death, with defendants having no rights. All the court had to decide was whether the defendant was an **enemy of the people**. Executions, which had fallen off in the spring, now suddenly rose once more. Of about 2,600 people guillotined in Paris between March 1793 and August 1794, over 1,500 were executed in June and July 1794. This period is sometimes referred to as the Great Terror. It was to be a final cleansing of the 'land of liberty' of the 'refuse' in its prisons, including a high proportion of nobles and rich men.

The definition of **enemy of the people** was so broadly drawn that almost anyone could fall within it.

A cartoon entitled 'Robespierre guillotining the executioner after having guillotined all the French'. What point is the cartoonist making? Consider carefully the details of the cartoon, including what Robespierre is standing on and the upside-down, burning cap on the spike behind him.

The Great Terror met with no great enthusiasm, and many began to feel that the CPS, apparently dominated by Robespierre, regarded any criticism as a threat to the republic. Robespierre had already lost the support of the *sans-culottes* by the purging of the Hébertists, the rise in prices sanctioned in March and, finally, by the attempt to impose the Maximum on wages in July. Robespierre's attempt in May to introduce a new kind of religion, the Cult of the Supreme Being, whether motivated by religious toleration or not, alienated both Catholics and atheistic patriots. He had also alienated the CGS by setting up a police bureau under CPS authority in April. Moreover, the Terror intensified at the very time when the rationale for it – rebellion, counter-revolution and invasion – had all but disappeared. On 26 June, French armies, on the offensive since the spring, secured a major victory over the Austrians at Fleurus. That opened the way to the reoccupation of Belgium.

Why had Robespierre lost support by July 1794?

Finally, on 26 July (8 Thermidor), the Convention listened to a speech from Robespierre in which he condemned a new conspiracy against liberty, of plots by the members of the CGS and even by members of the CPS. Enough people felt threatened by these vague accusations to persuade the Convention to act. On 27 July it ordered Robespierre's arrest, along with his closest allies Saint-Just and Couthon. On 28 July they were arrested and executed. Later, about a hundred followed them to the scaffold.

Aftermath: return to moderation

Although the machinery of Terror was not immediately dismantled, the Coup of Thermidor effectively marks the beginning of the end. In the subsequent months the powers of the great committees were reduced and spread amongst other bodies. The Revolutionary Tribunal was disbanded, the Law of 22 Prairial revoked, the commune abolished and the Jacobin Club closed. The Thermidorians, as the members of the Convention have been called after the coup, set to work on a new Constitution which would avoid the possibility of a dominant executive power and would secure power in the hands of the bourgeoisie; there would be no return to the CPS and popular democracy would be avoided by the return to a tax-paying franchise and indirect elections. Under the new **Constitution of the Year III**, an executive of five directors would govern under laws passed by a two-chamber parliament. All in all, it was an attempt to ensure a system that would avoid both the extremes of a Jacobin republic and a royalist restoration and would ensure the dominance of the moderate bourgeoisie.

The **Constitution of the Year III** included numerous checks and balances to ensure that the executive could not become too strong. For instance, one of the directors would be replaced each year by lot and one third of the members of each of the two legislative chambers would be elected each year.

However, not everything went smoothly. In December 1794 price controls were abolished, leading immediately to rapid inflation. The rise in prices was all the more severe because of the effects of a particularly bitter winter, the printing of more *assignats* to pay for the war effort and the effects of a poor harvest. Hunger and unemployment led to a final armed *sans-culotte* rising in May 1795 (Prairial), demanding bread. After an armed stand-off at the Convention, the crowds dispersed. The regular army was then used by the government to surround the *sans-culotte* areas and force them to give up their weapons. About six thousand were arrested and six leaders executed. It proved more than anything else that the *sans-culottes* were a spent force; they were never to rise again, even when conditions deteriorated once again in 1796.

Meanwhile revenge (known as the **White Terror**) was taken on some Jacobin terrorists in a number of areas, especially in the west and to the north and south of Lyons. The violence could be extreme. In the south-east gangs of youths killed as many as two thousand in 1795 and sporadic violence was to continue into 1796 and 1797. In the Vendée there was some guerrilla activity but the most serious threat came in Brittany, where a royalist movement known as the **Chouannerie** took shape. Roving bands of up to a hundred men attacked grain convoys and murdered government officials. Law and order effectively broke down outside the towns. The movement was supported in June 1795 by about three thousand *émigrés* who were landed at Quiberon Bay by the British. This revolt was swiftly crushed by General Hoche and about 750 rebels were shot. Thereafter flying columns were sent to root out all revolt in Brittany and the Vendée.

White was the colour of the Bourbon royal house. Those involved in the **White Terror** were royalists and also a range of others who had suffered persecution during the Terror. The objects of their attacks were those associated with the Terror regime.

The origin of the term '**Chouannerie**' is obscure, but it may be derived from a dialect word for owl, referring to the hoot of an owl, imitated by the rebels as a means of communication.

In Paris there was also a reaction. Bands of middle-class youths adopted extravagant fashions (hence their nickname, *la jeunesse dorée* – 'gilded youth') and confined their activities largely to beating up Jacobins and *sans-culottes*. There was a supposed royalist rebellion in Paris in October 1795 (the Vendémiaire rising), but the nature of this rising is not clear. It appeared to have as much to do with economic discontent as support for the restoration of the Bourbon monarchy. Whatever its causes, it was bloodily repressed when the army – commanded by one Napoleon Bonaparte – opened fire, with cannon killing or wounding over three hundred. His 'whiff of grapeshot' was enough to crush the rising. The people of Paris would not rise again until the revolution of 1830.

Some historians have interpreted the years of extremism between 1792 and 1794 as a period when the revolution was 'blown off course'. It was an aberration, but the Thermidorian reaction returned the revolution to its original course – a revolution in the hands of the bourgeoisie and in the interests of the bourgeoisie. Certainly, the revolution of 1789 had left power in the hands of the notables, the liberal bourgeoisie and nobility; and certainly their control of the revolution was threatened by the crisis of 1792 which brought the *sans-culottes* to the forefront. But even then political leadership at the centre was in the hands of bourgeois politicians. Although the Convention bowed to *sans-culotte* demands in autumn 1793, central control was restored by the Law of 14 Frimaire and the purging of the Hébertists early in 1794. The Coup of Thermidor against Robespierre was not a revolt of the moderate majority, but a coalition of convenience by all those who felt threatened by Robespierre's search for purity. Only over the succeeding months did a consensus emerge that allowed a constitution aiming at avoiding both Jacobin extremism and royalist reaction.

What was the role of the Jacobins, Paris and the *sans-culottes*?

The Jacobins and other political clubs

Even before May 1789, literary and political societies had developed amongst the middle and upper classes, from the salons of society ladies, through the more modest small-town literary societies, to the propagandist Society of Thirty which had done so much to promote the interests of the Third Estate during the winter of 1788/89. From the moment deputies gathered at Versailles in May 1789, political clubs and societies began to develop to discuss the issues of the day. One of these was the Breton Club, where deputies met to discuss a common approach towards the Estates-General and to issues raised in the National Assembly. This club changed its name to the Friends of the Constitution in January 1790 and became popularly known as the Jacobin Club because of its meeting place in an ex-Jacobin monastery.

The Jacobin Club acted as a pressure group and sounding board for 'patriot' opinions and sought to link up through correspondence with clubs in towns across France. Its membership was restricted partly by the process of nomination and partly by high fees, but its sessions were open to the public. This ensured that proceedings were well reported in the growing revolutionary press and that would-be politicians could make their influence felt. There was no unified opinion in the early years and moderates mixed with more radical members. However, the aftermath of the Flight to Varennes changed all that. The republican rhetoric of some radical members, like Robespierre and Pétion, was too much for moderates. The majority therefore left the club and set up the rival Feuillant Club. The rump left in the Jacobin Club, however, maintained their popularity in Paris and the provinces.

In the autumn of 1791 the club supported the Girondins and their war policy, despite the opposition of Robespierre. The Jacobin Club became increasingly republican and in the summer of 1792 supported the overthrow of the monarchy, even if members took little direct part in the action. After the events of August the club became an important centre of political leadership. Its dominant voices were Montagnard and in the autumn of 1792 the

Girondin members were increasingly sidelined. The club became one of the main power bases of the leaders of the Terror, including Robespierre.

Meanwhile, sister Jacobin clubs had developed across France. By June 1791 there were about nine hundred and in general they took their lead from Paris. They acted as centres of patriotic opinion, as propagandists for the revolution and as the training grounds for would-be local and national politicians. Just as the Jacobin Club in Paris exerted its influence over the National Assembly, Legislative Assembly and National Convention, so local Jacobin clubs tended to have great influence over local affairs.

There was one other very important political club in Paris, the radical Cordeliers Club set up in May 1790. Politically it was more radical than the Jacobin Club and more populist in its outlook. Its membership was open and fees were low. During the Terror it acted as a forum for *sans-culotte* opinion and attracted radical leaders like Danton and Marat. It saw itself as a means of political education for the people, as a protector of popular leaders, as openly democratic and as a forum for keeping watch on the authorities. It denounced the distinction between active and passive citizens, advocated a republic after the Flight to Varennes and played a key role in organising the *journée* of 10 August 1792.

The political clubs in Paris had a great influence on the course of the revolution, partly because their prominent members were also members of important institutions like the Legislative Assembly, National Convention, Paris Commune and the CPS. At a local level too, the clubs played a significant role, providing a forum for activists and a platform for propaganda. The king felt the clubs were the source of a conspiracy against him. As early as May 1789 members of the court were referring to their influence. In 1791 the king laid great stress on the idea that the French people had been led astray by the Jacobin clubs and that they, in effect, operated as a state within the state.

Paris and the provinces

Many histories of the French Revolution focus on events in Paris, and tend to view the revolution as an essentially Parisian affair. Certainly many of the decisive events occurred there, from the Storming of the Bastille to the over-throw of Robespierre in July 1794. It was there that the king was an effective prisoner from October 1789 and the various revolutionary assemblies met. Provincial Jacobin clubs took their lead from the Parisian Jacobin Club. From the summer of 1792, the people of Paris had a decisive impact and influence on the course of events.

However, to see the revolution in exclusively Parisian terms is to ignore the role of the provinces. Many **revolutionary leaders** were not Parisian at all. The overturning of the social system based on privilege came in great part from the

In what ways did the Jacobin clubs influence the course and nature of the French Revolution?

Among the **revolutionary leaders**, Robespierre was from Arras, Danton from Arcis sur Aube; and influential leaders in the early stages were from Brittany, Grenoble and the Gironde.

pressure exerted by the Great Fear of the summer of 1789 and, of course, from the evidence of the rural *cahiers*. The arrival of radical *fédérés* in the summer of 1792 helped overthrow the monarchy and defend the revolution at Valmy.

The spirit of the revolution before the Terror was one of decentralisation. Local officials were elected from below, not imposed from Paris. Resentment at the influence of Paris provoked the Federal Revolt in the summer of 1793 and contributed to the reign of Terror instigated that autumn. In many ways the Terror was at its most extreme in the provinces, not Paris. The *noyades* at Nantes, the *mitraillades* at Lyons and the revolutionary justice meted out in Marseilles, Toulon and Bordeaux were all on a scale at least equal to the worst excesses in Paris. Watch committees were as active in many provincial towns as in Paris. Dechristianisation was a feature of the revolution in provincial France as it was in Paris. Indeed, in the provinces it continued for months after it had been brought under control in the capital. The overthrow of Robespierre by the Convention in July 1794 was not only a reassertion of middle-class control over the revolution, it was also to some degree a rejection of the influence of Paris over it. Perhaps most significantly of all, it was not in Paris that counter-revolution threatened most, but in the west.

Sans-culottes

The term *sans-culotte* literally means 'without breeches'. Although originally it was used to describe someone caught with his trousers down, during the French Revolution it was used to describe politically active citizens of the lower middle class and skilled working class who formed the bulk of the crowds involved in the popular demonstrations that marked decisive moments in the course of events. They wore trousers rather than the knee breeches of the middle and upper classes. They were small employers, tradesmen, shopkeepers, journalists, clerks and skilled workers like cabinetmakers, stonemasons, tailors and metalworkers. To be a *sans-culotte* was to be a patriot, to be an ardent supporter of the revolution and, after 1792, to be zealous in defence of the republic against foreign and internal enemies. *Sans-culottes* wore their tricolour cockades and red caps of liberty with pride, resented the early distinction made between active and passive citizens, and believed in direct democracy and direct action – the people were the true source of sovereignty and the right of insurrection therefore was vital.

It was such people who stormed the Bastille in 1789, formed the crowd on the Champs de Mars in 1791, attacked the Tuileries in August 1792 and overthrew the king, carried out the September Massacres, forced the expulsion of the Girondins in June 1793, compelled the National Convention to adopt the Law of the General Maximum in September 1793, and took the Terror into the countryside. Although the *sans-culottes* came to be particularly influential in

In this painting an actor has posed as a *sans-culotte*. What image of the *sans-culottes* is being conveyed here? How reliable a view is this painting?

Paris after 1789, they were also important in the provinces. They, like their Parisian counterparts, formed the ranks of the provincial revolutionary armies and provincial *sans-culottes* (such as the Marseillais) gathered in Paris in the summer of 1792 to defend the revolution.

However, in Paris *sans-culotte* influence had a decisive effect on the course of the revolution. The Parisian crowd (not termed *sans-culottes*) that stormed the Bastille saved the National Assembly on 14 July 1789. Once the king and the assembly were brought to Paris in October 1789, the *sans-culottes* had an increasing influence on the revolution until their power began to be broken from December 1793. They were not a political party, but looked to popular leaders like Marat, Danton and later Hébert whose power base was in the Cordeliers Club, and to the Jacobin Club after the Feuillants seceded in the summer of 1791. In 1792 *sans-culotte* leaders came to dominate many of the Paris sections and the revolutionary commune that asserted its power that summer. From that summer no revolutionary grouping was able to rule effectively without their support. Jacobin leaders like Robespierre realised this and were willing to make concessions towards *sans-culotte* concerns, like the Maximum, in order to win their support. Robespierre brought the Jacobins to support a republic in the early summer of 1792 and was willing to accept (if not openly endorse) extreme measures in the summer of 1792 and to use *sans-culotte* pressure to overthrow the Girondins in June 1793. However, the

Jacobins did not control the *sans-culottes*, and *sans-culotte* pressure exercised through the sections, their leaders in the Cordeliers Club and the commune ensured that two leaders (Collot d'Herbois and Billaud-Varenne) were put on the CPS in September 1793 and that Girondin leaders were put on trial and executed in October 1793. The *sans-culottes*, and leaders like Hébert and Ronsin, advocated and perpetrated dechristianisation in the autumn of 1793. However, their influence, perhaps at its peak during this period of Terror, was short lived. In December, the Law of 14 Frimaire began to re-establish central government control, and the purging of the Hébertists and the closing of radical clubs in early 1794 was to mark the end of their effective influence.

In what ways and with what success did *sans-culottes* influence the course of the revolution?

What was the impact of war, economic crisis and religious division on the course of the revolution?

War

It should be clear that the onset and course of war had a decisive impact on the way the revolution developed. This section picks out a few key ideas.

In part the Legislative Assembly declared war in the first place to unify the French behind the revolution, but its effect was to divide France deeply and to make the revolution more radical. Its first victim was the monarchy, overthrown as Prussian forces advanced on Paris amidst accusations of betrayal. The chief proponents of war, the Girondins, were ironically to be amongst its victims when victory turned to defeat once more in the spring of 1793 and the Girondin General Dumouriez went over to the enemy. Thereafter the emergency created by defeat in war and counter-revolution at home was to justify the introduction of Terror. When defeat turned to victory once more, especially with the victory at Fleurus in June 1794, the rationale for the Terror finally disappeared and its leader, Robespierre, was overthrown.

So there was a pattern to events. Defeats in war radicalised the revolution as scapegoats were sought and cries of betrayal were raised. In August 1792 the victim was the king; in September the victims were the 'suspects' massacred in the prisons. The euphoria of victories after Valmy that September led the assembly to pass the Edict of Fraternity, which effectively declared revolution was for export, and by taking war beyond French frontiers widened its scope. France in the spring of 1793 found itself at war not only with Austria and Prussia, but with the Dutch, the Spanish and the British. The demands of the war, through conscription, helped provoke the revolt in the Vendée. On the defensive, threatened with invasion and internal rebellion, the revolutionary government introduced an early version of total war – the *levée en masse* of August 1793 – that was to change the nature of warfare and ensure the tide turned once more to victory. But whilst the emergency lasted, the

Montagnards were forced to accept some of the demands of the *sans-culottes*. Victory in the spring and early summer of 1794 brought calls for moderation and the Terror was reined in after July 1794.

Economic crisis

In general, there was a coincidence between times of economic hardship and significant turning points in the revolution. Bread prices reached their peak in Paris between 12 and 14 July 1789; the Great Fear coincided with this time of great hardship. A shortage of bread in Paris provoked the march of the women and the National Guard to Versailles in October that same year. Renewed economic problems and inflation caused by the depreciation of the *assignats* coincided with the emergency provoked by war in the early summer of 1792 which led to the eventual overthrow of the king. Renewed hardship in spring 1793 led to *sans-culotte* calls for the Maximum. The Montagnards sought to exploit this economic discontent to overthrow the Girondins at the end of May. Economic demands were central to *sans-culotte* demands in September which led to the increased rigour of the Terror and the revolutionary armies of the autumn of 1793. Similarly relative economic stability was accompanied by relative political stability, best illustrated by the celebrations of the first anniversary of the revolution in the Fête de la Fédération in July 1790.

> Draw up a timeline showing periods of economic crisis. How far do the periods of crisis coincide with major *journées*?

It was not economic crisis alone that provoked radical shifts in the course of the revolution. The economic crisis of 1789 was, of course, accompanied by a political crisis. The events of the summer of 1792 also coincided with defeat in war, and those of 1793 with both war and counter-revolution. Whilst economic issues were of great importance to the *sans-culottes,* they were also concerned about the course of political developments, and sought a political system that would more readily reflect their needs.

Religious division

The Civil Constitution of the Clergy and the associated oath, coupled with the rejection of the revolution by the pope, began to persuade many in France to work against it. The overthrow of the king in August 1792 hardened attitudes. Suspects were rounded up and many were massacred in the First Terror of September 1793. At this point fear of counter-revolution was probably much greater than its reality. The demands of war provoked the first outbreak of popular counter-revolution. The attempt to raise troops in the spring of 1793 finally provoked the outbreak of resistance in the Vendée and other parts of western France. The causes were a combination of relatively high taxation and urban versus rural **tensions**.

> These **tensions** included the purchase of *biens nationaux* by urban bourgeoisie, religion and conscription.

These issues merged in rejection of the revolution and support for the Catholic church and royalism. This popular resistance tended to be local in character. Rebels were not prepared to move much beyond their local districts, and the revolutionary forces were in the end able to deal with the revolt piecemeal, with a final defeat of rebel forces in December 1793. Civil war in the west was accompanied by excesses on both sides; there was a campaign of total destruction by the army led by General Westermann and the terrible excesses of the representative-on-mission Carrier at Nantes. Despite these extreme measures, or perhaps because of them, counter-revolution and resistance remained endemic in western France for the rest of the 1790s.

What were the main features of counter-revolution during the period 1789–95?

Conclusion

Explaining the course of the revolution is not straightforward. A range of factors play a part – the actions and decisions of individuals, ideas, attitudes to religion, political groups and clubs, fear of counter-revolution, economic crisis, war, reactions to different styles of government, the ordinary people of Paris and the provinces and so on. These and other factors all combine in different ways at different times to affect the course of the revolution. The radicals of 1789 were the moderates of 1792, the radicals of 1791 were the moderates of 1792–93, the various radicals of the autumn of 1793 became the enemies of the revolution in 1794. By 1795 moderates were once more in charge, seeking to contain threats from both the right and the left, a difficult balancing act that, in a state of war, was perhaps inevitably going to lead to the increasing involvement of the army in politics. The army was used by the government to crush disorder and then to purge the new elected assemblies during the years 1795–99. In the end, Robespierre's prediction that war would lead to the domination of France by a 'Messiah in army boots' was to prove prophetic. In a *coup d'état* in November 1799 Napoleon Bonaparte effectively seized power in France.

Summary questions

1 Give *two* main reasons why the king was overthrown in August 1792.

2 Compare the importance of *three* main causes of political instability in France between August 1792 and July 1794.

3 Napoleon and Europe: France, 1799–1815

FOCUS questions

◆ How did Napoleon come to power?

◆ What was the nature of Napoleon's reforms in France under the Consulate?

◆ How did Napoleon make his position secure?

◆ To what extent was Napoleon a dictator?

Significant dates

1769	Birth of Napoleon in Corsica.
1793	Napoleon helps relieve the siege of Toulon.
1796	Napoleon appointed commander of the army of Italy.
1798	Napoleon's expedition to Egypt.
1799	Coup of Brumaire brings Napoleon to power.
1800	Constitution of the Year VIII, Napoleon is first consul.
1801	Concordat with the pope.
1802	Revision of the Constitution makes Napoleon first consul for life.
1804	Napoleon becomes hereditary emperor; the Civil Code is published.
1807	Napoleon abolishes the Tribunate.
1814	Napoleon abdicates.
1815	Napoleon's Hundred Days.

Overview

In 1840 Napoleon's remains were brought back from St Helena where, on his defeat in 1815, he had been exiled and had died. They were interred with great ceremony in a specially constructed crypt at the Hôtel des Invalides in Paris. His massive **tomb** (inside the grand sarcophagus are six coffins, one inside the other) is surrounded by tributes to his great military victories and also to his supposed domestic achievements in law, religion, education and so on. This

This **tomb**, like the Arc de Triomphe and other monuments around Paris, is a physical representation of the Napoleonic legend.

chapter is concerned with the Napoleonic legend in so far as it relates to his rule of France. The legend suggests Napoleon was the man who brought stability and unity back to France and was an enlightened ruler anxious to bring lasting reforms beneficial to the French people and to consolidate the gains of the revolution.

How far is this picture of Napoleon as the great reformer, the healer of divisions and the heir to the revolution accurate? What was the true nature of his achievements? Was he a military dictator or an enlightened statesman who had the interests of the French people at heart? To what extent should Napoleonic France be seen as a police state?

How did Napoleon come to power?

Napoleon's rise to power, from son of a minor Corsican noble to first consul of France at the age of 30, is remarkable. He had his share of good fortune and favourable circumstances, and he had the talent, ambition and energy to take best advantage of the opportunities that emerged. He was born in 1769, soon after France acquired Corsica from Genoa. His status as the son of a noble enabled him to win a place at a preparatory school in Brienne and then to train as an artillery officer in Paris. Though not directly involved in the central events of 1789, Napoleon – like a number of young officers – welcomed the revolution. When war came in 1792 and the king was overthrown, Napoleon remained loyal to the regime, while many of his fellow officers chose to emigrate. In late 1793 he proved his potential by helping to secure victory over the British in Toulon. As a reward for his bravery and leadership he was promoted to brigadier general at the age of 24. He was careful to keep on good terms with the revolutionary authorities in Paris during the Terror, and was lucky not to suffer like others when Robespierre was overthrown in 1794 (see page 66). From then on, his star was in the ascendant. He won the gratitude of the regime for his crushing of the **Vendémiaire rising** in Paris in 1795 and in 1796 was given command of the French forces fighting in Italy. It was here that he proved his generalship by securing a number of victories over superior Austrian forces and forcing them to make peace on his terms at Campo Formio in 1797. Napoleon was hailed as a hero in France. It was perhaps in Italy that he began to show his wider ambition, because he acted in making peace with the Austrians without authority from the French government. The government was presented with a *fait accompli* so beneficial to France that it could not object. He had also, in 1797, sent one of his generals to help purge the assembly of royalists. The use of armed forces in this way inevitably increased the political role of the army and indicated the increased risk posed by an ambitious general. It was partly out of concerns about Napoleon's ambitions

The **Vendémiaire rising** was a popular royalist movement in Paris that Napoleon crushed with his 'whiff of grapeshot' – by blasting away the rioters with cannon and musket fire. It was the last popular rising on the streets of Paris until 1830. This and similar events Napoleon had witnessed earlier in the revolution explain his great fear of the mob.

that the French government agreed to send him on his Egyptian campaign in 1798.

His victories there, talked up in the bulletins he sent back to France, increased his reputation at a time when France was once more hard pressed, by the forces of the Second Coalition (Austria, Britain and Russia). News of French defeats, and his own increasingly perilous position in Egypt, persuaded Napoleon to return to France. By the time he returned, the danger posed by the Second Coalition had receded but a number of leading politicians, led by Abbé Sieyès, were looking for a general to help them force a reform of the Constitution to strengthen the government and protect it from both extreme republicans and royalists. Having failed to persuade any other leading general, they approached Napoleon. He agreed, but was not to prove the tame general the conspirators had envisaged.

The Coup of Brumaire was carefully prepared. Napoleon was placed in control of the Paris garrison and his brother Lucien made president of one of the two legislative bodies. Both were moved away from the centre of Paris to Saint-Cloud to avoid any possible crowd trouble. It was then Napoleon's role to declare the assembly suspended. He very nearly bungled this, but the coup succeeded. The army remained loyal and Paris quiet. **Abbé Emmanuel Sieyès** was now free to devise and implement his revised Constitution. However, it was not to be. Napoleon refused to retreat into the background and instead forced Sieyès to make concessions.

What was the nature of Napoleon's reforms in France under the Consulate?

Napoleon's changes to government and administration

When Sieyès invited Napoleon to help him overthrow the **Directory**, he intended that after the coup Napoleon would stand aside and let him redraw the Constitution. But this was never Napoleon's intention. He was not about to give up the political prominence the coup had given him. However, he had to tread carefully. The coup was not secure, even if Paris was quiet. He had sought to win acceptance by claiming the coup was intended to secure the gains of the revolution, and to win over the army he had to pose as the defender of liberty. He therefore negotiated with Sieyès on the basis of the latter's proposals. Napoleon agreed with **Sieyès's concept** of the general nature of the Constitution, but whereas Sieyès envisaged political authority being shared between three consuls, Napoleon wanted political authority concentrated in his own hands. In the end he agreed to three consuls, but the second and third consuls would only have the right to be consulted over policy; they would have no independent executive authority. He himself would be first consul. Neither

Abbé Emmanuel Sieyès (1748–1836) was a Catholic priest whose essay 'What is the Third Estate?' was influential in provoking the debate over the demands for constitutional government that recognised the principle of popular sovereignty in early 1789. He was a constant figure during the revolutionary years, helping to frame the 1791 Constitution, and a prominent politician during the Directory. Frustrated at French political instability, he was a major instigator of the *coup d'état* that brought Napoleon to power in November 1799. Whilst his influence helped shape the Constitution of the Year VIII (the Consulate) he was unable to prevent Napoleon from making himself effective ruler of France, but he did chair the Senate. On Napoleon's defeat he was exiled to Brussels.

The **Directory** was the name given to the government under the Constitution of the Year III devised after the end of the Terror. There was a legislature made up of two elected assemblies and an executive comprising five directors. The powers of the directors were limited.

Sieyès's concept was that there should be 'authority from above and trust from below'.

Sieyès nor Napoleon wanted the legislature to have a dominant place in the Constitution. Sieyès wanted the legislative process to be divided between different bodies. In the event it was to be shared between four bodies: the Council of State which would draw up legislative proposals, the Tribunate which could discuss legislation but not vote on it, a legislative body which could vote on legislation but not discuss it, and the Senate which would consider whether the proposed legislation conformed to the Constitution. Sieyès and Napoleon recognised the need for the Constitution to acknowledge the principle of popular sovereignty, but also wanted to ensure that the common people were largely excluded from effective political power. They therefore agreed that the principle of universal manhood suffrage would be accepted, but ensured the **system of election** would be indirect and of limited influence on the legislature and executive.

The details of the Constitution of the Year VIII were hammered out over six weeks of negotiation. What emerged gave Napoleon most of what he wanted: effective political power in France. To lend legitimacy to the new Constitution it was put to the people in a **plebiscite** in 1800. The Constitution was endorsed by a margin of over 3 million votes to around 1,500.

As first consul Napoleon had immense influence over the membership of the various legislative bodies. From the national list he selected the second and third consuls and the members of the Council of State, and indirectly influenced the choice of senators, tribunes and legislators. He was to consolidate this power over the succeeding years.

In 1802 a revised constitution was issued (the Constitution of the Year X) that did away with the system of election but not the lists – eligibility for inclusion on them was now determined by tax liability. The Tribunate was purged of troublesome elements and Napoleon was made first consul for life (under the previous constitution the term of office was ten years). He could also name his successor. In 1804 a further revision was made (the Constitution of the Year XII) which recognised Napoleon as emperor. Both revised constitutions were endorsed by the people in plebiscites whose results were similar to that of 1800.

By 1804, however, the normal constitutional channels for making law were often being ignored. Napoleon preferred the constitutional device of the *senatus consultum* to issue decrees. In this way he could ensure speed of execution and avoid the potential embarrassment of criticism by the various legislative bodies. One reason for the purging of the Tribunate in 1802 had been criticism by some members of his proposals for the Civil Code (see page 81).

Napoleon quickly established, therefore, effective control over the legislative process. He established a similar control over the executive. Under the Constitution he could appoint the second and third consuls, government

The **system of election** was that in each commune the electors voted 10 per cent of their number to be on a communal list. These then elected 10 per cent of their number to be on a *département* list, who in turn elected 10 per cent to be on a national list. From the names on this final list, the members of the various legislative bodies were chosen.

A **plebiscite** is a popular vote, a referendum.

The Latin term *senatus consultum* means 'the Senate having been consulted' and described a device for issuing decrees which avoided the necessity of going through the normal legislative process. Napoleon made increasing use of this means from early on in the Consulate.

Napoleon as first consul. In what ways does this painting by Ingres stress Napoleon's role as a civilian ruler?

ministers, the prefects of the *départements* (counties) of France and the mayors of larger communes. The first three were appointed from the national list and the last from the communal lists. At the centre there was no cabinet system – individual ministers reported directly to Napoleon. All effective decision making was concentrated in his hands – no minister or prefect, for instance, could take action unless sure that it was authorised by Napoleon. This was top-down government, centralised and authoritarian. Even at the local level, holders of government posts were appointed from above, not elected from below. Napoleon's control of the government system was more absolute than that of the monarchy that ruled France before 1789.

Overall, by 1804 Napoleon had effectively established a dictatorship. The gestures towards revolutionary notions of **popular sovereignty** were largely without substance. Napoleon himself would have denied this. He might have pointed to the evidence of the plebiscites to support that. However, analysis of the massive votes in favour has undermined their credibility. The organiser of the 1800 plebiscite, Napoleon's brother Lucien – perhaps worried at the Jacobin sympathies of many soldiers – simply added 500,000 votes to the 'yes' column for the army. Many local officials similarly doctored the results, and a

In what ways can the Constitution of the Year VIII be seen as upholding the revolutionary principle of popular sovereignty?

In what ways can it be seen as undermining this principle?

Napoleon said: 'My policy is to govern men as most of them wish to be governed. It is in this way, I believe, that **popular sovereignty** is acknowledged.'

truer figure for the 'yes' vote has been estimated at about 1.5 million, a quarter of the total electorate. What is more, the system of voting was open rather than by secret ballot and the question in the plebiscite only sought approval for a decision that had already been taken. But, whatever the doubts about the process, the plebiscites did lend **legitimacy** to Napoleon's rule and at least suggest a lack of mass opposition. Some historians have referred to Napoleon's rule as 'plebiscitary dictatorship'.

The power of the plebiscite to give **legitimacy** was recognised by twentieth-century dictators. Hitler, for instance, used a plebiscite to justify his annexation of Austria in 1938.

Reforms under the Consulate

Much of the claim that Napoleon was more than a dictator rests on the nature of the reforms he introduced into France under the Consulate. Not only the Constitution was reformed, but also religion, the judiciary, the legal system, education, the finances and the economy.

Although no friend, **Pope Pius VII**, writing after the final defeat of Napoleon in 1815, paid tribute to Napoleon's religious policy. The Concordat (agreement) with Pius VII was certainly a major achievement and arguably a masterstroke in reconciling many French Catholics to the Napoleonic regime. Ever since the seizure of church lands in 1789, the imposition of the Civil Constitution of the Clergy in 1790 and the introduction of an oath of loyalty to the revolution the same year (see page 46), Catholicism had been a divisive factor in France. Once the pope had denounced the revolution in 1791 it became associated with counter-revolution and support for a restoration of monarchy. Napoleon seized the opportunity offered by the election of a new pope, Pius VII, in 1800 to seek reconciliation between France and Rome. His **motives** were not born from religious conviction, but from political calculation. If he could win papal endorsement of his regime, the link between Catholicism and royalist unrest would be broken and the vast majority of French people would have one fewer excuse for opposition. What is more, the priest in every parish could become a vehicle for Napoleonic propaganda. But Napoleon wanted more than this. His price for reconciliation was high – effective state control of the church and church appointments, a clerical oath of loyalty to the state and acceptance of the loss of church lands during the revolution. In return he was willing to offer recognition of Catholicism as the 'religion of the majority of Frenchmen', the restoration of Sunday worship and state responsibility for the payment of clergy. Pius VII would have liked more, but his negotiating position was not strong – the French army had effective control of Italy. After long deliberation, the Concordat was eventually agreed in July 1801, more than a year after the opening of negotiations.

It was a remarkable achievement, but not one without its dangers for Napoleon, for many in France saw the Catholic church as fundamentally anti-revolutionary. Partly to assuage such concerns about the new religious

Pope Pius VII wrote: 'The pious and courageous initiative of 1801 moves us to forget and pardon the subsequent wrongs. The Concordat was a Christian and heroic act of healing.'

Napoleon's **motives** were made clear when he said: 'In religion I do not see the mystery of the Incarnation but the mystery of social order.'

framework, Napoleon – without papal agreement – added the 'Organic Articles' to the Concordat in April 1802. These guaranteed the revolutionary principle of religious toleration and made the Protestant and Jewish churches similarly subject to state authority. In the shorter term the Concordat did reconcile the Catholic church to the regime, help to pacify unrest in the Vendée and help secure the Napoleonic regime. The effective control of the church was a clear advantage to Napoleon. Bishops became public servants – 'prefects in purple' – whilst the village *curé* said prayers for Napoleon and exhorted his flock to be loyal. Napoleon was able to persuade Pius VII to attend his imperial coronation in December 1804. Although the new emperor crowned himself, the presence of the pope symbolised the Catholic church's endorsement of the new title.

Just as prefects and bishops were Napoleon's appointees, so were judges. Judges of the criminal and civil courts and magistrates were chosen from the *département* lists, whilst the members of the single Supreme Court of Appeal were elected by the Senate from the national list. Alongside this system of justice were special courts set up in 1801 to deal summarily with those suspected of sedition. Consisting of army officers and magistrates, the courts, without the help of a jury, tried defendants who were denied any right of appeal.

The legal system inherited from the *ancien régime* and the revolution was chaotic. Attempts during the 1790s to bring together the laws into a single uniform code that applied equally across the whole of France had failed, but Napoleon was to achieve it. In 1804 he published the **Civil Code** that still forms the basis of French law. The code, followed by codes for civil procedure (1806), commerce (1807), criminal procedure (1808) and punishment (1810), was the product of a committee of legal experts, whose work was considered in over a hundred sessions of the Council of State, often chaired by Napoleon personally. The code, whilst enshrining many of the achievements of the revolution, included a number of illiberal measures. On the one hand, it confirmed the abolition of feudalism, equality before the law and freedom of conscience, and gave fixed title to those who had bought church and *émigré* lands during the 1790s. On the other, it reintroduced slavery to the French colonies, gave employers the upper hand in wage disputes and compelled workers to carry a passbook or *livret*, effectively limiting their freedom of movement. It also reflected Napoleon's views about the subordinate position of **women** and children. Whilst a man could imprison an adulterous wife or disobedient child, a married woman had few property rights and could only sue for divorce if a husband insisted on his mistress sharing the family home.

A similar sentiment informed his attitude towards **education**. Napoleon was otherwise convinced of the necessity of education: 'Public education should be the first object of government. Everything depends upon it, the

What advantages were there for Napoleon and the pope in agreeing to the Concordat?

What disadvantages were there?

In exile on St Helena after 1815, Napoleon was to claim: 'My glory is not to have won 40 battles – what nothing will destroy, what will live eternally, is my **Civil Code**.'

A flavour of Napoleon's attitude to **women** is given by his view that: 'In France women are considered too highly. They should not be regarded as equal to men. In reality they are nothing more than machines for producing children. Disorder would be introduced into society if women abandoned the state of dependence which is their rightful position.'

Napoleon said: 'Public **education** does not suit women, as they are not called upon to live in public; manners are everything for them: marriage is their whole estimation.'

In what ways did Napoleon's education and legal reforms follow the principles of the revolution? In what ways did they go against them?

The **Imperial University** was in some respects a kind of early nineteenth-century Ofsted, to oversee the curriculum and inspect schools. As in other areas, this was a centralised system based on authority and control from above.

Review the last two sections (pages 76–82). What evidence can you find to support the view that Napoleonic government was highly centralised and authoritarian?

present and the future. Above all we must secure unity: we must be able to cast a whole generation in the same mould.' For the masses Napoleon viewed education as only necessary in this respect. Obedience to the regime was required and he left the task of inculcating this attitude to the church. He also recognised the need to ensure a steady flow of well-trained and loyal servants to fill both the officer corps of his army and official positions in the administration. In 1802 he instituted a system of state-run *lycées*, or secondary schools, for the sons of officers and notables. In these 37 schools the curriculum was closely supervised. Free thinking was discouraged. Schools taught a utilitarian curriculum based around French, mathematics, history, science and geography and inculcated both military values and loyalty to the regime. Alongside this state system, independent and Catholic schools continued to flourish, despite high fees. In order to bring such schools under closer government supervision, in 1806 Napoleon set up the **Imperial University**.

The tightening of control by the centre was also a feature of financial reforms introduced during the Consulate. Throughout the 1790s revolutionary governments had failed to balance the government books. Napoleon was determined to do so. He began by bringing tax collection under the control of the Ministry of Finance, developing a hierarchy of paid tax collectors and building up a comprehensive tax register. He ensured the flow of credit at reasonable rates of interests by guaranteeing the payment of interest on government debt. This was partly organised through the Bank of France founded in January 1800, which became responsible for the management of government bonds. The credit and credibility of previous governments had been undermined partly by the inflation associated with paper currency. Napoleon also increased financial confidence by reintroducing a metal currency (with a gold and silver content). By these measures he was able to balance the budget by 1802.

Successful financial management was aided by a range of other factors. Military victory in 1801 brought plunder whilst peace in 1802 reduced costs. Similarly, economic policies such as the offer of credit to businesses, the buying-up of foreign grain stocks to ensure bread-price stability and then a series of good harvests all contributed to the healthy economic climate of the Consulate.

How did Napoleon make his position secure?

Opposition to Napoleon

Napoleon was faced with two problems: he needed to deal with opposition to the new regime and had to win support for (or at least acceptance of) it. Some of the policies pursued in relation to one problem would have an effect on the other.

There were three main areas of opposition to the regime. The first was the Jacobin left. One of the reasons why Sieyès had come to the conclusion that the Directory needed reforming was the threat from the left – the Jacobins wanted a more democratic and radical republic. On his return from Egypt in October 1799, Napoleon had been approached by Jacobin leaders to lead a left-wing coup but had declined. The Jacobins had much potential support in the army and amongst the lower classes in the towns. The second source of opposition was the royalist right. Royalist unrest had been an endemic feature of the 1790s, strong in the west of France and helped by *émigrés* abroad and occasionally foreign powers. While Napoleon was seizing power in Paris royalist unrest had broken out in the west, especially in **Brittany**. The third source of opposition was liberals like **Benjamin Constant** and **Madame de Staël**, who resented the dictatorship Napoleon was establishing and wanted the restoration of a constitution in which the power of the executive was more clearly limited by the legislature and which would guarantee such rights as freedom of speech and of the press. Criticisms from such people were stifled by the censorship policies described below and the purging of the Tribunate in 1802.

Napoleon adopted a range of policies to eliminate opposition which can broadly be characterised as a combination of carrot and stick. The most immediate threat appeared to be from the royalists, given the rebellion in the west. In the immediate term Napoleon offered the carrots of amnesty if the rebels laid down their arms, **concessions on religion** and an end to laws which attacked *émigrés*. These measures of reconciliation were backed up by the stick of military repression. When the amnesty ran out in January 1800, Napoleon ordered the army under General Brune to adopt a hard policy towards the rebels: 'If it comes to action be active and severe: it is the only way to shorten a war, and to make it deplorable to mankind.' By April the Chouannerie had been crushed – there was no more widespread royalist unrest during the Napoleonic period.

There was still a royalist threat, but that strategy was now effectively limited to assassination attempts and reliance on foreign support. Two examples illustrate Napoleon's approach. In 1804 the government became aware of a plot involving the Chouan leader Cadoudal, dissident generals (Pichegru and Moreau) and a member of the Bourbon royal family, identified as the duc d'Enghien. The duc was captured in Baden, brought to Paris, summarily tried and executed. Cadoudal suffered the same fate, Pichegru 'committed suicide' in his cell and Moreau was banished. The execution of the duc d'Enghien shocked Europe and arguably persuaded the British that a Bourbon restoration was the only alternative to Napoleon.

It was the last royalist assassination plot. That of 24 December 1800 was one of the first. A bomb was meant to kill Napoleon on the way to the Opéra.

The rebels in **Brittany** were known as Chouans and the unrest as the Chouannerie.

Benjamin Constant (1767–1830) was a moderate republican during the Revolution and became a liberal critic of Napoleon's regime. This led to his going into exile in 1803. He was the lover of Madame de Staël. He returned to France during the first restoration and was the author of Napoleon's proposed liberal constitution – the *Acte additionelle* – (see page 93) during the Hundred Days. After Napoleon's fall he remained in France as a liberal deputy in the assembly.

Madame de Staël (1766–1817) was the daughter of Louis XVI's Swiss finance minister, Necker (see page 17). An educated and intelligent woman, she was a supporter of the revolution in 1789, but left France during the Terror. During the Directory she hosted an influential salon (where intellectuals and politicians met to discuss the issues of the day). Whilst welcoming Napoleon at first, she became one of his sharpest critics after 1802, regarding him as the oppressor of Europe. This led to her exile between 1804 and 1814.

The **concessions on religion** allowed Christian worship on a Sunday.

It exploded, killing and maiming between 39 and 78 people, but missed Napoleon. Although Fouché, the minister of police, knew better, the plot was blamed initially on the Jacobins. Napoleon used the assassination attempt as an excuse to deport 129 Jacobin leaders and arrest many more. The example was enough to neutralise the threat from extreme republicans.

In the longer term, containment and repression of opposition depended on the efficiency and effectiveness of local government, directed from the centre by the Ministry of the Interior, and also on the work of the Ministry of Police. The crucial officials at the *département* level were the **prefects**. These 'little emperors' were the link between the centre and the provinces. They were the eyes, ears and hands of the government at a local level, and took their instructions from the Ministry of the Interior and Napoleon. In relative terms, this system was both efficient and effective.

In relation to subversion, the Ministry of Police – first under **Joseph Fouché** and, after 1810, under Savary – was most important. 'Police' in this context refers to the idea of national security, rather than the 'bobby on the beat'; indeed one of its arms was the Sureté, still the French equivalent of the Special Branch. There was a gendarmerie of regular police which grew to a strength of around 20,000 men. The ministry's main purpose was to keep a close watch on all forms of subversion. It did this through the use of spies and informers. Fouché reported daily to Napoleon on the state of public opinion. Napoleon also had his own personal spies who acted as a check on Fouché's reports. *Département* prefects also had a responsibility to keep a watch on public opinion and similarly sent reports to Napoleon. Those suspected of subversion could be tried before special courts, imprisoned, sent to penal colonies or kept under house arrest. The Ministry of Police also had responsibility for censorship, prison surveillance and monitoring of food prices.

The effective police operation prevented opposition from becoming open, and increasingly strict censorship helped deny critics and opponents the oxygen of publicity. However committed he was to revolutionary principles like equality before the law and careers open to talents, Napoleon certainly did not believe in freedom of the **press**. From the start he wished to control the flow and nature of information reaching the public. In January 1800 the number of newspapers in Paris was reduced from 73 to 13, and in 1810 to 4. The press bureau of the Ministry of Police kept a close watch on all publications, and editors were forbidden from printing anything defamatory about the regime. Increasingly they relied on official bulletins or articles written in the government newspaper *Le Moniteur*. Not only were newspapers censored, but plays, books and art as well.

The other side of censorship was, of course, propaganda. A deliberate attempt was made to ensure that the right messages got full publicity in all media. Napoleon had shown a keen grasp of news management from his early days as a general. As he said: 'The truth is not half so important as what people think to be true.' His army bulletins, which he ensured reached Paris first, made sure his message was propagated. For instance, the Battle of Marengo was not a near disaster but a planned and decisive victory. Napoleon also recognised the power of imagery. He employed a number of painters – David, Ingres, Gros and others – to paint him in various modes (see below, page 86 and front cover), as the statesman, the romantic military hero, the Roman emperor. The Arc de Triomphe, begun in 1808, is a celebration of his victories.

Punishment, police, censorship and propaganda are all features we associate today with the notion of a police state. These elements were all important in containing opposition and securing obedience to the regime. Napoleon also sought to bind people positively, to win their active loyalty. In his own mind he was a latter-day Charlemagne or Alexander, a ruler who combined military prowess with enlightened rule and a desire to reconcile all to the regime. In relation to domestic policy, therefore, repression was to go hand in hand with reform and reconciliation. The 1790s had been racked with division and political instability, factional politics, disorder and economic problems. On the one

Napoleon visiting the plague victims of Jaffa, by Gros. What does the picture show Napoleon doing? (The title is a clue.) What impression of Napoleon is the painter intending we should have from his actions here? Who might Napoleon be compared to here? (Think about what he is doing and where he is.) Why was such a picture painted? See also the cover picture, *Napoleon crossing the Alps*, by David. Look at the way Napoleon and his mount are painted. What image of Napoleon is conveyed here? Consider also the names on the stone in the bottom left-hand corner. With whom is Napoleon being linked and why?

The coronation of Napoleon I, by David. The title of this painting is a little deceptive because Napoleon was not crowned by the pope but by himself. What message is this painting aiming to convey? Look closely at the people around Napoleon. Who are in attendance? Where are they looking? Look at the clothes. What do they convey?

hand, Napoleon wanted to solve the problems facing France; on the other, he sought to unite the French people under his rule.

How did Napoleon aim to reconcile the people to the regime? The policy was called *ralliément*. Napoleon portrayed himself as standing above the factions and divisions in French political life. He would forgive and forget what people had done in the past so long as they were loyal to the regime. For instance, he allowed *émigrés* home if they were willing to accept his authority. His appointments as second and third consuls, Cambacérès and Lebrun, were an ex-member of the National Convention and an ex-servant of the *ancien régime*. This policy was followed through in his appointments throughout the government and administrative machine. His ministers and prefects, the members of the Council of State and the Senate, the deputies of the Tribunate and the Legislative Body, together represented a mixture of political backgrounds: some were new men, some nobles, some were ex-royalists and some ex-regicides. The same was true of ecclesiastical appointments: 16 ex-**refractory** bishops served alongside 12 ex-constitutionals and 32 new appointees. What appeared to matter to Napoleon was ability to do the job and loyalty, not past political affiliations.

Ability mattered. Napoleon followed the revolutionary principle of meritocracy, careers open to talents. Although he appointed judges, for example, there is no real evidence of political bias or interference in their work. They were appointed for life on the basis that they could do an effective job. Of course, eligibility for positions in state service required inclusion on the various communal, *département* and national lists. After 1802 that eligibility was linked closely to wealth – to tax liability, to be precise. Herein lies another secret of Napoleon's domestic success. He aimed to bind men of property, both bourgeois and noble, to his regime. The attractions of office – which carried salaries, status and other benefits – were one incentive dangled in front of the propertied elite. Another was a conscious effort to look after the interests of the propertied classes (often referred to as the notables) and so give them a vested interest in the maintenance of the regime. Napoleon had one distinct advantage here. The vast majority of the men of property in 1799 feared both a royalist restoration and a Jacobin republic. A royalist restoration would threaten the property (*biens nationaux*) they had acquired from the sale of church and *émigré* noble lands; whilst a democratic, egalitarian Jacobin republic carried the threat of mob rule and a similar attack on property.

In what ways did Napoleon seek to look after the interests of the middle classes and why?

Napoleon sought to allay notables' fears and protect their interests. His **proclamation** accompanying the Constitution of the Year VIII set the tone. In particular, both in the Civil Code and even more reassuringly in the Concordat with Pius VII, Napoleon guaranteed the propertied classes possession of their *biens nationaux*. Interestingly, when he became emperor in 1804 he took an oath to uphold 'equality of rights, civil and political liberty [and] the irrevocability of the sales of *biens nationaux*'. Napoleon was, quite literally it seemed, the security for the wealth of the notables. Many men of property were also the holders of government bonds; and one of Napoleon's first acts was to guarantee the payment of interest on such bonds. There would be no repudiation of debt. Napoleon also restored law and order within France. One of the features of the latter years of the 1790s had been the growth of brigandage in the countryside. Through the use of the army and special courts this problem was virtually eliminated. Education at the Napoleonic *lycées* was open to the sons of officers and men of property. Napoleon's economic and financial measures were geared to bring social and economic stability, and rises in taxation were confined to indirect taxes rather than the direct tax on land.

In the **proclamation** Napoleon said the Constitution was 'based upon the principles of representative government, and on the sacred rights of property, equality and liberty. The power it sets up will be strong and lasting. Citizens, the revolution is stabilised on the principles which began it. The revolution is over!'

For the wealthy, the Napoleonic regime offered security at the least, status and jobs for many and advancement and further wealth for some. The notables were given a strong vested interest in maintaining the regime and were crucial to its stability.

The nature of Napoleonic rule under the empire

Between 1799 and 1804 Napoleon tightened his grip on France. His coronation as emperor in 1804 suggested his position was secure and he felt less need to shelter behind revolutionary rhetoric and republican forms. But the nature of Napoleon's rule in some ways changed fundamentally after 1804.

By making himself emperor, albeit with the endorsement of the Senate and legislature and of the people in a plebiscite, Napoleon was attempting to join the club of kings, to found a dynasty bearing his name. The Napoleonic court began more and more to resemble that of an *ancien régime* monarch. His brothers and sisters were made princes of the empire in 1804, a new title of grand dignitary was introduced and in 1808 an imperial nobility was instituted, with titles ranging from count to duke. As final confirmation of this change from republican consulate to imperial dynasty, in 1810 Napoleon married Marie-Louise, the daughter of the Austrian emperor. In 1811 the dynasty appeared secured on the birth of a son.

However, this was not quite a return to *ancien régime* forms. Title depended not on birth but on wealth, and could be given as a reward for service. Napoleon created 3,263 nobles between 1808 and 1814; 60 per cent of them were military men, the rest prefects, bishops, senators, mayors and so on. A duke had to command an income of at least 200,000 francs, a baron only 15,000. Napoleon often granted estates and pensions to those who were ennobled to provide them with the necessary income. In this sense the imperial nobility links back to the notion of meritocracy and the **Legion of Honour**. The aristocracy of wealth and merit created might reconcile the old nobility with the notables (22 per cent of the new nobility were from the old). If this is what Napoleon intended, he miscalculated. According to historians like Jean Tulard, the increasing resemblance of the Napoleonic regime to an absolute monarchy aroused fears of a return to feudalism and offended a deep attachment to revolutionary rhetoric about equality, even amongst the notables.

These changes were accompanied by other developments. Revolutionary national festivals, such as that of 21 September commemorating the establishment of the republic in 1792, were gradually phased out and replaced by days to celebrate **anniversaries** related to Napoleon and his military victories. The institution of St Napoleon's Day (16 August) was a religious change that placed emphasis on Napoleon. There were others: a new catechism was issued to be taught to children and said in church. It emphasised the duty of loyalty and obedience to Napoleon and suggested that the empire's creation was God's will. A kind of cult of the emperor was developed and reinforced by the work of artists like David and Ingres, the official bulletins and the work of the poets and playwrights who were allowed to be published.

In general, after 1804 the regime became more obviously authoritarian and restrictions on freedom increased. In 1810 a system of imprisonment without trial was introduced to deal with political suspects and others. This smacked

The **Legion of Honour** was instituted in 1802 to recognise service to the regime.

The **anniversaries** included the Battle of Jena (14 October), the Coup of Brumaire (9 November) and the Battle of Austerlitz with the imperial coronation (2 December).

of the old royal power exercised under a *lettre de cachet*, but it was used selectively – even in 1814 there were just 640 such prisoners. The criminal and penal codes issued in 1808 and 1810 respectively reintroduced harsh penalties such as branding and mutilation for certain crimes. Censorship was tightened – in 1811 the number of Parisian newspapers was limited to four, with only one in each *département* (from 1810). All were dependent on the official news contained in *Le Moniteur*. The number of theatres in Paris was reduced from 33 to 8 in 1807 and any production challenging the regime was banned. Censorship had been a feature of the Napoleonic regime from the start, and it became more rigorous during the empire. Official censors were appointed, half the printing presses in Paris were closed down and publishers were required to obtain a licence and swear an oath of loyalty (1809). Writers critical of the regime faced persecution and were sometimes, like Madame de Staël, deported. Control over education (see page 82) became more direct with the creation of the Imperial University.

The retreat from republican forms towards more overtly authoritarian rule is reflected in the fate of the legislature. As early as 1802 Napoleon had purged the Tribunate; in 1807 it was abolished. The **Legislative Body** remained, passing all it was required to pass, but was called to meet less and less frequently. Napoleon preferred rule by imperial decree or *senatus consultum*.

In 1814 Napoleon was defeated by the forces of the Fourth Coalition (see page 96) and forced to abdicate. He was exiled to the island of Elba in the Mediterranean, but escaped and returned to France in March 1815. His return to power in the Hundred Days was brief but seemed to indicate a different style of rule.

To what extent was Napoleon a dictator?

The nature of Napoleon's rule has been an issue for debate ever since he seized power. Some have seen him, as Napoleon saw himself, as the saviour of France whose enlightened rule brought benefits to the French people and created institutions and reforms that would endure. Others have portrayed him as little more than a tyrant motivated by cynical self-interest who exploited France in pursuit of his personal ambitions. He has been interpreted as both the heir to the revolution and its betrayer, as both an **enlightened despot** and a military dictator, as a latter-day Charlemagne and a precursor of Hitler and Stalin. Few writers of **books and articles** about him have remained neutral.

A dictionary might define a dictator as someone who exercises sole, complete and unlimited authority within a state. Dictatorship is often associated with repression and the **machinery** of a police state. An examination of Napoleon's rule might suggest the presence of all or most of these features to

The **Legislative Body** met for only 17 days in 1811 and not at all in 1812.

The term '**enlightened despot**' was invented by historians to describe the rule of certain eighteenth-century absolute rulers who were influenced in one way or another by the Enlightenment (see page 25). 'Despot' refers to the absolute nature of such rulers' authority – they recognised few or no institutional checks. 'Enlightened' refers to the style and substance of their rule. Enlightened despots portrayed themselves less as divine right monarchs and more as the servants of their people, ruling for their benefit. Frederick II of Prussia, a patron of Voltaire, one of the great enlightened *philosophes*, described himself as the 'father of his people'.

There have been over 250,000 **books and articles** about Napoleon. The number is constantly increasing.

This **machinery** includes arbitrary infringement of civil liberties, arrest of political opponents and a secret police.

some degree. His position as first consul and then emperor certainly gave him a great deal of power within the state. The centralised nature of government and administration also supports the notion of authority from above. Moreover, he did enforce censorship and made great use of propaganda. In addition, his Ministry of Police and the use made of spies and informers, special courts and arbitrary imprisonment would support the notion of a police state. But is this a fair representation of Napoleonic rule? He maintained, even through the empire, bodies like the Senate and the Legislative Body which could limit his freedom of action. He introduced the Civil Code, which guaranteed legal rights, and he introduced a number of reforms that arguably brought real benefits to the people. Perhaps to describe him as merely a dictator fails to do him justice.

So was Napoleon an enlightened despot? He sought to portray his rule as directed towards the interests of the French people and as consolidating the gains of the French Revolution. By the Constitution of the Year VIII, he appeared to recognise limitations to his power. But was this any more than propaganda? Was Napoleon a dictator who sought to conceal his power behind a constitutional façade?

Did Napoleon's policies introduce **enlightened** reforms? It is possible to argue that in many areas Napoleon's rule at least appears enlightened, but what was the motive behind the reforms? Was it to benefit the people or to secure loyalty, obedience and the resources to pursue his wider ambitions abroad? There were certainly some unenlightened aspects to his rule – such as the denial of a free press – and there was perhaps some pretty unenlightened thinking behind the details of the supposedly enlightened reforms. Were his education reforms motivated by a concern for the people and academic freedom or by a desire for loyal subjects and trained servants? How enlightened were his legal reforms? The codification of the law, the confirmation of the abolition of feudalism, the principle of equality before the law all seemed to be enlightened; but what of his view of women, attitude to workers, reintroduction of slavery and of arbitrary arrest, and use of inhumane punishments in the Penal Code? If the label 'enlightened despot' doesn't quite fit, perhaps the description of him as the 'heir to the revolution' fits better.

Robespierre warned in the 1790s that if the French Revolution went to war, the consequences would be that France would eventually be ruled by a 'Messiah in army boots'. His prediction seemed to come true in November 1799 in the Coup of Brumaire. In this sense, Napoleon can be seen as the direct heir to the revolution: here was a general who portrayed himself as the saviour of a France at war, divided, disorderly and weak. However, the issue is wider and usually seen in terms of the ideas and principles of the French Revolution. Whether he is regarded as a dictator will depend on the ideas and principles

The key **enlightened** ideas are:

government and administration should be rational – both efficient and uniform in application;

religious toleration – people should have 'freedom of conscience' and freedom to practice their chosen religion;

people have equal rights – particularly equality before the law and freedom from arbitrary arrest;

freedom of speech and the press – censorship was wrong because it prevented the exchange of ideas and the progress of mankind;

promotion of education;

in the sphere of economics, free trade and equal taxation (the preference was for direct taxes on property rather than indirect taxes on essentials like salt which disproportionately hit the poor);

'careers open to talents'.

one associates with the French Revolution. Broadly, those include popular sovereignty, property, equality and liberty; but they changed and developed through the 1790s. The centralisation and democracy based on universal suffrage associated with the republic of 1792–94 were very different from the indirect democracy, federalism and constitutional monarchy of 1789–92.

Popular sovereignty is the idea that at root all political power in the state is derived from the people. It means that government must in some way be answerable to the people. During the revolution this was achieved through some kind of elected assembly which made law and to which government was answerable. Napoleon could claim to have elected bodies which were involved in the law-making process. Under the terms of the Constitution of the Year VIII, the law-making institutions – the Council of State, the Senate, the Tribunate and the Legislative Body – were all chosen from the national list, whose members were all elected from below, initially via universal manhood suffrage. All the major constitutional changes (1800, 1802, 1804 and 1815) were put to the people in plebiscites. However, this was hardly popular sovereignty in action; effectively political power was concentrated in the hands of the first consul. Universal manhood suffrage and the elections were a fairly transparent façade for Napoleon's authoritarian rule. The plebiscites, whilst producing overwhelming majorities in favour of each constitutional innovation, were more or less fixed (see page 79). Napoleon himself tacitly acknowledged that popular sovereignty, as normally understood, was being ignored when he said that he believed that popular sovereignty consisted in ruling people as they would wish to be ruled. He believed he had a particular insight into this. In relation to the nature of government, Napoleon rejected the decentralised bottom-up approach adopted in the early years of the revolution; his style was more in tune with the centralised, authoritarian model applied during the Terror to cope with the emergency of civil war and foreign invasion. On the count of popular sovereignty and accountable government, the claim that we was the 'heir to the revolution' seems spurious.

In terms of liberty, it could be argued that Napoleon fundamentally violated revolutionary principles. Whilst he allowed religious freedom by tolerating all religions (as expressed in the Organic Articles), the hierarchies of the various churches were under his control. What is more, there was no freedom of speech. Censorship was a key element of Napoleonic rule of France, and those suspected of sedition could be tried and punished outside the normal framework of the law. Nor was there freedom of movement for workers compelled to carry their *livret* (passbook).

In the area of equality, the Napoleonic regime does in some respects seem to have confirmed the ideas of the revolution. The principle of equality of taxation was maintained – all citizens were liable. This reflected a confirmation of the abolition of feudalism and an expressed belief in 'careers open to talents'. There was to be both formal legal equality and equality of opportunity – holding office would depend on ability, loyalty and experience, not accident of birth. But opportunity became increasingly restricted to the families of the middle class, and the notables in particular. Eligibility for government posts depended on being named on the communal, *département* or national lists and eligibility to be on these lists depended on the amount of tax one paid. Secondary education was largely restricted to the middle classes and sons of officers in the army. As for equality before the law, the answer is not clear cut; women were effectively discriminated against and slavery was reintroduced.

Rights of property were upheld, however. It was a key feature of both the Concordat and the Civil Code that the lands purchased by wealthier peasants and the middle classes from the *biens nationaux* taken from the Catholic church and *émigrés* were secure.

What conclusions can be drawn from this? One view would be that Napoleon preserved only those elements of the revolution that suited his purposes – to bind the propertied classes to his regime and to secure himself in power. Where a revolutionary principle – such as free speech – might threaten him, it was refused or modified (as in the exceptions made in respect of possible political sedition). Where a revolutionary principle might help him – as with careers open to talents – he was willing to maintain it. Additionally, he may have felt compelled to maintain some elements of the revolution, whether he wanted to or not. To challenge the abolition of feudalism, for instance, might have provoked mass peasant unrest. Certainly, as he felt more secure in power, Napoleon's attachment to certain revolutionary ideas seemed to wane. The lip-service paid to popular sovereignty by the Constitution of the Year VIII largely disappeared during the empire, and his creation of an imperial nobility seemed to contradict any commitment to equality. Napoleon was not a philosopher or even a politician with definite principles. His approach was practical and pragmatic; he would do whatever was necessary to secure his ends. If that meant buying support or acquiescence with bribes, pensions and lands, so be it. If it meant presenting himself as the heir to the revolution, so be it. If policies to secure order and obedience could be portrayed as enlightened, so much the better. What he would not do was to follow policies that might threaten his power or position. Religious toleration was one thing, freedom of the press quite another.

Napoleonic rule during the Hundred Days

Napoleon's rule of France during the Hundred Days lent some credibility to his claim on St Helena that he was aiming at a liberal France, with constitutional government and an executive answerable to the people. When he reached Paris in March 1815, he consulted with erstwhile liberal critics like Benjamin Constant over changes to the governance of France. The result was the *Acte additionnelle*, which introduced a liberal constitution guaranteeing freedom of the press, ministers responsible to the legislature and universal suffrage. As before, the constitutional changes were put to the French people in a plebiscite. Only about one fifth voted, and the result was over 1.5 million votes in favour with fewer than 6,000 against.

The likelihood is that the *Acte additionnelle*, like his Constitution of the Year VIII, was not to be a permanent solution, nor did it represent a significant change of heart on Napoleon's part. It was what was necessary to give his renewed seizure of power some credibility and some chance of support from the notables in France. Napoleon was later to confess that he considered the constitutional changes as nothing more than a temporary expedient. It would have taken more than this to convince liberals of his intentions. Most remained suspicious and aloof. His power base in the Hundred Days lay not in the notables, but in the veterans of the army and amongst the peasants and other landowners who feared a royalist restoration presaged an attack on their acquisition of *biens nationaux*.

The Hundred Days came to an abrupt end with Napoleon's defeat at Waterloo. A second abdication was followed by a second restoration. This time Napoleon's defeat was to be final and he was to serve out his days on St Helena, where he was to dictate his memoirs and so help create his own legend.

Summary questions

1 Explain *two* ways in which Napoleon dealt with opposition.

2 How far did Napoleon's rule of France change after he became emperor in 1804?

4 Napoleon and Europe: Napoleon's rise and fall

Focus questions

◆ Why was Napoleon so successful in Europe (to 1807)?

◆ Was Napoleon a great general?

◆ What factors help explain Napoleon's downfall?

Significant dates

1793	Napoleon's command of the artillery at the siege of Toulon wins him promotion to brigadier general.
1796	Napoleon is appointed commander of the army of Italy. Victories at Lodi, Castiglione, Arcola.
1797	Victory at Rivoli. Napoleon secures a victorious peace with Austria at Campoformio.
1798	Second Coalition between Great Britain, Austria and Russia against France. Napoleon invades Egypt, wins Battle of the Pyramids.
1799	Napoleon returns to France and secures power in the Coup of Brumaire.
1800	*June* Napoleon wins Battle of Marengo.
1801	Treaty of Lunéville with Austria.
1802	Treaty of Amiens with Britain.
1805	Third Coalition (Britain, Austria, Russia) against France. French fleet defeated at Trafalgar. Napoleon wins battles of Ulm (October) and Austerlitz (December). Treaty of Pressburg with Austria.
1806	Creation of the Confederation of the Rhine by Napoleon. *October* Napoleon wins twin battles of Jena and Auerstadt against Prussia. Napoleon's Berlin Decrees institute the Continental System.
1807	Indecisive Battle of Eylau against Russia. *June* Napoleon wins the Battle of Friedland against Russia. Treaties of Tilsit with Russia and Prussia; creation of grand duchy of Warsaw. French army invades Portugal. Milan Decrees extend Berlin Decrees.
1808	Spanish resistance against French starts; defeat of French army at Baylen.
1809	Napoleon wins Battle of Wagram against Austria (July); Treaty of Schönbrunn with Austria.

1810	Napoleon marries Marie-Louise of Austria.
1811	Napoleon's son, the king of Rome, is born.
1812	Napoleon invades Russia.
1813	*October* Napoleon is defeated at the Battle of the Nations at Leipzig.
1814	Paris falls and Napoleon abdicates.
1815	Napoleon returns to France.
	Napoleon is defeated at Waterloo (June) and is exiled to St Helena.
1821	Napoleon dies, possibly poisoned.

Overview

The foundation for Napoleon's rise to power, whatever other factors were involved, was his military success. It began with his command of the artillery at Toulon in 1793, when he drove the British from the port. His Italian campaign of 1796–97, when he defeated the Piedmontese and Austrian armies in a series of victories, was to make his reputation in the army and in France. He crowned this success with an Egyptian campaign in 1798 that captured the imagination of France. Once he was in power, further success came, at Marengo (1800), Ulm and Austerlitz (1805), Jena–Auerstadt (1806), Friedland (1807) and Wagram (1809). These were the major battles in a series of campaigns that saw him defeat the Great Powers of continental Europe (Austria three times, Prussia and Russia) and establish French control of the continent through direct annexation of territory and the establishment of satellite and allied states. By 1810 Napoleon's control extended from Spain in the west to St Petersburg in the east and from Denmark in the north to Naples in the south. He had redrawn the map of Europe and made kings out of brothers and relatives (see map on page 99).

What can be said in favour of regarding 1810 as the high point of Napoleon's power in Europe? What can be said against?

But Napoleon's empire was always unstable and, as he understood himself, his authority rested on his military might rather than on any legitimising principle such as hereditary monarchy. That is why he set so much store by his second marriage to Marie-Louise of the royal house of Austria, the Habsburgs, in 1810 and the birth of a son in 1811. He hoped that by marriage he would win acceptance from the established crowned heads of Europe.

Napoleon probably regarded 1810 as the high point of his empire, and in territorial extent this was justified. However, the cracks were already appearing in the fragile edifice he had built. Master of the continent he may have been, but he had not succeeded in defeating his most consistent opponent – Britain. Britain's navy controlled the seas, a fact forcefully brought home to Napoleon by the crushing defeat of the combined Franco-Spanish fleet at Trafalgar in 1805. Napoleon therefore tried to strangle Britain economically

A **coalition** is an agreement between two or more powers to act together. The French revolutionary and Napoleonic wars feature a number of different coalitions against France. We shall refer to the Second Coalition of Britain, Austria and Russia, which fought against France in 1798–1802; the Third Coalition consisting of Britain, Austria and Russia in 1805, but from 1806 of Britain, Prussia and Russia (Austria having been defeated in 1805); and the Fourth Coalition which took shape in 1813 and included all the Great Powers. Apart from the Fourth Coalition, formalised as the Quadruple Alliance by the Treaty of Chaumont in 1814, the coalitions were weak associations bound together by specific and different agreements between individual powers.

What were the key events in Napoleon's downfall?

by preventing her from trading with the continent. This so-called Continental System, whilst damaging to Britain, was not fatal and created resentment in many areas across the continent that depended on British trade. In trying to seal off the continent, Napoleon was to invade Spain and Portugal, to invade the Papal States and imprison the pope, and finally to invade Russia (1812). The first and last of these actions played a crucial role in his downfall: the so-called 'Spanish ulcer' was to prove a long-term drain on French resources, men and morale, whilst the invasion of Russia was to break the back of Napoleon's military might and encourage the development for the first time of a **coalition** of all the Great Powers against France.

The coalition armies defeated Napoleon at the Battle of the Nations in 1813, paving the way for the invasion of France and the abdication of Napoleon in 1814. His exile by the coalition powers to the island of Elba off the coast of Italy was short-lived. He returned to France in March 1815, re-established his authority in Paris and set off on an unsuccessful last bid for military glory. Such was the impact of his life that his name continued to arouse either fear and loathing or admiration and respect across Europe for the rest of the nineteenth century and beyond. The Napoleonic legacy affected French history directly through that century and arguably the next.

This chapter sets out to explain why Napoleon was so successful in Europe for so long, to consider his reputation as a general and to explain his downfall. It concludes by briefly examining the nature of the Napoleonic legend and the historical controversy about him.

Why was Napoleon successful in Europe (to 1807)?
Events between 1799 and 1807

One reason why Napoleon left Egypt in the autumn of 1799 was that he had received news of military defeats imposed on France by the Second Coalition of Britain, Austria and Russia. It seemed as though France was on the verge of being invaded. By the time Napoleon managed to get back to France by a circuitous route along the north African coast to avoid the British navy, France was no longer in immediate danger and the Second Coalition appeared to be falling apart as Russia withdrew. That said, France had lost most of its Italian conquests and faced strong Austrian forces in both northern Italy and Germany.

Trumpeting his victories in Egypt helped win Napoleon acclaim. Many saw him as a potential saviour of France, even if they were not expecting his seizure of power in the Coup of Brumaire of November 1799. Napoleon felt that if he was to secure himself in power in the aftermath of the coup and make his personal control of France a reality, he needed to bring peace – not peace at any price, but peace with honour. A decisive defeat of Austria would enable Napoleon to dictate terms and bring him support and security in France. It would also leave Britain without a continental ally and might bring it, too, to the peace table.

During 1800 Napoleon sought to play on Russian difficulties with Britain, hoping to woo Russia into taking up arms. Meanwhile, he offered peace terms that he knew Austria and Britain could not accept, to justify a military campaign. This was the second element in his strategy. Napoleon needed a quick and decisive victory. The most straightforward option would have been an attack across the Rhine against the Austrians. Instead he chose to take his army across the Alps to cut off the Austrian army currently besieging the French in Genoa from their line of communication with Vienna. The strategy worked splendidly in so far as the difficult crossing of the Alps was achieved. However, Napoleon dispersed his forces to be able to march forward more quickly and unexpectedly ran into the main Austrian army at Marengo with his force divided.

Fortunately for Napoleon, he was saved from a potentially disastrous defeat by the timely arrival of extra forces under General Desaix. Desaix's attack, which cost him his life, turned the battle into the decisive French victory Napoleon needed to secure his position in France. This victory on its own was not enough to bring the Austrians to the peace table, but their defeat at Hohenlinden in Germany at the hands of General Moreau in December did. The result was the Treaty of Lunéville (1801), in which the Austrians effectively gave up Italy to the French. Without a continental ally and exhausted by nine years of constant warfare, Britain was also willing to make peace, at **Amiens** in 1802.

Some historians would mark this as the high point of Napoleon's career. He was now secure and popular at home, having delivered peace with honour. However, the peace was to be short lived. The harsh terms imposed on Austria at Lunéville made it likely that it, too, would consider taking up arms again. British diplomacy was also active in wooing the Russians under Tsar Alexander II.

By 1804 disputes over Naples and Malta and British involvement in conspiracies against Napoleon were sufficient to provoke war once more. Napoleon prepared a new army which gathered along the Channel coast around Boulogne for an invasion of England. Meanwhile he ordered his admirals to secure control of the Channel to enable a crossing. Napoleon had little conception of the difficulties and uncertainties of naval warfare. His navy, bottled up in various ports, would need to break out, pass the British squadrons keeping watch, concentrate and then try to win at least temporary control of the Channel from the British fleet. Villeneuve managed to elude Nelson, break out

How did Napoleon combine diplomacy and warfare to win 'peace with honour' against the Second Coalition?

Amiens was no more than a truce and its terms gave both Britain and France ample excuse to find a reason for war.

from Toulon and eventually gather a sizeable Franco-Spanish fleet at Cadiz. His attempt to set out from there was intercepted by Nelson, who inflicted a decisive defeat on the French off Cape Trafalgar in October 1805.

By this time, however, Napoleon had already given up his invasion plans and instead was marching to fight the Austrians and Russians in Germany. British gold, nicknamed 'Pitt's Cavalry' (see page 108), and diplomacy had persuaded Austria and Russia to join a Third Coalition against France. Napoleon had managed to keep Prussia from joining his enemies by dangling the prospect of acquiring territory in Germany, namely the British territory of Hanover.

What ensued over the next three years proved to be the high point of Napoleonic warfare. Napoleon's *grande armée* inflicted a series of decisive defeats on his enemies. At Ulm, just as Nelson was annihilating the Franco-Spanish fleet at Trafalgar, Napoleon surrounded an Austrian army under General Mack and forced its surrender (October). He then took on a superior combined Austrian and Russian force in perhaps his greatest battle, at **Austerlitz** in December. The victory was crushing and forced Austria to make peace once more at Pressburg, on humiliating terms. Austria gave up its Italian territories and lost lands in Germany (Bavaria and Württemberg) to French allies. The following year Austria was forced to accept the territorial reorganisation of Germany, including the creation of the kingdom of Westphalia and the Confederation of the Rhine. By these acts the ancient institution of the **Holy Roman Empire** was destroyed.

Meanwhile, Prussia had joined the coalition. Its army had been the premier fighting force of the eighteenth century but it proved no match for the French. At the twin battles of Jena–Auerstadt Napoleon caught the Prussian army split into two and was able to defeat both elements so convincingly that thereafter Prussian resistance collapsed. Napoleon was able to march victoriously to Berlin.

That left the Russians. A bloody encounter took place at Eylau in a blizzard in February 1807. Although Napoleon claimed victory, it proved indecisive. However, he went on in the summer to inflict a major defeat on the tsar's forces at Friedland (June). This was sufficient to bring peace after face-to-face negotiations between Napoleon and Alexander II on a raft in the middle of the River Niemen. The result was the treaties of Tilsit (July 1807). By the first of these Russia and France became allies, Russia agreed to the creation of the grand duchy of Warsaw out of Prussian Polish lands and Russia recognised the territorial changes Napoleon had made in Holland, Germany and Italy. The second humiliated Prussia, which was forced to pay an indemnity, lose territory, accept a French army of occupation and limit the size of its own army to 42,000.

The victory at **Austerlitz** coincidentally took place on the anniversary of Napoleon's coronation as emperor.

The end of the **Holy Roman Empire** was a fact recognised by the ruler of Austria, who adopted a new title, emperor of Austria, in place of that of Holy Roman emperor.

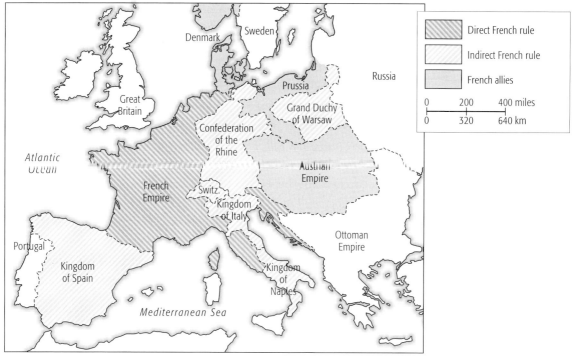

Map of Napoleonic Europe, c.1810.

By the summer of 1807, Napoleon was master of Europe and his army appeared invincible.

The reasons for Napoleon's success

Napoleon's phenomenal and rapid success has three broad elements:

- the nature of the French army;
- Napoleon's generalship;
- the relative weaknesses of Napoleon's enemies.

These three are not mutually exclusive. The relative strengths France and Napoleon enjoyed are mirrored by the relative failings of their enemies. Napoleon's generalship would not have been so successful if the quality of his forces had not been relatively high, and he would not have had the freedom to act as he did if France had been unable to provide the resources necessary or if he had not also been ruler of France.

The nature of the French army

David Chandler, a prominent military historian and admirer of Napoleon, argues convincingly that Napoleon inherited an armed force that was already superior to that of his enemies. The French army had undergone fundamental reform for two reasons. Humiliating defeats for France in the War of Austrian

List the key evidence in this section that would support the claim that Napoleon was invincible.

In **David Chandler's** words, 'the weapon was ready forged'.

Gribeauval was inspector general of the artillery in France after the Seven Years' War (1756–63). He drove through a series of reforms that improved the quality and manoeuvrability of artillery, whilst also standardising calibres and developing different cannon for different purposes.

Chevalier **Du Teil** was an artillery expert who advocated a greater role for artillery in battle. Not only should artillery open the battle, it should also be moved in the battle to continue to mow down enemy positions. He also advocated the concentration of artillery fire on particular targets. The reforms of Gribeauval made Du Teil's tactics a practical possibility.

Count **Guibert** wrote the influential *Essai général de tactique* published in 1772. In this he advocated

How did the reforms of Gribeauval and Guibert change the French army?

Succession (1740–48) and the Seven Years' War (1756–63) had led to technological, organisational and tactical developments that would improve its fighting capacities. Then the French Revolution totally overturned the nature of the army and its officer corps.

A key technological development under the guiding hand of **Gribeauval** was the manufacture of lighter, more manoeuvrable and standardised cannon. This facilitated the supply of munitions and allowed the development of new artillery tactics under **Du Teil**. The development of horse artillery, for instance, allowed the movement of cannon around the battlefield so that cannon fire could be concentrated where it was needed. Light horse artillery, in particular, could be manoeuvred to support infantry and cavalry attacks. But the favourite artillery weapon of the infantry was not the light four and six pounders, but the heavy twelve pounders, nicknamed Napoleon's 'little daughters', which used together in 'grand batteries' could have devastating effects on enemy forces. Indeed, the use of the concentrated artillery barrage was to become a notable feature of Napoleonic warfare.

Meanwhile, **Guibert** had examined the organisation of the army and promoted the use of divisions of about ten thousand men as the key unit, rather than the much smaller regiment. The divisional structure allowed flexibility and speed of movement (different divisions could move along separate lines of advance) and simplified communication and command (the commanding general needed only to communicate with a few divisional commanders rather than a large number of regimental officers). In addition Guibert examined the tactics of eighteenth-century warfare, which generally involved the movement of troops in columns and their deployment on the battlefield in lines to maximise the effectiveness of volley fire. Guibert developed a more flexible system that would allow commanders to adopt column (*ordre profond*) or line (*ordre mince*) or a mixture of both (*ordre mixte*) according to circumstances (see below). The shock and momentum of a column attack could therefore be combined with the firepower of the line on the battlefield.

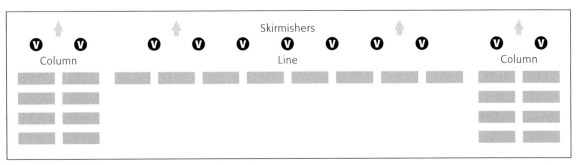

The mixed order (*ordre mixte*) formation, here applied to three battalions; those on the right and left are in columns, while that in the centre is in line. The *voltigeur* companies (V) from all the battalions form a skirmish row at the front.

The crucial developments came during the French Revolution. As a result of the revolution many officers (who were nobles) left France, leaving the officer corps severely depleted. Meanwhile, the revolution enshrined the principle of 'careers open to talents' or meritocracy. This coincidence of circumstances enabled **young officers** of talent to rise rapidly through the ranks.

Perhaps even more important was the military potential the revolution released. As a result of the pressures of foreign invasion and civil war in 1793, the revolutionary government in Paris introduced the *levée en masse*. Effectively this involved the organisation of the state for war and introduced the principle of universal conscription (it was therefore an early version of 'total war'). From 1793 France was a nation in arms. It was the duty of every citizen to contribute to the war effort; for young men this meant service in the armed forces. They served as citizen soldiers in defence of France and the revolutionary ideas of liberty and equality. Universal conscription meant that France by the mid-1790s was approaching a million men under arms. Losses could be replaced by further conscription. Napoleon was to boast that he could afford to lose 30,000 men a month.

The problem of absorbing the constant stream of raw recruits was resolved by the policy of the *amalgame* – of mixing in regiments veterans with new conscripts. The conscripts could be trained on the march and be helped by their more experienced colleagues. In this way, too, something of the martial spirit, the common *esprit de corps* was passed on.

Along with the increased size and motivation of French revolutionary armies came a change in the purpose and nature of warfare. At times the French were fighting for the survival of the revolution, at others they were threatening to overturn the European states system by wars of conquest and liberation. In the wake of victories states were annexed, frontiers redrawn, new social and political systems imposed. French armies actively sought battle and were willing to bear heavy losses to achieve victory. Because these armies were less well trained but better motivated than traditional eighteenth-century armies, reliance was placed on the shock of the column attack and the use of the bayonet rather than on the disciplines required of sustained volley fire in lines. Guibert's ideas about deploying light infantry – skirmishers – in front of the main force were developed and employed effectively by revolutionary armies.

Finally, revolutionary governments were not capable of keeping the larger revolutionary armies supplied and, although previously advocated by Guibert, almost by force of circumstance the policy of living off the land developed. Such an approach was possible because the new divisional structure allowed the army to move along separate lines of advance and the main arenas of fighting in the 1790s – northern Italy, the Low Countries and Germany –

l'ordre mixte, flexibility of formation according to need, the divisional structure (which Pierre de Bourcet had advocated for mountain warfare) and living off the land. He also speculated about the strength of an army based on a citizen soldiery. His ideas became the basis of the French army's drill book issued in August 1791.

The early career of Napoleon is a good example of the opportunities available to talented **young officers** (at the age of 27 he controlled the French army fighting in Italy), but he had had the advantage of officer training before the revolution because of his noble status. It is an exaggeration to suggest that each soldier carried a marshal's baton in his knapsack, but many of his senior officers were of modest birth. Murat, who became a marshal and king of Naples, was the son of a Gascon innkeeper; Ney, 'the bravest of the brave' (see page 120), was the son of a barrel maker; Augereau was the son of a stonemason; Jourdan was the son of a surgeon; Lannes the son of a stable-keeper; and Massena the son of a wine merchant.

How did the French Revolution change the nature of warfare?

were fertile. The effect of this policy was to give French forces the advantage of mobility over their enemies.

Was Napoleon a great general?

The army Napoleon inherited as first consul in 1799 was one army he was to hone into a supreme instrument of offensive warfare. As commander-in-chief, he was to lead it to a series of glittering victories. His talents as a general were many, although he was not without flaws. He was a born leader of men, with immense personal magnetism. He had a quality of natural authority and could charm almost anyone he met. He made effective use of his abilities to get his way. One of his aides reported him as saying, 'If I want a man sufficiently badly I would kiss his arse.' With his men, officers or rank and file, he had a familiar style that made him highly popular. He had a memory for names and faces which he put to good effect when reviewing troops and would tweak the ear of favoured soldiers.

Napoleon believed that 'a general's principal talent consists in knowing the mentality of the **soldier** and in gaining his confidence'.

He also had a keen sense of what motivated the **soldier**. For instance, when taking command in Italy of a semi-mutinous army in 1796, he promised to pay them in silver rather than the worthless paper currency. He also played on the prospect of plunder. However, it is the creation of a sense of *esprit de corps* and regimental pride that helped make the French army such a formidable force. By rewarding success and bravery and punishing failure or weakness, he played to soldiers' higher ideas of honour. The award of the Legion of Honour, other decorations and titles or swords for bravery or outstanding service all helped. His presence amongst his men on the eve of and during battles was significant, as was the impression he gave of sharing the privations of his men on campaign. His bulletins and orders of the day praised, cajoled and exalted as necessary. Overall, he created a sense of deep personal loyalty amongst his men and helped replace the motivation provided by defence of the revolution with a motivation directed towards military glory – *la gloire*. It was partly his personal impact on army morale that made the duke of Wellington remark that Napoleon's presence on the battlefield was worth 40,000 men.

Why was the ability to motivate men so important in generalship?

The remark was also a tribute to other aspects of his generalship. Napoleon's intellectual capacities were impressive. He was clear thinking, had a phenomenal memory for detail without being bogged down in it, and had so organised a mind that he could dictate to four different secretaries simultaneously. At his peak he was able to **work** up to 20 hours a day. It was this impressive intellectual capability that enabled him to combine the command of the whole army with control of the government of France and its empire. It was also why he was able to direct all his military campaigns personally without delegating significant authority to subordinates. Practically every

Napoleon claimed, '**Work** is my element. I was born and made for work.'

important decision was taken by Napoleon. The concentration of power in his hands reflects his view that 'in war men are nothing; one man is everything'.

Napoleon was master of his men. But he was also a supreme strategist and military planner. In this he was no innovator, but he was able to apply lessons he had learned from studying the great **generals** of the past and the writings of military thinkers like Guibert, Bourcet and Du Teil. His skill was not in developing a new theory of war, but in selecting from others and putting ideas into practice. He was above all a great executor. His approach to warfare was offensive. His aim was almost always to locate and destroy the enemy's main army and break the spirit of resistance. The emphasis was on a war of movement, typically involving a single, short, sharp and decisive **campaign**.

Building on the idea of autonomous divisions able to fight on their own, Napoleon developed the **corps** system. On manoeuvre, corps would advance along separate routes, moving relatively quickly and living off the land. The aim was that each army corps should be within a day's march of at least two others. Each was individually strong enough to engage a superior enemy until neighbouring corps 'marched to the sound of the guns' and took up the fight.

The ideal formation was the *bataillon carré*, a diamond formation of four corps which, as the diagram (see below) shows, was flexible and allowed a rapid concentration of force. The flexibility and speed of the corps system was brilliantly displayed in the rapid march from the Channel coast into Germany and down to the Danube in October 1805. Napoleon got news of the Austrian concentration at Ulm on 20 September. His advance was so rapid and the surprise so complete that General Mack and the Austrians were surrounded and forced to surrender on 20 October. A soldier is rumoured to have commented after the Ulm campaign: 'The emperor had found a new way of waging war; he makes use of our legs instead of our bayonets.'

Among the **generals** Napoleon took as models were Alexander the Great, Hannibal, Julius Caesar, Gustavus Adolphus and Frederick the Great.

Perhaps the best example is the **campaign** of 1806 in which the defeat of the Prussian army in the twin battles of Jena and Auerstadt resulted in the rapid collapse of Prussian resistance. Napoleon's organisation of the army and his strategy were directed to maximising the possibility of rapid victory.

The army was divided into separate **corps** typically 15,000–30,000 men strong and containing elements of cavalry, artillery and infantry. Each corps was a 'little army' able to fight effectively on its own or in combination with other corps.

How did the corps system complement Napoleon's campaign and battle strategies?

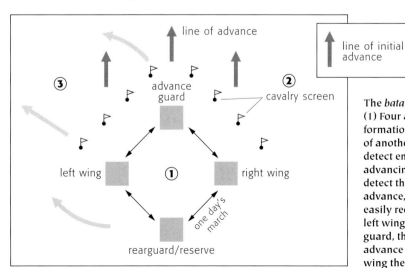

line of advance

line of initial advance

possible change

advance guard

cavalry screen

left wing

right wing

one day's march

rearguard/reserve

The *bataillon carré* and the corps system. (1) Four army corps advance in a diamond formation, each corps within a day's march of another. (2) A cavalry screen both seeks to detect enemy forces and shields the advancing army. (3) If the cavalry screen detect the enemy to the left of the line of advance, for example, the *bataillon carré* can easily redeploy and change direction. The left wing would now become the advance guard, the rearguard the left wing, the advance guard the right wing and the right wing the rearguard/reserve.

Part of the reason for the success of the corps system was the detailed planning and command exercised by Napoleon. His understanding of the rate of movement of his forces enabled him to calculate when and where they should be even when they moved dispersed so that they could concentrate at a particular point. At Austerlitz in December 1805 Napoleon knew that his apparent weakness would be strengthened by the arrival of Davout's corps and the bringing-up of extra forces from Vienna in time for the battle.

In terms of campaign strategy, Napoleon also aimed to achieve local superiority so that he had a good chance of inflicting a decisive defeat on his opponent. His favourite strategy, and that employed when he enjoyed superiority of numbers, was envelopment (see below). This involved using part of his forces to pin the enemy down in a certain position whilst manoeuvring the bulk of his troops behind his opponent to cut his lines of communication and surround them. This strategy is best demonstrated by the Ulm campaign, when Murat's cavalry was used to launch feint attacks across the Rhine in southern Germany in order to keep the Austrians there. Meanwhile, the bulk of Napoleon's forces, moving rapidly in separate corps, crossed the Rhine to the north and closed on the Austrians who were concentrated at Ulm from the rear. The Austrians, finding themselves surrounded, surrendered.

In battles, Napoleon looked to achieve local superiority. He hoped to spot or create a weakness in the enemy formations which he could exploit. At Austerlitz, he planned to dupe the combined Austro-Russian force into weakening their centre. Once it was weakened, he would attack with forces held back from the initial attacks. He tried to convince the Austro-Russian forces of his weakness on his right flank in order to tempt them to attack there. The plan worked. The Austrians and Russians did as predicted, transferring troops

The Ulm campaign:
The strategy of envelopment

① Murat's cavalry feint towards Ulm to keep the Austrians there.

② Two army corps used to watch/prevent any Russian advance.

③ Remaining corps envelop the Austrians around Ulm. With no way out, the Austrians are forced to surrender.

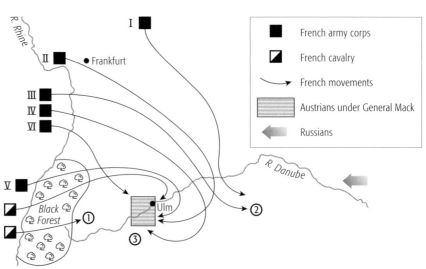

The Ulm campaign, October 1805.

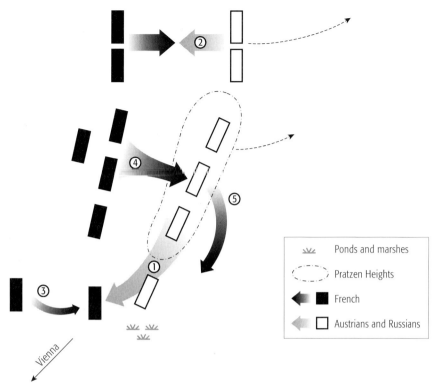

Vienna

The Battle of Austerlitz, 1 December 1805. The numbers relate to the main events.
(1) Napoleon, having exposed the weakness of his army to the Austrians and Russians, withdrew from the Pratzen Heights into the valley beyond before the battle. He deployed leaving his right wing deliberately weak. Meanwhile, the Austrians and Russians had occupied the heights. As Napoleon had hoped, when the Austrians and Russians realised Napoleon's weakness on the right, they decided to attack there – weakening their centre. (2) The Austrians and Russians mounted a secondary attack on Napoleon's left wing which was repulsed. (3) Meanwhile, extra forces that Napoleon had called up from Vienna stiffened resistance against the attack on his right wing. (4) Once Napoleon was convinced the Austrians and Russians had weakened their centre, he mounted a massive attack against it with troops that had been hidden in the low-lying morning mist. The attack was successful. (5) Once counter-attacks had been repulsed, Napoleon was able to turn and envelop the Austrians and Russians and achieve a complete victory.

from their centre to attack his right. At this point he sent his reserves forward. They broke the enemy centre and were able to inflict a crushing victory.

In other circumstances, Napoleon would attempt to engage the enemy whilst mounting a concealed move on their rear to cut off their line of retreat and prevent reserves being drawn up. This he attempted at Jena. Once his cavalry had located the Prussians at Jena, he turned the bulk of his force on to them whilst sending **Davout**'s corps and **Bernadotte**'s corps to cut off the lines of communication. In fact, Napoleon had run into only part of the Prussian forces, which he was able to defeat through his superior numbers. Meanwhile, Davout had run into the other main Prussian force at Auerstadt. Although outnumbered by nearly three to one, Davout was able to defeat the

Louis-Nicolas **Davout** (1770–1823), although a noble by background, served in revolutionary armies and earned promotion to divisional command after serving Napoleon in Egypt. He led the cavalry in the Italian campaigns of 1800 and was promoted to marshal in 1804. His most famous victory was at Auerstadt in 1806, and his loyalty and ability earned him the title of duke of Auerstadt in 1808 and prince of Eckmühl in 1809. He played a prominent role in all Napoleon's military campaigns and never lost a battle.

Jean-Baptiste **Bernadotte** (1763–1844), son of a lawyer, rose rapidly through the ranks during the revolution. He was a general by 1794 and briefly served as minister of war in 1799. He was not involved in the Brumaire coup, but accepted a place in Napoleon's Council of State. He was made a marshal in 1804 and prince of Pontecorvo in 1806. He distinguished himself in the Ulm–Austerlitz campaign of 1805 and redeemed his inactivity during the battles of Jena and Auerstadt by his rapid pursuit of the Prussians thereafter. He was never trusted by Napoleon and was disgraced after Wagram in 1809. However, in 1810 he became heir to the Swedish throne and thereafter was to move to the allied side, playing a part in the defeat of Napoleon in Germany in 1813. He became king of Sweden in 1818.

Joachim **Murat**
(1767–1815), son of a
Gascon innkeeper, rose
through the ranks to
become a cavalry officer in
1792. By 1797 he was
respected as a brave
cavalry commander and
supported Napoleon in the
Coup of Brumaire. He
married Napoleon's sister
Caroline in 1800. Like
Davout, he became a
marshal in 1804, and he
was rewarded with the title
prince after his contribution
to the victory at Austerlitz.
His cavalry charge at Eylau
(1807) was vital in
ensuring Napoleon was
not defeated in that battle.
He was made king of
Naples in 1808. His
attempts to hold on to this
kingdom after Waterloo led
to his capture and
execution in October 1815.

What do you notice
about the backgrounds
and ages of
Napoleon's marshals?

Prussians decisively, partly because the Prussians believed they were fighting Napoleon.

The years 1805–07 were years of impressive campaigns and decisive victories, yet some historians have questioned Napoleon's greatness as a commander. They have suggested that he was lucky, as at Marengo in 1800 when Desaix's timely arrival turned defeat into victory. Napoleon would not have denied that luck was important. It was the first quality he looked for in his subordinates. Some have suggested he was often reliant on the skill and leadership of his more able subordinates. **Murat**'s cavalry charge at Eylau arguably saved the French from defeat in February 1807, while Davout's timely arrival at Austerlitz potentially saved Napoleon's right wing and enabled the fabulous victory that followed. He took great risks that could easily have turned to disaster. For instance, as his army corps moved to the Danube in the Ulm campaign their lines of communication were vulnerable to a northward thrust by Mack in Ulm, a possibility almost realised by the battle at Haslach. His reconnaissance was often poor, as in the advance that led to the Battle of Marengo. He was lucky that his opposition was mediocre both in terms of troops and generals. Mack was certainly poor, and Prussian generals were old and cautious. However, Kutusov, Blücher and Archduke Charles were able commanders. Finally, some argue, his victories owe more to the quality of the French army than his leadership of it.

Other critics point to a lack of innovation. There was nothing new and revolutionary about Napoleon's strategies. He would have admitted this himself – he learned his generalship from his study of the great commanders of the past. The developments he did make tended to be ones of scale rather than design. The corps system was an extension of the divisional system advocated by Guibert, for instance. There was also nothing particularly revolutionary about the use of the massed battery, which became a feature of Napoleon's later battles. He eschewed the use of newer weapons like rockets. However, innovation is not necessarily a quality of great generalship. Napoleon's defenders argue that whilst he used others' ideas he put them into practice expertly. As he himself said, 'everything is in the execution'. More serious, perhaps, is the argument that Napoleon became predictable, so that his enemies came to know what to expect and began to counter his strategies effectively.

Before considering the relative weaknesses of his enemies, it is worth stressing one final important advantage Napoleon had over his enemies. He was not only commander-in-chief of his army, he was also head of state. This supreme unity of command meant there was never any conflict between the home and the battle fronts. If Napoleon wanted troops, they were raised. If he needed supplies, they were organised. His reorganisation of the war ministry ensured relative efficiency. The lack of domestic opposition to his rule meant he could concentrate on his foreign ambitions. As his empire expanded, so did his resources. His allies and satellite states were obliged to contribute heavily and frequently to his war chest with resources and men.

The relative weaknesses of Napoleon's enemies

A final argument to support the view that Napoleon was not truly a military genius is that his enemies were weak and divided. In relative terms this was true. Their weaknesses tend to be the corollaries to his own strengths. Whilst the French army had been transformed by developments after the Seven Years' War and the revolution, those of his enemies remained largely as they had been in the mid eighteenth century. They tended to be made up of a mixture of mercenaries and press-ganged subjects drawn from the lowest ranks of society, to require harsh discipline in order to secure obedience, to have an almost exclusively aristocratic officer corps, to move slowly in long columns dependent on enormous supply trains, and to fight according to eighteenth-century methods (marching in column, deploying for battle in line). Napoleon's enemies had divided command structures and separation of control between army and state. This last was demonstrated clearly at **Austerlitz**. Napoleon could plan and issue his orders without fear of interference; Austrian and Russian generals had to agree and co-ordinate their activities and needed the agreement of their rulers.

The Battle of **Austerlitz** is sometimes known as the 'Battle of the Three Emperors'.

How did the nature of allied coalitions hinder attempts to defeat Napoleon?

This example also illustrates another of his enemies' weaknesses. They tended to fight in loose coalitions, without a strong sense of united aims. These coalitions were fragile. The Second Coalition (Britain, Russia and Austria) had broken down in 1799 partly because Russia could not co-operate effectively with Britain or Austria. Coalition partners were often willing to make separate treaties with France. Austria pulled out of the Third Coalition after Austerlitz and made peace with Napoleon at Pressburg; and Russia pulled out after Friedland, leaving Britain to fight alone. What is more, Napoleon was sometimes able to prevent all his potential enemies coming together at once. He played on Prussian desires to annex Hanover (which belonged to the British royal family) to keep it out of the Third Coalition until after Austria had been defeated.

Finally, Napoleon could normally rely on the practical difficulties of effective co-operation and mutual rivalries between coalition partners to provide him with the opportunity for victory. His ability to take on the Austrian army at Ulm before the Russians arrived was partly explained by the fact that Austria worked on the basis of a different **calendar** from Russia. Napoleon's chance of a quick victory over the Prussians in 1806 was provided partly by the Prussian desire to try to take the laurels for defeating Napoleon before their Russian allies arrived.

The Russians operated on a **calendar** that was 12 days behind that of Austria.

What factors help explain Napoleon's downfall?

The opposition of Britain and the Continental System

In 1805 the French and Spanish navies had been decisively defeated at the Battle of Trafalgar. Although Napoleon had abandoned his plan to invade England before the battle took place, it convinced him that Britain's control of the sea made direct action against it impossible. Yet Napoleon was obsessed with the need to defeat Britain if he was to achieve his aims on the continent. Britain had been France's most consistent enemy since the outbreak of war in 1793 and constantly threatened the French position through its willingness to subsidise France's enemies through the distribution of '**Pitt's Cavalry**'.

Napoleon determined to beat Britain by cutting it off from the sources of its wealth: the huge trade with the continent. What historians refer to as the Continental System evolved. This comprehensive attempt at economic warfare was rooted in Napoleon's belief that the 'nation of shopkeepers' was on the verge of economic collapse.

The rationale for the Continental System went something like this:

1 If Britain could be prevented from trading goods on the continent for cash, its supply of gold would dry up, leading to bankruptcy and the inability to pay for the continuance of the war directly or by subsidising its allies.

2 Britain could also be forced to pay for imports from the continent (such as grain and naval stores) in gold, thus draining its reserves even more.

3 Without gold Britain would be unable to pay the interest on its massive national debt or to back its paper currency. This could lead to inflation and economic collapse.

4 Closing off trade would cause commercial bankruptcy, unemployment and possible political unrest, forcing Britain to the peace table on French terms.

5 France could replace Britain as the continent's supplier of manufactured goods and textiles.

The idea of economic warfare was not new. The French revolutionary government in 1793 had ordered the exclusion of British goods from French markets. But it was the Berlin and Milan Decrees of 1806 and 1807, which applied to all territories controlled by or allied to France, that established a blockade across the continent. The **Berlin Decrees** declared Britain to be in a state of blockade. Under the treaties of Tilsit the blockade was extended to Prussia and Russia, and later to Denmark, Sweden and Austria. The Milan Decrees of 1807 extended the blockade by including neutral shipping that had called at a British port.

In response, Britain took counter-measures in 1807 that prohibited seaborne trade between France and its allies and attempted to force all

Millions of pounds in gold, known as '**Pitt's Cavalry**', were handed out to pay for continental armies. Britain had been the paymaster of all the coalitions against France since 1793, and that, combined with British naval superiority and occasional expeditionary forces, meant that until Britain had been brought to its knees France and Napoleon could not be secure.

Under the **Berlin Decrees**, all trade with Britain was forbidden and all British goods were liable to seizure.

seaborne trade with France to pass through British ports. Meanwhile the Royal Navy blockaded French ports.

In general terms, Napoleon overestimated the French ability to enforce the blockade and underestimated the resilience of the British economy. After the Milan Decrees there was a dramatic initial downturn of 30 per cent in British exports, but the effect was short lived. Britain found new markets (especially in South America) and new ways into the continent.

There were serious problems for Britain in 1810–11 after Napoleon's defeat of Austria and the annexation of Holland and the north German ports. This coincided with a glutted market in South America and a flood of colonial imports. Britain's trade with Europe virtually disappeared. Economic problems stimulated industrial unrest in Britain with a wave of industrial violence, rising unemployment, inflation, shortage of gold and a depreciation of the pound by over 40 per cent on the money markets. Moreover, French privateers managed to sink or capture 619 British merchant ships in 1810.

However, overall the Continental System failed. Economic measures can only be successful if applied consistently, fully and over a long period of time. This proved impossible. Its effectiveness rose and fell according to the strength of French control of the continent. It was effective in 1807–08 and 1810–11, but was breached during the wars with Austria in 1809 and Russia in 1812.

> What factors limited the effectiveness of the Continental System?

France never had the resources to enforce the system rigorously, relying on the co-operation of allies and satellite states which was not always wholehearted. One reason why Napoleon decided to annex Holland was because it was not enforcing the Continental System. The essential point was that the continent (and France) needed British goods, from its textiles and manufactured products to its colonial supplies of sugar and coffee. Napoleon himself connived at breaching the blockade by issuing licences to import **British goods**.

The system also had a disruptive impact on France and the continent. For example, restrictions on trade affected French commercial and industrial interests. Whilst the Lyons silk industry benefited to some degree through the ban on imports of British textiles, the colonial and wine trade of the western seaports like Bordeaux dried up. Measures were taken to try to protect French industries because Napoleon hoped France would replace Britain economically. This had a damaging effect elsewhere on the continent as traditional trade routes were closed off and French goods were given preferential treatment. Eastern Europe suffered because it was unable to sell its grain, timber and naval stores to Britain.

> Ironically, the French army in the Eylau campaign (1807) wore **British goods**: overcoats made in Leeds and shoes in Northampton.

Most importantly, the desire to defeat Britain by means of the Continental System was a major factor in Napoleon's decisions to invade Portugal and Spain in 1807 and Russia in 1812. Failures in both areas were to be major reasons for his eventual downfall.

The Peninsular War and Austria

In exile on St Helena, Napoleon commented, 'This unfortunate **Spanish war** has been a real sore, the prime cause of the misfortunes of France.'

Napoleon referred to the **Spanish war** as the 'Spanish ulcer', a constant and painful drain on the resources, manpower and morale of France.

The Peninsular War began in October 1807 when Napoleon secured Spanish agreement to the passage of a small French army across its territory to Portugal. His initial aim was to defeat Britain's ally Portugal and force it to comply with the Continental System. Marshal Junot was able to advance on Lisbon and the Portuguese royal family only managed to escape through the good offices of the Royal Navy.

However, Napoleon decided not only to deal with Portugal but also to bring Spain more closely under French control. He exploited divisions in the Spanish royal family to justify French intervention. In early 1808 French forces occupied key northern fortresses and in March Murat entered Madrid. However, on 2 May Murat's bloody suppression of the **Dos de Mayo** in the capital stimulated resistance across Spain. The abdication of Charles IV and the proclamation of Napoleon's brother Joseph as king in June did nothing to stem the growth of opposition. Provincial councils (*juntas*) organised armies and on 20 July a French army was forced to surrender at Baylen. This was the first time a French army had been defeated and it served to stimulate resistance to Napoleon not just in Spain, but also in Portugal and Austria. The immediate consequence was that Joseph abandoned Madrid and the French retreated to the north of Spain. In Portugal Junot was isolated by the revival of Portuguese resistance. In August a small British force under **Sir Arthur Wellesley** landed and defeated Junot at Vimeiro.

The *Dos de Mayo* was a popular rising.

This collapse of the French position both in Spain and Portugal led to Napoleon's direct intervention. He marched south with veteran troops. In a series of battles the Spanish were defeated and Napoleon entered Madrid in December. However, the British had sent further forces to Portugal under Sir John Moore, who advanced into Spain threatening Napoleon's lines of communication. This was a crucial move. In order to deal with Moore Napoleon had to break off offensives against the Spanish. While Moore retreated towards Corunna, Napoleon left his final destruction to Soult while he returned to France to deal with the growing threat from Austria. Soult, however, failed to stop Moore, who managed to evacuate his forces on Royal Navy ships even though he himself was killed in fighting off the French (January 1809). Moore's campaign gave the Spanish time to reorganise and saved Portugal from immediate attack.

Sir Arthur Wellesley (1769–1852) was made duke of Wellington in 1814 for his role in defeating Napoleon. He had joined the army in 1787, bought himself a lieutenant colonel's rank in 1793, and served with distinction in India. In 1805 he had begun a political career and briefly served as chief secretary for Ireland before returning to the military. In 1809 he took command of the British forces in Portugal and was to lead them to a series of victories over the French between 1809 and 1814, when the British army entered France. His most famous victory was at Waterloo in June 1815. After the Napoleonic wars he resumed a political career, becoming prime minister in 1828.

Meanwhile, Napoleon had to face renewed opposition from Austria, encouraged by the strength of resistance in Spain and Napoleon's diversion of veteran troops from Germany. Austria had some grounds for optimism. It had been rebuilding and reorganising its armed forces since 1805, copying French measures such as the corps system and opening up the officer corps. It had some able commanders, like Archduke Charles, and hoped to exploit resentment at French depredations in Germany by appealing to German nationalism. In this last it was unsuccessful. Prussia would not act if Russia did not, the Confederation of the Rhine stayed loyal to Napoleon and other German states even contributed forces to the French. Even so, Austria's frontline strength was around 350,000 men and 750 guns in 1809.

Napoleon was well aware of the dangers, and had sought to get positive help from Russia when he met the tsar at Erfurt in 1808. He was to be disappointed as the tsar would make no firm commitment. In spring 1809 Napoleon cobbled together a force of 275,000 men to face the Austrian offensive, managing to beat them at Eckmühl, though this was not a decisive blow. Napoleon advanced along the Danube in the hope of securing a quick, decisive victory. Poor reconnaissance and preparation led to almost total disaster at Aspern–Essling in May. Napoleon attempted to cross from the south to the north bank of the Danube across a single pontoon bridge erected by his engineers but unexpectedly ran into the main Austrian army. A bloody and hard-fought battle ensued in which both sides lost about 20,000 men, but the victory was Austria's. Fortunately, Napoleon managed to withdraw intact.

Stung by this reverse, Napoleon hurriedly called up reserves and prepared for a second battle. This time the ground was well prepared. By crossing the Danube further to the east than expected, he caught the Austrians by surprise at Wagram in July 1809. Battle was joined. Although the initiative lay with the French and the battle was won, resistance had been strong and French losses were again very heavy – 32,000. It proved a decisive victory, however, and the Austrians were once again forced to make peace on French terms. By the Treaty of Schönbrunn (October 1809) the Austrians gave up more territory, paid a huge indemnity and accepted arms limitations. They also agreed to enforce the Continental System and the emperor agreed to the marriage of Napoleon to his daughter Marie-Louise in 1810. In 1811 a son was born; the master of Europe had an heir. For Napoleon this probably marked the high point of his career, despite the continued problem of Spain.

What evidence is there in the war against Austria in 1809 that Napoleon was finding it more difficult to secure victories? How do you explain this?

The Peninsular War 1809–14

The year 1809 saw more French victories in Spain, but also one significant defeat. In May 1809 Sir Arthur Wellesley had forced the French out of Portugal once more and made to advance on Madrid. He defeated the French at Talavera (for which victory he was made Viscount Wellington), but was then forced to retreat into Portugal. The French still did not have effective control of Spain, and Portugal remained secure.

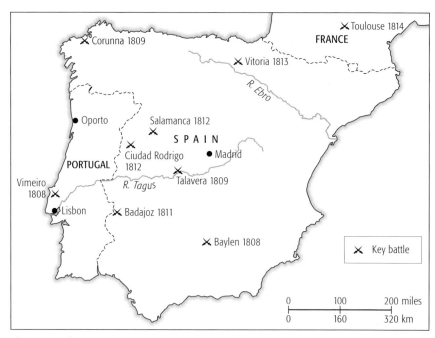

The Peninsular War, 1808–14.

This was to be the pattern for the next three years. The French could win battles against the Spanish armies, but were unable to control the countryside. Their columns were harried by guerrilla forces and Wellington's Anglo-Portuguese forces prevented success in Portugal. In 1812 Wellington felt strong enough to advance into Spain. Although the French had 300,000 troops in Spain, garrison duties and the threats from guerrillas meant that they could never concentrate more than about 70,000 to face Wellington in the field. After securing the fortresses of Badajoz and Ciudad Rodrigo, the British advanced and defeated the French at Salamanca, forcing them to evacuate Madrid and retreat north.

In June 1813 the French forces, weakened by the demands of the Russian campaign and the influx of raw recruits, were defeated decisively by the now clearly superior Anglo-Portuguese forces at Vitoria. This forced a French retreat to the Pyrenees and gave Wellington the initiative. Desperate defence delayed Wellington's advance but during the winter of 1813/14 he forced his way into France. The final battle took place at Toulouse on 10 April 1814 before news of Napoleon's abdication on 6 April reached there.

The French failed in Spain for several reasons. These include:

1 Napoleon's initial underestimation of the scale of resources needed to conquer Portugal and Spain, coupled with his overestimation of the degree of French support in Spain.

2 The revival of Austrian opposition to France caused Napoleon to leave Spain

before Spanish resistance and Sir John Moore's army had been decisively defeated.

3   The decision by Britain to maintain a small army in the peninsula under the able command of Wellington stiffened Spanish and Portuguese resistance and enabled battle victories over the French.

4   Spanish control of the countryside required French forces to be diverted into maintenance of strong garrisons and escort duties for ensuring supplies and communications. Whilst French field armies could secure victories they failed to crush resistance.

5   Napoleon divided command of French forces in the peninsula. This meant that French efforts were left in the hands of different commanders (Junot, Soult, Massena, Marmont, Joseph and others) whose mutual rivalries and jealousies diluted French efforts.

6   Napoleon had to divert veteran troops away from Spain at vital times to fight in central Europe and Russia, crucially in and after 1812.

The Peninsular War is important in explaining Napoleon's eventual defeat for several reasons. First, the defeat of a small French army at Baylen was significant because it punctured the image of French invincibility. Secondly, Spanish resistance encouraged the Austrians to take up arms in 1809, causing Napoleon to leave Spain at a crucial moment. Thirdly, the Spanish and Portuguese resistance provided the British with a continental theatre of operations against France. The constant guerrilla attacks and lack of a decisive victory sapped French morale, required the maintenance of a force of over 200,000 men in the peninsula which strained French resources and increased the levels of conscription and taxation at home. This served to undermine French support for Napoleon. The war cost France over 300,000 casualties and 3 billion francs. The need to maintain forces in Spain meant that there were fewer for operations elsewhere and that in 1809 and 1812 Napoleon was fighting on two fronts. Taken together, these reasons help explain Napoleon's own admission about its prime role in his downfall. If the consequence of the Peninsular War was to be slow death, the Russian campaign hastened the final crisis.

In what ways does the history of the Peninsular War support Napoleon's view of it as the 'Spanish ulcer'?

The Russian campaign, 1812

Despite the apparent harmony at Tilsit in 1807, relations between France and Russia were characterised by mutual suspicion. Differences emerged over the fate of the Ottoman Empire and Poland. France proved lukewarm in support of Russian ambitions in the former, whilst Russia was concerned about whether the French creation of the grand duchy of Warsaw might presage the recreation of the kingdom of Poland. Friction was also caused by Napoleon's annexation of the lands of the tsar's brother-in-law, the duke of Oldenburg, in

Why did Napoleon invade Russia in 1812?

Before approaching the Austrians, Napoleon had hoped to secure a **marriage** with 15-year-old Grand Duchess Anne, a member of the Russian royal family. His hopes were dashed by the tsar, who claimed that Anne was too young to marry. In fact the tsar's court was hostile to Napoleon and his advisers already realised that the Continental System would bring France and Russia into conflict. Another factor may have been the rumour that Napoleon was impotent. Napoleon was therefore forced to turn to his second choice – the 19-year-old Marie-Louise of Austria.

The **army** had lost 55,000 men before Napoleon reached Vilna. By the time he entered Smolensk in August he had lost a further 100,000 and still had not brought the Russians to battle.

What was the state of the Napoleonic army by the time it reached Moscow?

1810. Meanwhile Napoleon was angry at the lack of support from Russia in the Austrian war of 1809 and Russia's rejection of his **marriage** to a Russian princess. Most importantly, perhaps, Napoleon was angry when Alexander relaxed the embargo on British trade, thus breaching the Continental System. Whatever the exact causes, Napoleon resolved to attack Russia in 1812. Victory would make him master of all Europe and might offer the opportunity for further conquests to the east.

Napoleon secured the support of Prussia and Austria, but failed in his attempts to win that of Sweden and the Ottoman Empire – partly through the diplomacy of Britain, which brokered a peace between Russia and the Ottoman Empire, and joined Sweden and Russia in coalition. Despite these setbacks, Napoleon appeared in a strong position in June 1812. He had gathered a force of over 600,000 men with which to attack Russia. He was faced with about 200,000.

As usual, his plan was to locate his opponents and bring them to battle. However, a combination of unusual lethargy on his part, poor roads and the huge size of his army meant that his forces moved too slowly to pin down the Russians. The two main Russian armies – without any preconceived plan – merely retreated before Napoleon, refusing to fight even when ordered to do so by the tsar. Napoleon's forces were drawn ever further into Russia and denied the quick victory Napoleon desired. The rigours of the march, the lack of adequate supplies and desertion eroded Napoleon's **army** more effectively than any battle. Caution should have dictated halting at Smolensk for the winter, but Napoleon marched on, still hoping for a decisive battle that would force the tsar to make terms.

In the end he got his battle, some 60 miles west of Moscow, when Kutusov – recently restored to command of the Russian army – turned and stood at Borodino. A bloody battle of artillery fire and frontal assaults by both sides ensued, leaving approaching 80,000 casualties. The French claimed victory because the Russians retreated, but the result was not decisive, even though Napoleon was now free to enter Moscow, which he did on 14 September. Even the taking of the city did not bring the tsar to terms. Napoleon stayed in Moscow a month, a crucial delay as it turned out, before deciding to cut his losses and retreat.

A combination of harassment by Cossacks, the occasional bloody encounter with Russian forces, starvation and the early onset of winter turned retreat into disaster. Forced by the Russians back along the routes by which he had advanced, by the time he reached the River Beresina Napoleon had fewer than 50,000 men left. Here a combination of heroism and desperation enabled about half his force to get across before the Russians arrived. In the ensuing panic thousands drowned in the freezing waters. Only about 25,000 made it back to the relative safety of the grand duchy of Warsaw.

The retreat from Moscow, 1812. Part of the mythology surrounding the disastrous Moscow campaign is that the army was decimated by the early onset of the harsh Russian winter – 'General Winter'. In fact, the bulk of the losses to Napoleon's force were incurred on the way to Moscow during the summer, not on the way back.

By this time in December Napoleon was already back in Paris raising new forces. But the damage done by the Russian campaign was vast. About 500,000 men were lost. In military terms, even more significant was the loss of artillery and **cavalry horses**. The lack of trained cavalry was to be a significant feature in Napoleon's defeat in 1813 because although he could still win battlefield victories he no longer had the means to follow them up.

The material damage was only one aspect of the impact of the Russian campaign. It finally blew the image of Napoleon's invincibility, severely damaged French morale and, most significantly, encouraged others – especially the Prussians – to take up arms against him. The defeat of 1812 more than anything else marked the decisive turning point in Napoleon's fortunes.

Men could, to an extent, be replaced, but **cavalry horses** needed extensive training.

In what ways does Napoleon's defeat in Russia contribute to his eventual downfall?

The War of Liberation and defeat of Napoleon, 1813–14

Although Napoleon had suffered an immense reverse in Russia, it was not a foregone conclusion either that Russia would continue the fight or that Prussia would join them. Austria was to stay out of the fight until the summer of 1813. Perhaps the decisive event that helped ensure that the fight would now continue was the decision of the East Prussian diet (assembly), encouraged by General Yorck, to raise troops to fight France. This pressure persuaded the fearful Frederick William III to call all Prussia to arms in February 1813, opening the way for the signing of the Treaty of Kalisch with Russia. Alexander I,

The **conscripts** were nicknamed 'Marie-Louises' after Napoleon's wife.

despite some advice to the contrary, had decided to form a European coalition against Napoleon. In March, as French forces retired into Germany, Sweden joined the coalition.

Napoleon gathered what strength he could. At this stage Italy, the Confederation of the Rhine, Saxony and Bavaria remained faithful to him. He managed to raise over 300,000 men, but many were young, raw **conscripts**. He was relatively strong in infantry and his artillery was adequate, but he could not make good the losses in cavalry from 1812. Napoleon was having to defend a long line against three main enemy armies. As always, he took the offensive, and although he was able to win victories at Lutzen and Bautzen in the spring he was unable to take advantage of the victories. He had also suffered losses he could ill afford and was short on supplies. However, he had forced the coalition armies to retreat and the coalition partners had the difficulties in working together that they had had in the past.

It suited both sides to call a truce in June 1813. It lasted seven weeks and in the end proved fatal to Napoleon. It gave the coalition powers time to reinforce their armies and to win over Austria. The decisive moment came when Napoleon rejected terms that would have left France with Italy, Belgium and the Rhine frontier, although he would have had to accept loss of the grand duchy of Warsaw and the Confederation of the Rhine. His rejection of the terms persuaded Austria to join the coalition, and war restarted in August. The coalition adopted a strategy of avoiding battle except when they had superior numbers. This approach frustrated Napoleon's aim of defeating each of the allied armies in turn, and gradually the coalition powers were able to converge on Leipzig. Meanwhile, Napoleon's allies began to melt away.

In October the decisive battle known as the 'Battle of the Nations' was fought over three days at Leipzig. Napoleon was heavily outnumbered and surrounded on three sides; 350,000 allies faced fewer than 200,000 French. On the third day Napoleon retreated, having lost some 70,000 men. The defeat signalled the end of the Napoleonic Empire. In its wake the rest of Germany, Italy and Holland rose against Napoleon. Even at this late stage, Napoleon was offered terms on the basis of France's natural frontiers. He refused them, and the decision was taken to invade France.

What difficulties faced Napoleon in 1813?

Despite the overwhelming odds, Napoleon was still able to win victories over the allies, but he lacked the resources to affect the inevitable outcome. British intervention ensured final defeat when on 1 March the allies signed the Treaty of Chaumont, by which they agreed to fight until Napoleon was defeated and accepted terms based on France's 1791 frontiers. Without support in Paris and with waning support from his marshals, Napoleon was persuaded to abdicate on 6 April 1814. He was exiled to the island of Elba, off the coast of Italy.

What Napoleon's enemies learned from their mistakes

The defeats of Austria and Prussia in 1805–06 certainly led those states to embark on reform. Prussia's defeat was a profound shock, reinforced by the harsh terms imposed at Tilsit when Prussia lost half its territory and was forced to pay 600 million francs over subsequent years. However, the defeat and French exactions helped foster unity and persuaded the government to embark on a programme of social and military reform to modernise the state. Education was reorganised under Humbolt, serfdom was abolished and local government reorganised under Stein. The army was reorganised by Scharnhorst. The obsolete tactics of the eighteenth century were abandoned, harsh disciplinary measures relaxed and promotion on merit was introduced to the officer corps.

In addition, these years saw the first flowering of a distinctive **German nationalism** that was to bear fruit in 1813 when some 'volunteer' forces were raised amongst students and artisans in the towns and gave a nationalist flavour to the 'War of Liberation'. Austria had tried to latch on to this nascent nationalism in 1809 when it appealed to 'the German nation' to rise against Napoleon. The appeal then fell on deaf ears, but once Austria began to re-organise its military, it was able to put up a more equal fight.

In terms of military strategy and tactics, the enemies of Napoleon had learned from past mistakes by 1813. This is reflected in the strategy adopted then to avoid battle with Napoleon as far as possible until the coalition armies had overwhelming numbers. In this way Napoleon's offensive strategy was to a great degree neutralised, even though he was able to force battle on a number of occasions. The strategy came to fruition at Leipzig in October 1813 when, in the Battle of the Nations, sheer numbers made up for any tactical deficiencies. Again, in the spring of 1814, although Napoleon had minor victories in a series of battles, the resources of his enemies told against him.

Napoleon's generalship after 1807

There was some personal decline in Napoleon over the years. This can be seen in paintings of him (see pages 79 and 118). The physical and mental strain of fighting constant wars, running France and an empire eventually told, even on a man of action with an immense capacity for work. The nervous strain of living on the edge and having to appear in command had its effects. There were outbursts of anger and hysteria, and occasionally something resembling epileptic fits. Physically he not only became increasingly corpulent, but also suffered from piles and from bladder and stomach problems. His character changed to some degree too. He grew more intolerant of others' views, more convinced of his own rightness, more obstinate in his decisions, and less able to distinguish the possible from the impossible.

Reorganisation of the **army** involved the requirement for every Prussian to serve in the army before entering the reserve. Prussia thereby built up a reserve of 150,000 trained men by 1812.

German nationalism was developing. Although Germany did not exist as a separate state in this period, writers and philosophers at the end of the eighteenth century had begun to talk of a distinctive German culture and spirit that united the people of the various states of central Europe north of the Alps. Partly as a result of the ravages and reforms associated with the conquests of French revolutionary and Napoleonic armies, writers, poets and thinkers like Arndt, Jahn and Fichte stressed the differences between German culture and French culture. German nationalism therefore began to take on a distinctly anti-French character and grew as a force for resistance to Napoleon. However, its real impact at this time was limited.

What factors contributed to the more effective allied military performance in 1813–14?

Napoleon in
decline.
Compare this
portrait of
Napoleon with
that on page 79.
What changes
do you see?

There is evidence that his
health – specifically
bladder and stomach
problems – may have
affected Napoleon's
effectiveness at Borodino
and Waterloo.

Problems of physical **health** may well have had an impact on Napoleon's generalship. Some historians have also detected a more general decline in the quality of his military leadership after the high points of 1805 and 1806. They point to the lack of sophisticated tactics adopted in many later battles. Borodino, for instance, involved no classic attempt to envelop the enemy by threatening its rear (as suggested by some of his advisers), merely the straight-forward bludgeoning of massed artillery and frontal assaults by infantry. They point also to Napoleon's apparent lethargy during the Moscow campaign. The army was slow to move and early chances to envelop the Russians were lost through inactivity or slow movement. Napoleon can be criticised for both lack of adequate reconnaissance and poor preparation for what was to be a long campaign. However, these features can be explained at least in part by other factors, such as general decline in the quality of the French army and its size.

The best army Napoleon commanded was that of 1805–06. Perhaps by 1809 and certainly by 1812 the quality of the army had been diluted by the loss of veteran troops through war and their replacement by raw recruits. Another factor was the ever increasing proportion of non-French contingents. Of the massive force Napoleon led into Russia only half was French. The flank commands were made up principally of Prussians and Austrians. The rawness and the mixture of forces brought a reduction both in reliability and in ability to adopt the flexible tactics of the *grande armée* at its peak. The size of his army and the poor roads in Russia hindered rapid manoeuvre. The logistics of moving and supplying a force of 450,000 men was beyond the capacity of a single commander with a small staff, especially in hostile territory where living off the land was practically impossible and the few roads made movement difficult.

The argument that Napoleon had lost his genius seems to be belied by the vigorous campaigns he fought in the springs of 1813 and 1814 and even by the strategic conception of his final campaign, which came to grief at Waterloo in June 1815.

More telling perhaps is that, whatever Napoleon's vigour or lethargy, he became predictable, and his enemies had successfully learned how to counter his strategies. Apart from increasing the scale of certain tactics and elements of military organisation, he was no great innovator. As he said, 'I have fought over 60 battles and I know nothing now that I did not know at the start.' Unfortunately for him, his enemies had learned.

The inevitability of Napoleon's downfall

Some have argued that Napoleon's eventual downfall was inevitable from the start. The qualities that brought him success were those that guaranteed his eventual failure. His ambition, egoism, sense of destiny and single-minded determination helped him to achieve remarkable feats both in politics and on the field of battle. The flaw was that he did not know when to stop. Securing frontiers developed into conquering an empire which further developed into ambition to establish some kind of universal monarchy in Europe, like those of his role models Charlemagne and Alexander the Great. His military success bred in him a self-belief that led him to ignore advice or not to seek it. The concentration of command in his hands left him with subordinates incapable of or unused to successful independent command, as the Peninsular War demonstrated.

He lacked the quality of statesmanship that could have enabled him to make peace treaties that had some chance of lasting. Having defeated his enemies in the field, he sought to defeat them again at the peace table. His peace treaties were usually harsh and one sided. The experience of Austria in this respect is perhaps most instructive, as it sought to reverse the effects of previous defeat and humiliation at Napoleon's hands every few years. Austria took up arms in 1798 after the humiliation of Campo Formio in 1797, only to be humiliated once more at Lunéville in 1801. It did the same in 1804, only to be crushed by the terms of Pressburg in 1805, and then again in 1809 at Schönbrunn. A final attempt in 1813 was to give Austria its reward at Vienna in 1815. In this sense, it can be seen that there was no real chance of lasting peace in Europe while Napoleon was on the throne. He had the opportunity to

What aspects of Napoleon's character and attitude contributed to both his success and his eventual defeat?

make peace in 1813 on terms that would have left France substantially more powerful than it had been in 1789, but was blind to such offers – partly perhaps because he believed he could still win, but partly because he was only interested in the fate of France in so far as it served his own ends.

Another sense in which the seeds of his downfall were there from the start could be said to be the constant opposition of Britain, whose material resources enabled it to fight on and subsidise allies until Napoleon was finally defeated.

The Hundred Days

Michel **Ney** (1769–1815), son of a cooper, benefited from the rapid promotions available to military men of talent during the revolution. A sergeant major in 1792, he was a brigadier general by 1796 and became one of Napoleon's first marshals in 1804. He played a distinguished role in the Ulm (1805) and Friedland (1807) campaigns and was rewarded with the title of duke in 1808. For his efforts in 1812 he was awarded the title of prince of the Moskva and nicknamed 'the bravest of the brave' by Napoleon. He was to suffer for his going over to Napoleon during the Hundred Days. After Waterloo, he was arrested, tried for treason and shot in December 1815.

Napoleon's final defeat, of course, did not occur in 1814. In exile on Elba, he kept a careful eye on events in France. The restored Louis XVIII, brother of Louis XVI, was insecure on the throne and reliant on the support of the coalition powers. In March 1815 Napoleon made what turned out to be a last bid for power. He escaped from Elba and landed in southern France with a few hundred followers. Troops led by Marshal **Ney** sent to capture him and bring him back to Paris in an iron cage defected to him. This led to a triumphal progress to Paris. His entry there was preceded by the sorry sight of Louis XVIII scuttling across the frontier to Brussels and the protection of coalition forces.

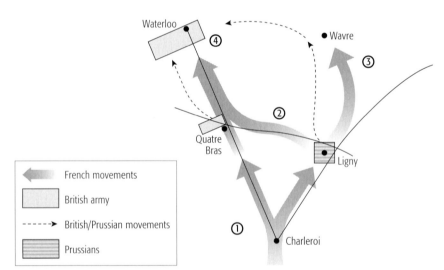

The Waterloo campaign, June 1815. Napoleon's strategy was to take the central position; the numbers relate to the main events. (1) Napoleon crosses into Belgium between the British and Prussian forces. He turns the bulk of his army to deal with the Prussians at Ligny. Meanwhile, some forces are detached to keep the British at bay. (2) Having defeated the Prussians at Ligny, Napoleon turns the bulk of his army to join the French at Quatre Bras to deal with the British. Meanwhile, he detaches some forces to pursue the Prussians. (3) Napoleon expected the Prussians to retreat from the British, but instead they retreated on a parallel line towards Wavre. The French pursuit therefore lost touch before marching to Wavre. (4) Napoleon engages the British at Waterloo, but the Prussians, marching from Wavre, are able to join them.

Once back in control, Napoleon knew he needed a quick and decisive victory to have any chance of persuading the coalition powers to accept his return. He chose to advance against the British and Prussians in Belgium, hoping that their defeat would persuade Austria and Russia to make terms. However unrealistic this plan was, his strategy revealed once more his military talent. He adopted the central position, aiming to get between the Prussians and British before they had the chance to join up. He could then defeat them each in turn.

After successfully achieving the first stage of the plan by crossing into Belgium at Charleroi, he sent Ney to keep the British at bay whilst he engaged and defeated the Prussians at Ligny. But from this point on his plans began to go wrong. He turned the bulk of his forces towards Wellington, leaving Marshal Grouchy with the task of pursuing the Prussians, assuming they would retreat from Wellington. Grouchy lost touch with the Prussians, who instead retreated parallel to the British. Wellington, relying on the prospect of Prussian help, took up position at Waterloo and waited. He had chosen his ground well. There were three fortified points in front of his main lines and a reverse slope where he could protect the bulk of his forces from French artillery fire. He was fortunate that heavy rain fell the night before the battle, turning the ground into a quagmire and restricting the manoeuvrability and effectiveness of artillery. Concerns over the artillery persuaded Napoleon to delay the start of the battle until the ground had dried out. Meanwhile, Wellington had sent word to Blücher, commander of the Prussians. Blücher duped Grouchy by keeping a diversionary force at Wavre while he marched to Waterloo with the bulk of the Prussian army.

As Wellington said afterwards, the battle was a close-run thing, but the final attacks of Napoleon's army were broken by the British and the arrival of the Prussians secured a decisive victory. Napoleon was pursued back to Paris, where he abdicated for a second time. This time he was exiled to the remote Atlantic island of St Helena, where he lived out the rest of his life dictating his memoirs and creating his own legend. He died in 1821. His name and reputation lived on, affecting the politics of France and Europe over the next century and provoking an incessant and unresolved debate amongst historians and writers about the nature of his rule and reputation.

Summary questions

1 Explain *two* main reasons why Napoleon was eventually defeated.

2 'The most important reason for Napoleon's military success was his generalship.' How far do you agree with this assessment?

5

France, 1814–48

Focus questions

◆ How successful was Louis XVIII?

◆ Why was Charles X overthrown in 1830?

◆ Why was Louis-Philippe overthrown in 1848?

◆ What were the key social and economic developments?

Significant dates

1814	Restoration of the Bourbons; Louis XVIII proclaimed king of France. Louis XVIII grants the Charter.
1815	Napoleon's Hundred Days and defeat at Waterloo. Second restoration of Louis XVIII. Harsh second Treaty of Paris. 'White Terror' and ultra assembly.
1820	Murder of duc de Berry.
1821	Villèle becomes chief minister.
1824	Death of Louis XVIII.
1825	Coronation of Charles X. Sacrilege Law.
1827	Fall of Villèle.
1829	Polignac becomes chief minister.
1830	Ordinances of Saint-Cloud. July Revolution overthrows Charles X. Louis-Philippe proclaimed 'king of the French'.
1831	Suppression of the Lyons insurrection.
1834	Suppression of unrest in Paris and Lyons.
1840	Mohammed Ali crisis and overthrow of Thiers. Appointment of Guizot as chief minister. Napoleon's remains returned to France.
1846	Onset of economic crisis.
1847	'Year of dear bread'.
1848	February Revolution.

Overview

In April 1814 and again in spring 1815 Napoleon was forced to abdicate. On both occasions his abdication in favour of his son was ignored and the allies imposed on the throne Louis XVIII, brother to Louis XVI who had been overthrown and executed during the revolution. Louis XVIII was to live out his brief reign, but his successor, Charles X, and the next monarch, Louis-Philippe, were to be overthrown by revolution. Their wishes on abdication were ignored. This chapter explains these events.

How successful was Louis XVIII?

Louis XVIII was first restored to the throne of France in 1814. He was 59 years old, fat, dull and uninspiring, and had spent the previous two decades outside France – hoping for the overthrow first of the French Revolution and then of Napoleon. When he returned to France in 1814 he did not do so by popular demand but 'in the baggage train of the allies'. He was restored by the force of arms of the Quadruple Alliance (Britain, Prussia, Austria and Russia) after the abdication of Napoleon in April 1814. Even the allies showed varying degrees of enthusiasm for his restoration. It was only the insistence of **Talleyrand** and of Britain, and the evidence of some pro-royalist demonstrations in places like

Charles-Maurice **Talleyrand** (1754–1838) was a French noble, liberal bishop who became one of the period's great survivors, with a reputation for corruption and cynicism. He welcomed the revolution of 1789, and in 1792 he gave up the church for a diplomatic career. He served Napoleon as foreign minister until 1807. Thereafter he largely stayed out of active politics, but in 1814 he worked for the restoration of Louis XVIII and went on to represent France at the Congress of Vienna. He was later to serve as ambassador to England under Louis-Philippe.

Compare this portrait of Louis XVIII with that of Louis XVI on page 16. How similar are they? Why might such a portrait anger many French people?

How would the nature of the restoration affect French people's attitudes to Louis XVIII?

Louis XVI's son was regarded by monarchists as Louis XVII.

Bordeaux when it was 'liberated' by the British, that persuaded them a Bourbon restoration had some chance of success.

The new king's first moves did little to win him friends in France. He insisted on the title Louis XVIII, in succession to **Louis XVI's son** (who had died in a revolutionary prison during the 1790s), thus symbolically denying the revolution. He restored the white Bourbon flag in place of the Tricolour and claimed to rule by divine right, denying the revolutionary ideal of popular sovereignty. Along with the king came a restoration of court ceremonial and of a royalist Household Guard and the demobilisation of much of the Napoleonic army and its officers. Such moves aroused fears of a royalist backlash and did little to endear Louis to a wary, if exhausted, French people.

On the other hand, Louis XVIII's government was not treated harshly by the allies. The Treaty of Paris signed on 30 May 1814 asked for no indemnity, allowed France to keep its 1792 frontiers and permitted looted art treasures to remain in France. Louis appeared aware of the dangers of his position and the need to win over those who were politically influential. Significantly, in 1814 he granted to his subjects a charter 'voluntarily, and by the free exercise of our royal authority'. Despite the language of a royal grant to subjects, this document seemed to declare there was to be no return to the absolute rule associated with the pre-revolutionary monarchy.

The Charter

The term *ancien régime* refers to the monarchical system of government prior to 1789 and the old social system based on aristocratic privilege.

Feudalism is the system whereby landlords or seigneurs exercised various rights over their peasants, such as requiring them to use the lord's mill and pay various dues.

The *biens nationaux* were lands formerly belonging to the church or to aristocrats, confiscated during the revolution and sold off, mainly to the bourgeoisie.

In many ways the Charter established a liberal basis for government. It confirmed almost all the legal and social changes since 1789. There was no attempt to restore *ancien régime* privileges and **feudalism**. It provided for a parliament of two chambers: a nominated Chamber of Peers and an elected Chamber of Deputies. Deputies had to be over 40 years old and substantial property owners. The limited franchise restricted the vote to around 100,000 of the wealthiest people in France (out of a population of 30 million). Equality before the law, no imprisonment without cause, careers open to talents, security for property (including the *biens nationaux* acquired during the revolution), apparent freedom of the press (subject to 'laws which must check the abuse of this liberty') and religious toleration ensured continuity with the liberal principles established during the revolutionary and Napoleonic periods.

Louis XVIII did reserve considerable powers for himself. He appointed ministers (although it remained unclear whether these ministers were responsible to parliament), initiated legislation, had the power of veto, could dissolve the Chamber of Deputies, nominated the Chamber of Peers and controlled all civil and military appointments.

The Charter can be seen as a compromise between the claims of divine right monarchy to rule and the liberal ideal of constitutional (limited) government.

As such, it was a promising foundation for the restoration monarchy. However, there were difficulties right from the start. The Charter was a royal grant, voluntarily given, and some feared it might be just as easily voluntarily withdrawn. The franchise, like the powers of parliament, was limited. Certain of the Charter's provisions, such as the relationship between ministers and parliament and the position on the freedom of the press, were ambiguous and could easily become sources of friction.

Whether the Charter could work would depend on the political will of the various parties involved in its operation to make it work and the strength of pressures for change (both conservative and more radical).

What features of the 1814 Charter might a French liberal welcome?

What concerns might they have about the Charter?

The second restoration

The restoration appeared short lived when in March 1815 Napoleon escaped from exile on Elba and returned to France. As he made his triumphal progress to Paris, Louis XVIII scuttled away to seek protection from the Quadruple Alliance. But this was a temporary setback and subsequent to Napoleon's final defeat Louis XVIII was once more restored to the throne by the allies.

This time, the allies were less inclined to be lenient towards France. The peace treaty of 1814 was replaced by a much harsher one in 1815. The extent of French territory was reduced to the frontiers of 1790, a huge indemnity was imposed and an army of occupation installed (the combined cost of which was well over a billion francs). More than ever, Louis XVIII appeared as a king imposed on France. The Bourbon monarchy was associated with humiliation and defeat and dependence on hated 'allies' whose soldiers billeted about France showed little respect for ordinary Frenchmen. However, this time the restoration was to stick and Louis was to live out the rest of his life as king of France.

Louis's situation in 1815 was by no means secure. On the plus side, whilst there was not much positive enthusiasm for the Bourbons, a war-weary France desired peace and stability. Many members of the middle and upper classes were willing to support the regime if it brought peace and respected their gains from the revolution. Additionally, Louis could look to support from those who had suffered most under the revolutionary and Napoleonic regimes: the Catholic church, the nobility and, to a degree, the peasantry – who had borne the brunt of conscription and high taxation and had in the final years of Napoleon experienced inflation and hunger again. The downside to this was that the church and nobility had expectations of Louis which he could fulfil only at his peril. This was because France was a divided society. Liberals, holders of *biens nationaux*, Napoleonic officers on half pay, demobilised soldiers, other beneficiaries of the Napoleonic regime – all had reason to be fearful. Any moves that seemed to appease the church and the nobility

Louis XVIII said: 'I must not be the king of two peoples.'

What advantages and disadvantages did Louis XVIII have as king after the second restoration?

The literal meaning of **Trestaillons** is 'three pieces'.

Une chambre introuvable means 'a matchless assembly'. It was so called by Louis XVIII because the success of the royalists in the elections for it far surpassed their highest hopes.

Elie Decazes, later the **duc de Decazes**, was a minor official under Napoleon, and became Louis XVIII's favourite and chief minister between 1818 and 1820. He was associated with the attempt to moderate the regime by purging the administration of ultra sympathisers. His pro-liberal policy was discredited by the murder of the duc de Berry and in the ultra backlash he lost power.

might well provoke opposition from these groups. **Louis XVIII** recognised the problem. Resolving it was another thing.

The omens in 1815 did not augur well. Many of the noble *émigrés* and clergymen who returned from foreign exile wanted revenge on those who had caused their misfortunes. Paradoxically, it was these 'ultra-royalists' who posed the greatest initial threat to the stability of the restoration. On Napoleon's final defeat in the summer, ultra-royalists in southern France launched a 'White Terror' (white for the Bourbons) against the supporters of Napoleon. This involved mass arrests, pillaging and massacring of prisoners by Catholic bands of peasants and workers, often encouraged by local nobility. In Nîmes, for instance, Catholics were led by the notorious brigand leader **Trestaillons** who, it was claimed, cut his enemies into three parts. The strength of this royalist backlash was reflected in the elections for the Chamber of Deputies in August, when a huge royalist majority was elected. Louis's hopes of a policy of reconciliation seemed destined to fail. He referred to the new Chamber of Deputies as *une chambre introuvable*. It demanded a more 'royalist' government and an official White Terror involving a purge of government and administration, both at the centre and locally. Louis was forced to dismiss the moderate government of Talleyrand and Fouché, to sack or punish about a third of the civil service and to remove about 15,000 army officers. Special courts punished a further 6,000 accused of sedition. Further problems for Louis were caused by economic disruption at the end of the wars, a flood of cheap British imports and harvest failure in 1816–17.

Louis managed to ride the storm, however. In September 1816 he felt strong enough to dissolve the chamber and seek a more malleable body of new deputies. Emotions had cooled somewhat since the summer of 1815 and this, combined with the effects of royal patronage and influence used against ultra candidates, resulted in a new chamber dominated by moderate 'constitutional' royalists. One of the new chamber's first acts, as directed by the new government headed by the duc de Richelieu, was to amend the electoral law to make it harder for ultras to be elected. The trend to more moderate government was continued when Richelieu was replaced in 1818 by the **duc de Decazes**, a moderate liberal or 'doctrinaire' who accepted the idea of a constitutional monarchy based on the Charter. He purged the administration of ultras and appointed a batch of liberal nobles to the Chamber of Peers. He also reorganised the army, introducing voluntary enlistment and promotion by merit, and relaxed some restrictions on the press. In Decazes, it seemed, Louis had found a minister committed to making the Charter work.

Decazes was opposed by the ultras and also by liberals, or independents, on the left who wished to further liberalise the regime by, for instance, extending civil liberties and the powers of the Chamber of Deputies. By 1819 these two groups represented a numerical majority in the chamber. Decazes considered modifying the electoral law once again, this time to weaken the liberals, but his plans were overtaken by the assassination of the **duc de Berry**. The murder, by a Bonapartist opponent of the Bourbon restoration, killed the second in line to the throne and destroyed the moderate policy Louis had attempted to pursue since 1814.

Baying for blood and blaming liberals, the ultras demanded a series of repressive measures. The reaction against the liberals was reflected dramatically in the elections of 1820, in which they received only 80 out of 450 seats. The victory of the ultras was also reflected in the birth of the duc de Berry's posthumous son, the 'miracle baby', which ensured a continuation of the Bourbon line.

In the light of these events, in 1821 Louis appointed the ultra-royalist leader the **comte de Villèle** to head the government, a position he was to hold for six years. Louis, aged and sick, increasingly left affairs in the hands of his chief minister. Villèle was no mere fanatic, but an able statesman who aimed to restore royal authority. His policy has been described as aiming to 'royalise the nation and nationalise the crown'. Playing on middle-class fears of revolution and conspiracy, he was able to pass further repressive legislation in 1822. Press censorship was imposed and detention without trial allowed. Liberals, like Guizot, were purged from universities. Schools were pressured to teach Catholicism and obedience to royal authority and teachers came under the authority of bishops. Finally, he persuaded the chambers to amend the electoral law so that deputies would be elected for a seven-year term. Other changes loaded the electoral dice in favour of ultras. In the 1824 elections the liberals won only 19 seats out of 434. In an echo of Louis XVIII's description of the 1815 chamber, this was called *la Chambre retrouvée*.

The success of Villèle's ministry between 1821 and Louis XVIII's death in 1824 was aided by a period of economic stability and growing prosperity, alongside a major foreign policy success when French troops intervened in Spain in 1823 to restore royal authority there. This was seen as a triumph against the British, who had opposed intervention.

It could be argued that Louis XVIII left a France slowly recovering from the impact of 25 years of revolution and war, a people slowly becoming reconciled to a restored monarchy which itself was willing to accept some constitutional limitations and to respect the rights gained by the people after 1789. The prestige of the monarchy and of France had to some extent been restored also by the removal of the allied army of occupation in 1818; by France's reacceptance as a great power, symbolised by its joining the other Great Powers in a quintuple alliance (1818); and by its successful intervention in Spain. Moderate monarchists and moderate liberals (*doctrinaires*) were willing to work on the

The **duc de Berry** was the son of the king's brother and heir, Charles, comte d'Artois.

The **comte de Villèle** was chief minister from 1821 to 1827, spanning the end of Louis XVIII's reign and the start of Charles X's. He was an ultra landowner from Toulouse, but no fanatic. He was an able administrator and able politician, but became associated with ultra policies like the Sacrilege Law of 1825 and the *milliard* (see page 129). Liberal opposition resulted in Villèle's defeat in the 1827 election and led to his fall at the end of the year.

How did government policy change after 1821?

La Chambre retrouvée means 'the assembly regained', indicating that the royalists had regained control of it.

basis of the 1814 Charter. On the down side, the ultras still wanted a return to pre-1789, liberals wanted to move further towards constitutional monarchy, and Bonapartists and republicans – few in number and at the margins of political life – wanted to overthrow the regime. In addition, governments had shown themselves willing to manipulate and change the electoral law and to attack press freedoms. If Louis had been succeeded by another such as himself, perhaps the Bourbon restoration would have survived. But Louis's heir was a man of a very different stamp.

Why was Charles X overthrown in 1830?

The **comte d'Artois** made his views clear when he said he would rather chop wood than be a king like the king of England.

Charles, **comte d'Artois**, brother to Louis XVIII, had a long history of counter-revolutionary activity behind him. He had been the first member of the royal family to flee France after the revolution, three days after the Storming of the Bastille, and had consistently worked against the revolution thereafter. His sympathies lay with the *ancien régime*, absolute monarchy, the Catholic church and the aristocracy.

The ultras had won the 1824 election, had an ultra chief minister and now had an ultra king. Louis XVIII had sought to reconcile, in however limited a fashion, the restoration with the revolution. Charles X sided with the ultras and clericals against it. From the start he indicated a desire to return to the

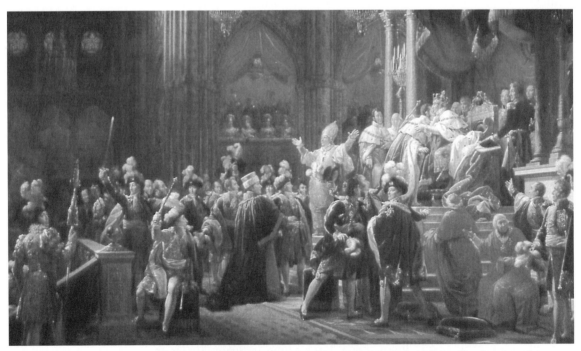

Charles X's coronation. Compare this painting with that of Napoleon's coronation as emperor in 1804 (page 86).

ancien régime. His coronation (May 1825) took place in the cathedral at Rheims with all the pomp and ceremony appropriate to divine right monarchy. Charles was anointed with the sacred oil of Clovis, supposedly brought down from heaven by a dove in 496, and proceeded after the ceremony to 'touch' a number of people suffering from the 'king's evil', scrofula.

There followed a series of laws that turned liberals against the regime. Whilst there was no attempt to seize back lands lost by *émigré* nobles during the revolution (which upset the ultras), a law was passed to compensate them. In 1825 a grant of a billion francs (the *milliard*) was to be raised by reducing the interest payments to holders of government bonds. This may have been a cost-effective way of raising the money, but it hit the wallets of the bourgeoisie who had invested in such bonds. It also roused revolutionary sensibilities: loyal Frenchmen were being asked to sacrifice income to pay those who had fought against France.

A major concern of the ultras was to reassert the importance and position of the Catholic church. In 1825 the chamber passed a **Sacrilege Law**. Nunneries were revived, and in 1826 Jesuits were allowed back into France and again taught in schools. A bishop was appointed minister for education. Such measures created a storm of protest in the liberal press and in pamphlets. There were anti-clerical popular songs and demonstrations and churches were attacked. The apparent growth of clerical influence was at odds with the secular, rational and tolerant principles of the revolution. It also provoked rumours of a return to the payment of the **tithe**.

In the face of protests and criticisms, the government also sought to restrict press freedom and introduced legislation requiring all publications to be submitted for royal approval. When, in 1827, this measure was resisted by the Chamber of Peers (many of whom were liberal, having been appointed before 1820), the government introduced the measure by royal ordinance and proceeded to create 76 new peers to counteract liberal opponents. Such actions seemed to presage an increase in royal power and a lack of respect for the Charter. Also in 1827, the government decided to disband the National Guard after Charles X had been greeted with anti-clerical and anti-government slogans at a review. The National Guard symbolised the revolutionary heritage of France. Its disbandment was interpreted as another sign that the king had no intention of respecting the liberties laid down in the Charter.

Meanwhile, ultras replaced liberals and others in public employment. This gave rise to the criticism that Jesuits controlled appointments and added further weight to the impression that Charles X wished to revive the power of the nobility and clergy in France.

The cumulative effect of these measures and others led to the revival of opposition to the regime. This came from a number of sources, and reflected

The **Sacrilege Law** revived *ancien régime* punishments of mutilation and death for profaning religious objects and restricted freedom of speech on religious matters.

The **tithe** was a tax paid directly to the church.

What were the main beliefs of the ultras?

In what ways did the policies of Charles's government go against liberal and revolutionary ideas?

a swathe of different opinions from moderate constitutionalists to revolutionary republicans, all united in opposition to the regime.

The growth of opposition and some criticism from within ultra ranks gave the government some concern and, trying to bolster its authority before opposition grew any further, Villèle called a general election in November 1827. Press freedom, allowed during the election campaign, opened a floodgate of criticism, not just of the king's ministers but of Charles X himself. Comparisons were made between him and **James II** of England. Despite government efforts, the election left Villèle with only a minority in the Chamber of Deputies. The results were welcomed with demonstrations in Paris and, ominously, riots in working-class districts.

Unable to win support, Villèle was replaced by a more liberal former minister, Martignac, who introduced minor concessions to liberal opinion by relaxing press controls, restricting Catholic schools and expelling Jesuits. Martignac's policies encouraged liberals to demand more and angered both ultras and Charles X. In August 1829 Charles X replaced Martignac with an alliance of royalists led by the **prince de Polignac**. It was not a politically wise move. Polignac personified ultra-royalism criticised by the liberals. His appointment of ministers confirmed the image of a deeply reactionary regime. Polignac could not command a majority in the chamber and there seemed little hope of compromise. When in March 1830 the king's speech criticised the opposition's 'blameworthy manoeuvres', the opposition responded with a condemnation of the government. Charles reacted by dissolving the parliament. It seemed the experiment in constitutional monarchy based on the Charter had run its course.

New elections were called for June–July 1830, but both the government and the opposition saw revolution or a *coup d'état* as a possibility. The king was urged by his ultra advisers to stage such a coup, but little was done. An attempt was made to rally France behind the king and his government by a more active foreign policy, the most tangible evidence of which was an attack on Algiers in north Africa. Though victorious, it had little impact on the electorate. The electoral campaign was fought in terms of a contest between the revolution and the monarchy, between liberty and equality on one side, and the church and king on the other. When the results came in, the government could only muster 145 seats against 270 for the opposition. The king had lost.

The issue was now clear to Charles X. Either he must, as urged by his royalist supporters, abandon parliamentary government; or he must give in, as his brother Louis XVI had done. If Charles took the latter route, he was warned, the road ended, as it had for his brother, on the scaffold. Charles chose the former. On 26 July Polignac issued four ordinances (royal decrees) which effectively meant the abandonment of the 1814 Charter. These Ordinances of

The **prince de Polignac** was a close friend of Charles X and an extreme ultra with a British wife. An *ancien régime* aristocrat, revolutionary *émigré*, anti-Napoleon conspirator and devout Catholic who was subject to visions from the Virgin Mary, he had little sympathy for the Charter. Appointed chief minister in November 1829, he was to support Charles X's attempt to assert royal authority with the Ordinances of Saint-Cloud in the aftermath of disastrous election results in June 1830.

What mistakes did Charles X make between 1829 and 1830?

Saint-Cloud (named after the palace where Charles was staying) declared the recent elections void and the new chamber dissolved, reduced the electorate to around 25,000 by means of a stringent property qualification, and imposed strict press censorship. Polignac and Charles (who went hunting) naively assumed there would be no major disturbance and made no effective provision to ensure the success of the coup – for that is what it was.

Their assumption was wrong. On 27 July there were demonstrations (but little violence) in Paris. On 28 July workers and students there grabbed the initiative by seizing arms, building barricades and attacking royal soldiers. They did so waving the Tricolour and shouting *Vive l'Empereur!* These events had no leadership from liberal politicians or journalists, although some republican and Bonapartist leaders were involved. Liberal leaders were busy drawing up protests and working out how to defy the ordinances; they were onlookers to the violence in Paris rather than participants. On 29 July the Parisians attacked the Tuileries and captured the Hôtel de Ville, killing some soldiers and sustaining several hundreds of casualties themselves. The Tricolour was raised. A revolution had taken place and the reign of Charles X was at an end. On 1 August, when it was clear there was no significant royalist support, Charles X abdicated in favour of his infant grandson.

Painting by Eugène Delacroix entitled *Liberty leading the people* (1830). The female figure represents liberty. Note the prominence of the bourgeois fighter (wearing the top hat) with workers behind him. Few bourgeois actually took part in the fighting of July 1830. Why do you think the painting depicts both the middle and working classes fighting together?

Why was Charles X overthrown? The immediate cause was the issue of the Ordinances of Saint-Cloud, which provoked the violence of the 'three glorious days'. Charles X and Polignac had attempted a *coup d'état* without ensuring that there were sufficient loyal troops in Paris to contain opposition – many of the troops who were available were sympathetic to the revolutionaries and the bulk of the army was in Algeria. It was the workers, mainly skilled craftsmen, who had taken to the streets. Their complaints were as much economic as political.

There had been relative prosperity in the early 1820s, but from 1825 onwards a series of bad harvests pushed up bread prices by 66 per cent, whilst economic slump and population growth combined to force down wages and increase unemployment. The frustrations caused by such circumstances gave an economic impetus to the politicisation of Paris (and other cities) that had accompanied the regime's unpopular policies. Journalists, popular-song writers, pamphleteers – all liberal and anti-clerical in sympathy – found a ready audience amongst the artisans and craftsmen of Paris. Liberal newspapers' circulation was over three times that of royalist papers. Some workers, of course, had a vested interest in liberal issues like freedom of the press – printworkers were among the first on the streets when the ordinances were declared. These developments show that the equation between reactionary policies and economic distress was convincingly drawn.

The workers' bosses were also disenchanted with Charles X, and there is evidence that some helped arm their employees. Owners of workshops and businesses were, like their workers, victims of the economic depression that set in after 1826. They were further angered by the disbanding of the National Guard in 1827 and a ban on Sunday trading. At the highest level, businessmen and merchants were increasingly excluded from political influence as the top positions in the state, both locally and at the centre, became increasingly dominated by the old aristocracy. Certainly some historians see the swing to the liberals in 1827 as the result of a loss of business confidence in the regime. The proposed restriction of the electorate in the ordinances would have excluded them from the right to vote altogether. The same applied to some extent to the professional middle classes, as promotion and prospects seemed to depend less on talent than on birth and ultra sympathies. By 1830, 70 per cent of prefects and 40 per cent of subprefects were ultras. The meritocratic principles of 1789 were being ignored.

The fragile guarantee of the gains of 1789 was the 1814 Charter. Louis XVIII had by and large stood by it, but Charles X felt no commitment to it; at best he regarded it as a temporary and undesirable necessity. Freedom of the press was violated and electoral law arbitrarily changed. Liberals feared a return of absolutism; constitutional monarchy could only work if Charles X went.

The feeling that Charles X was not committed to a constitutional regime was reinforced by religious policy. The king's alliance with the Catholic church and the insensitive policies that resulted from that alienated a largely anti-clerical middle class and aroused fears amongst holders of *biens nationaux*, as did the sympathy shown to *émigrés*. Some historians emphasise the importance of anti-clerical sentiment in the rising unrest. Clergy were easy targets for popular violence, scandal-mongering and popular abuse in songs, pamphlets and broadsheets.

All this suggests that Charles X carried much of the responsibility for his own downfall. He sided with the ultras and made no effort to make the constitutional system work. In this sense he was divorced from the political realities of restoration France. He said himself that he had not changed since 1789. He believed he should rule France, but the reality was that although he could appoint ministers they could not survive without commanding a majority in parliament. He believed in a France where social and political status depended on birth and land, but a generation of Frenchmen had grown up believing in the virtues of meritocracy, equality and wealth. He believed in a society where the Catholic church was dominant and the ally of the crown, but for many French people the church was the enemy of liberalism and progress.

Certainly, Charles X's narrowness of vision, lack of political acumen and intransigence play a central role in explaining the revolution of 1830, but there were longer-term factors that made political stability in nineteenth-century France difficult to achieve. One legacy of the years of political, religious and social upheaval was that there were always alternatives to the existing regime and that revolution or a *coup d'état* was a justifiable way of changing it. On the political right there was the option of royalism (ultras), which supported the restoration of absolute rule, the Catholic church and aristocratic privilege. There was also clericalism, whose aim was – more narrowly – the restoration of the power and prestige of the Catholic church. Clericals therefore tended to support the royalists.

In the centre there were Orléanists who pressed the claims of the duc d'Orléans as a constitutional monarch, willing to accept liberal principles, the Tricolour and an elected assembly. Liberals did not necessarily espouse the Orléanist cause, but felt that a truly constitutional monarchy was the best solution for France. They believed that government should be left to ministers who would be answerable to a parliament elected by men of property.

Bonapartism was particularly strong amongst ex-army officers, especially those 'purged' during the restoration. Bonapartism, by definition anti-restoration, began to grow in the 1820s as memory of the glories Napoleon brought to France grew and memories of suffering faded. The release of Napoleon's memoirs and the publication of some histories helped develop the myth.

> In what ways had Charles X alienated the middle classes?

Republicanism represented the most obvious, if not the strongest, threat to the restored monarchy. Republicans wanted an end to the restored monarchy and a democratic republic in its place. Republicanism tended to be strongest amongst workers in towns, but aroused fears of mob rule and attacks on property amongst the middle classes. It had prominent supporters like the marquis de Lafayette, who was to play a crucial role in securing Parisian consent to a constitutional monarchy under the duc d'Orléans in the wake of the July Revolution.

Marxist historians have pointed to class conflict as a cause of the revolution. In this analysis Charles X's ultra-royalism represented an attempt to return the landed aristocracy to power in France. This was out of step with the interests of the bourgeoisie, who sought political and social power and a state responsive to the interests of capitalism. Both the aristocracy and the bourgeoisie feared the lower orders – peasants and urban workers – but the bourgeoisie were willing to exploit unrest to achieve their own political ends.

Was the overthrow of the Bourbons inevitable in 1830? Some might argue that the difficulties facing the restored monarchy in 1815 were such that long-term survival was unlikely unless the monarchs were willing to embrace the idea of constitutional monarchy wholeheartedly. Even then, the likelihood of political stability was remote because of the divided nature of French society, the mutually antipathetic heritages left by the revolutionary and Napoleonic eras and periodic economic crisis. After 1830 Louis-Philippe was unable to make constitutional monarchy work, resulting in another revolution in 1848. On the other hand, Louis XVIII had survived and left France prosperous in 1824. This would suggest the downfall of the Bourbons had much more to do with the character and policies of Charles X and the short-term economic crisis which hit France after 1826.

Why was Louis-Philippe overthrown in 1848?

The abdication of Charles X left open the question of who or what would replace him. There seemed three main options:

- A regency for Charles X's 9-year-old grandson, favoured by the royalists.
- A constitutional monarchy under Louis-Philippe, the duc d'Orléans, favoured by liberal politicians.
- A democratic republic, favoured by many of the Parisian revolutionaries.

The first was never a serious possibility, even though Charles X believed Louis-Philippe could be persuaded to act as guardian of royal interests, and he and royalists (henceforward referred to as legitimists or Carlists) felt betrayed when Louis-Philippe accepted the crown. The last option could not command much support amongst the politicians of the parliament or the middle classes more widely. A fourth option, rule by **Napoleon's son** – reflected in popular cries of *Vive l'Empereur!* and *Vive Napoléon II!* heard in the streets of Paris and other towns – was never a serious possibility. For the leading politicians, the best solution was a constitutional monarchy that would make government answerable to parliament. The key problem in the short term was winning the acceptance of the republicans and workers of Paris who had taken over the Hôtel de Ville. Louis-Philippe, persuaded at this stage to accept the post of lieutenant governor of the kingdom by the parliament, took the brave decision to go to the Hôtel de Ville. There he met the marquis de Lafayette, the hero of the Parisian revolutionaries. Together, wrapped in the Tricolour, they appeared on the balcony and embraced, to public acclaim. Meanwhile, liberal journalists like Adolphe Thiers organised a poster campaign advocating the claims of Louis-Philippe, by emphasising his revolutionary credentials as the son of **Philippe Egalité**, a hero of the early French Revolution, and as a veteran of the revolution's first battles against foreign monarchs at Valmy and Jemappes. Die-hard republicans may not have approved, but the majority appeared to give at least their temporary approval.

In the short term, then, Louis-Philippe appeared to be the solution that divided the French least. On 9 August he was proclaimed 'king of the French by the grace of God and the will of the nation'. The title made it clear that he did not claim to rule by divine right but by popular consent – a ruler of citizens, not subjects. He deliberately distanced himself from the style of the Bourbon monarchy, reducing court ceremonial, adopting the dress of the bourgeoisie and walking the streets of Paris. The spin was that he was the 'citizen king', representing the *juste milieu* (middle way) between the anarchy of republicanism and the despotism of absolute monarchy. Whatever the style, it would be the substance that in the end would count.

One of the first issues for the July Monarchy to settle was the nature of the new Constitution. A revised charter was drawn up which removed the king's power to suspend laws and rule by decree and gave the assembly the right to propose legislation. Censorship was abolished. The **franchise** was extended to those who paid 200 francs in tax a year and who were 25 or over. The minimum age for a deputy was lowered from 40 to 30. Effectively it brought more liberals into the political process, but still under 3 per cent of the population had the vote. Additional measures included the adoption of the Tricolour and the loosening of the ties between the Catholic church and the state – the Napoleonic formula that recognised Catholicism as the religion of the majority of Frenchmen was employed.

This was followed by a purge of the administration. The majority of prefects and subprefects – mainly ultras, many noble – were sacked and replaced

Napoleon's son was kept at the Austrian court; he died in 1832.

Philippe Egalité was the name adopted in September 1792 by Louis-Philippe, duc d'Orléans (1747–93). He was a junior member of the royal family whose liberal sympathies and support of the revolution of 1789 led him to change his name after the overthrow of the monarchy. Although he voted for the king's execution, he came under the suspicion of the Paris Jacobins and was guillotined during the Terror, on 6 November 1793. He was the father of Louis-Philippe, whose liberal sympathies also stretched back to the revolution (he had fought against the Austrians in the Battle of Jemappes, November 1792).

Having overthrown Charles X, why did France emerge from the July Revolution with another king?

The extension of the **franchise** was a relatively modest change, according to the historian Robert Tombs, merely increasing the electorate 'from 90,000 extremely rich elderly men to 170,000 very rich middle-aged men'.

How liberal was the revised Constitution of 1830?

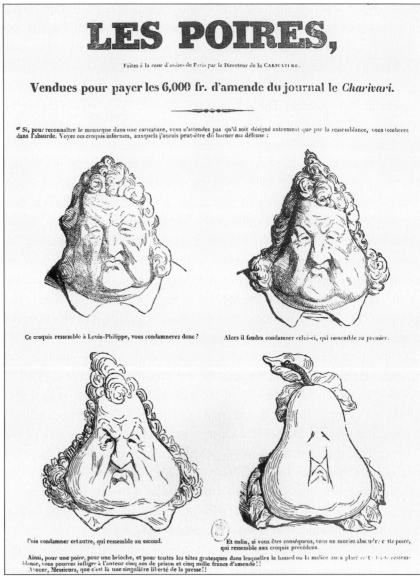

A very famous caricature of Louis-Philippe from the newspaper *Le Charivari*. From this point on Louis-Philippe's nickname was *La Poire* – the pear. How damaging do you think such imagery was to the July Monarchy?

The **changes** were commented on by the leading politician Casimir Périer, who was Louis-Philippe's second chief minister. He remarked: 'There has been no revolution; there has merely been a change in the person of the head of state'.

by bourgeois officials, many of whom had served previous regimes. The character of the new assembly and the new civil service was predominantly that of the wealthiest, propertied middle classes. Here, too, the **changes** were not great. The ship of state was to be held steady in the hands of a slightly expanded propertied elite.

However, the 'three glorious days' of July 1830 had raised all kinds of expectations amongst the people. The revolution had spawned new ideas, demands and hopes of change. In the atmosphere of freedom, the number and range of political clubs and societies exploded, accompanied by street demonstrations and a flood of journalistic and literary publications. Liberals, republicans, Bonapartists, socialists, democrats and others all found a voice. Revolutionary fervour and excitement were not sated by the imposition of a compromise king. The outbreak of revolution in Belgium, Poland and Italy led to demands that France should support these revolts and revive the national glories of the revolutionary and Napoleonic past. Here was a chance for France to overturn the Vienna settlement and for the new regime to secure its reputation in France. The internal pressure for a revolutionary and nationalist foreign policy, however, was at odds with the reality of the international situation and the natural caution of Louis-Philippe and much of the political elite.

However attractive the annexation of Belgium and the seizing of the Rhine as France's 'natural frontier' might be, Louis-Philippe recognised that any attempt at aggression by France would be met by the concerted opposition of the other Great Powers. In any case, the French army was in no state to fight, despite a flood of volunteers. Louis-Philippe, therefore, sought to negotiate over Belgium and intervened in Italy only in so far as to send a force to Ancona in the Papal States to counteract the influence of Austria. It was not enough to excite or appease the nationalists and the tone had been set for an unadventurous and cautious foreign policy that was to help undermine support for Louis-Philippe's regime.

For the workers and peasants suffering from the continued effects of bad harvests and economic crisis, the expectation was of relief and improvement of their condition. The workers who had produced the revolution wanted the new regime to respond to their demands for guaranteed wages, fixed hours, banning machinery and so on. There were strikes and demonstrations in Paris and other towns and cities and in November 1831 a major insurrection erupted in **Lyons**. Not only was the idea of fixed wages against the liberal principles of the 'bourgeois' monarchy, but social disorder could not be tolerated. Military force was used to suppress the rising. Economic unrest remained endemic in France for the next three years, often merging and being stirred up by republican sympathisers. Against the background of a cholera epidemic that killed 20,000 in 1831–32, barricades were thrown up in the working-class districts of Paris in June 1832. In 1833 and 1834 strike activity continued and in April 1834 there was another major rising in Lyons and Paris. The military suppression of the Paris rising involved the shooting of several innocent civilians in the so-called 'rue Transnonian Massacre'. Instead of winning over the urban workers, the regime had alienated them. It did nothing in the succeeding years to appease them or relieve their distress. It was to reap the consequences in 1848.

Silk workers in **Lyons**, demanding guaranteed wages, temporarily took over the city.

What evidence is there in his handling of the workers that Louis-Philippe was truly a 'bourgeois monarch'?

The failure in these early years of the regime to appease nationalists and workers, and the tendency to blame unrest on republican extremists and conspirators, helped push these groups into sympathy for republicanism. Republican movements such as the Society of the Rights of Man – often led by intellectuals and professional men – attracted increasing support in these years, mainly from skilled workers in the cities. A left-wing press also flourished. The line between economic unrest and political opposition was a fine one, and certainly the response of the authorities to strikes and protest was to prosecute left-wing newspapers and arrest leaders of republican societies. Following the risings of 1834 there were mass arrests of society members. In 1835 the worst of numerous assassination attempts on Louis-Philippe was carried out when an 'infernal machine' exploded near him at a review of the National Guard, killing 14. This event led to a series of repressive measures known as the **September Laws**.

The **September Laws** effectively banned the left- and right-wing press and outlawed their societies.

In what ways can Louis-Philippe's policies towards opposition be seen as a success?

What dangers were there in such policies?

As the scope of the September Laws indicates, whilst the threat from the left was the more serious, the threat from the right still existed. For example, in May 1832 the duchesse de Berry landed in France with her son, whom legitimists referred to as Henri V, to stir up revolt in the traditionally royalist Vendée region. She attracted only limited support and the revolt was crushed. More typically, perhaps, events involving legitimists provoked republican and popular unrest – such as the trial of Charles X's ministers and the riots following a commemoration service for the duc de Berry in February 1831. Royalism was a relatively minor threat to the regime; repression was enough in this case to reduce it still further.

The approach of Louis-Philippe's government to this unrest was a combination of repression of disorder at home and caution abroad. These were the policies of the so-called 'party of resistance' in the assembly and the king's chief minister, Périer. The party of resistance saw the July Revolution as an end point. There would be no further change and the job of government was to ensure stability. They were opposed by a 'party of movement', which viewed the 1830 revolution as the beginning of a period of further political and social reform and which desired a more active foreign policy. Louis-Philippe sided in the early 1830s with the party of resistance, and this was clearly where his sympathies lay. However, he did not want to be a mere puppet king, and after the mid 1830s, when disorder died down and he felt more secure, he sought to take a more active role in politics – by, for instance, appointing ministers he thought he could control. He was helped in this by the rivalry between various leading politicians in the assembly. But Louis-Philippe's hands-on approach led to criticism from the assembly and in 1840 he was forced to call on the ambitious **Adolphe Thiers** to form a government.

Thiers sought to win support from the left in the assembly by employing

Adolphe Thiers (1797–1877) was a historian, journalist, parliamentary deputy and minister during the restoration. He strongly supported the claims of Louis-Philippe in the July Revolution and was to become a prominent minister thereafter. He led two short-lived ministries (in 1836 and in 1840). In the latter his ambitious foreign policy, which threatened war, brought about his downfall. During the 1840s he was prominent in opposing Guizot.

the rhetoric of reform at home and pursuing a more independent and 'national' policy in foreign relations. Whilst the left was pleased with various pieces of economic legislation, such as the first state guarantee of interest on railway bonds (to secure investment for railway building), there was to be no electoral reform. Thiers instead hoped to revive some of the enthusiasm of 1830 by stimulating patriotism. He did this by playing on the Napoleonic legend, in particular by arranging for the return of **Napoleon's remains** to France from St Helena. Such moves only served to raise expectations and to revive support for Bonapartism.

Thiers also sought to follow a more nationalist policy abroad. He found his opportunity in the so-called Eastern Question, the future of the Turkish Empire. Britain and France had tended to co-operate in the past to prop up the 'sick man of Europe' as a bulwark against **Russian expansion** into the Mediterranean. In 1839 a threat to the stability of the Turkish Empire came from within its own frontiers when Mohammed Ali, the ruler of pro-French Egypt, fought a successful campaign in Syria against his overlord, the Turkish sultan. In 1840 Britain and the other Great Powers decided to intervene to save the sultan and threatened to use force unless Mohammed withdrew from Syria. The threat to France's friend raised nationalist opinion in the French press on both the left and the right, united for a while in sabre rattling against France's hereditary enemy, Britain. Thiers sought to wrest international advantage by exploiting the warlike atmosphere, threatening to invade the German Confederation in pursuit of French interests and the liberation of oppressed peoples. Whilst this French bluster roused nationalist anger in Germany and persuaded some foreign politicians to argue for compromise with France, Palmerston, the British foreign secretary, called the French bluff and went ahead with action against Mohammed Ali, who was forced to withdraw.

The French reaction to this humiliation was to increase the demands in the press for war. The atmosphere of 1830 seemed truly to be reawakened as nationalist demonstrations were accompanied by strikes and demands for electoral reform. The left employed the rhetoric of revolution and a war of liberation. Even Louis-Napoleon, Napoleon's nephew, sought to exploit the situation by landing at Boulogne, hoping to start a military revolt. The expedition proved a farce, and Louis-Napoleon was arrested and imprisoned. The prospect of war and revolution had alarmed the conservatives, who looked to Louis-Philippe to save the situation. Louis-Philippe was thoroughly alarmed and decided to ditch Thiers in October, a popular move amongst the majority of the limited electorate if not amongst the people as a whole. Thiers's policy of attempting to conciliate the left and pursue a nationalist foreign policy was abandoned. Once again Louis-Philippe had shown himself to be out of touch

Napoleon's remains were buried in a massive tomb, built at the Hôtel des Invalides on the bank of the Seine.

Russian expansion in the Mediterranean would threaten French trading interests in the Levant (eastern Mediterranean) and Britain's strategic interests by way of routes to its empire in India.

In what ways does Thiers's foreign policy differ from that pursued earlier in the reign?

What evidence is there that Louis-Philippe and his government were out of touch with public opinion?

The **placemen** were the numerous civil servants who sat as deputies.

with popular opinion. However prudent his abandonment of Thiers may have been, disillusion with his regime was growing and the number of his friends declining.

Louis-Philippe replaced Thiers with the more conservative **François Guizot**, who was to remain chief minister until the revolution of February 1848. There was to be no more dabbling with aggressively nationalist or reforming policies that might let the left into power. Whilst this pleased the conservative elite, it gave the left the opportunity to accuse the king, Guizot and the right of betraying and humiliating the nation by bowing to foreign pressure. This attitude merely served to convince the king that the alternative to conservative policies was war and revolution.

Guizot believed that political power was the prerogative of the upper classes. He made it clear that there was to be no lowering of the property franchise which restricted the right to vote and to stand for election. His answer to the advocates of reform was dismissive – *Enrichissez-vous!* He meant that if you wanted the vote, all you needed to do was become rich enough to qualify. He was deaf to the argument that an extension of the franchise to more of the middle class would widen the basis of support for the regime. He totally rejected the notion of universal suffrage, viewing it as a recipe for disorder and chaos. The limited extent of the franchise (fewer than a quarter of a million Frenchmen had the vote in 1848) and the government's powers of patronage ensured that Guizot could rely on a majority in the assembly. The use of patronage, bribery and office to ensure support led inevitably to accusations of corruption which undermined the political system still further in the eyes of an ever wider literate public. As the 1840s progressed, opposition grew more vociferous and united in the assembly itself.

After the storms of 1840 came a relative calm supported by a period of relative economic prosperity, ministerial stability and a revival of harmonious relations with Britain. Whatever the apparent political calm, the sources of criticism and opposition remained. But it was not until after 1845 that the regime was to experience renewed instability when issues of foreign policy, electoral reform and government corruption took centre stage against a backdrop of severe economic and financial crisis.

When French naval officers claimed a protectorate over Tahiti in 1842 and expelled a British missionary called Pritchard in 1844, Guizot apologised to the British government and agreed to pay compensation. The debate over the issue in 1845 produced harsh criticism in the assembly over what was interpreted as a weak surrender to Britain, and the government was only able to win the vote by reliance on its **placemen**. This led to demands for parliamentary reform and the debarring of civil servants; it also united the various strands of opposition in the assembly into an anti-Guizot alliance. The demand for parliamentary reform was revived further with accusations of government corrupt practices in securing a majority in the 1846 general election. Guizot remained unmoved and unmoveable in his belief that any relaxation of the franchise might open the door to anarchy and revolution. The opposition argued that to reject all change and ignore public opinion was to encourage, not discourage, revolutionary forces.

In 1846 also, Anglo-French relations turned sour once more. This time the issue was the **marriage** arrangements of the Spanish queen and her sister. The British, when they discovered them, accused the French of double dealing, and this 'victory' over Britain did not go down well in France. The shabbiness of the affair and its dynastic overtones led to the accusation that Louis-Philippe was putting the interests of his family before those of the nation. The government made things worse by the mildness of their protest over Austria's annexation of 'Polish' Cracow in 1846.

French diplomacy helped secure the **marriage** of the queen to an ageing relative, which was unlikely to produce an heir, whilst her sister was to marry one of Louis-Philippe's sons.

How did Guizot's foreign policy help to undermine support for Louis-Philippe?

Guizot had promised prosperity. In 1846 it disappeared. France, like most of Europe, suffered a combination of disastrous grain and potato harvests and a financial and industrial slump. In autumn 1846 share prices fell and industrial workers in railways, iron and steel were laid off. Bread and potato prices rose steeply. Because workers were paying more for basic foodstuffs, they had less to spare for manufactured goods. The result was a slump in demand that led to further lay-offs and unemployment alongside bankruptcies and debt. As share prices fell, investors lost their money and economic confidence collapsed. Whilst workers and peasants struggled through the 'year of dear bread', businessmen blamed government policies for the financial and industrial crisis.

In this atmosphere the campaign for parliamentary reform, copying the tactics of the successful Anti-Corn-Law League in Britain, took off once more. The parliamentary opposition organised reform banquets to circumvent the restrictions on public assembly. Over 20,000 people attended such banquets and as the campaign proceeded republicans became more prominent and began to speak of revolution. The government was roundly condemned for its corruption, its elitism and its failures. In this atmosphere scandals involving **ministers** were a gift and a duke committed suicide after murdering his wife.

Two former **ministers** were convicted of corruption in July 1847.

Louis-Philippe remained blind to the situation. He insisted that the reform campaign was 'a storm in a tea-cup', that the opposition was divided and that the government majority was secure. He refused to consider any measure of parliamentary reform. Guizot backed his judgement. Whatever the government's situation in the assembly, it was out of touch with public opinion. Revolutions tend to be made on the streets, not in debating chambers.

Government complacency perhaps partly explains why it was taken by surprise by the events of 22–24 February 1848 that toppled Louis-Philippe from

PUT OUT!

Louis-Philippe's candle extinguished by the red cap of liberty. The red cap was a symbol used during the French Revolution in the 1790s. The revolutionaries took it from ancient Rome, where such caps were presented to freed slaves. Of what fruit does the shape given to Louis-Philippe make you think? What is the significance of this shape? What can you tell about the nature of the revolution from this cartoon? This is a cartoon by John Leech from the British magazine *Punch* in March 1848.

his throne. The trigger was the banning of a proposed reform banquet in Paris. While the parliamentary opposition protested but accepted the decision, workers and students took to the streets. Little was done to disperse them and on 23 February the barricades went up. National Guards refused to act and instead shouted for Guizot's dismissal and parliamentary reform. It appeared the government had lost the support of the working classes and of the unenfranchised middle classes. The seriousness of the situation at last became apparent to Louis-Philippe and he dismissed Guizot in the hope of restoring order. The sacrifice of his minister, however, proved too little, too late.

By this time events were getting out of hand. Celebrations on the streets of Paris led to fighting in which 20 civilians were killed by royal troops. As a result, armed mobs manned the barricades whilst agitators demanded a republic. Paris was ungovernable. Louis-Philippe, unwilling to attempt force, instead left Paris (allegedly in a cab), abdicating in favour of his grandson, the 10-year-old comte de Paris (his son had died in 1842 in a traffic accident). It was too late. The demonstrators occupied the Hôtel de Ville and declared a republic with a provisional government made up of opposition deputies from the assembly. France's second experiment with constitutional monarchy since 1815 had failed; it was time to try a democratic republic.

The reasons for Louis-Philippe's downfall

The account of Louis-Philippe's reign clearly indicates a number of factors that together help to explain his overthrow. Part of the explanation must lie with the personality, attitudes and actions of the king himself. Like Charles X, Louis-Philippe wanted to rule as well as reign, and became associated with unpopular policies pursued by his ministers. Like Charles, he became associated with a particular group of politicians, especially after the appointment of Guizot in 1840. Like Charles, he failed to recognise the true state of public opinion and was taken by surprise when the revolution came. In addition, the bourgeois lifestyle of the 'citizen king' did little to add romance and glamour to his reputation.

The combination of all these made him an easy target for political and personal attack by a vociferous and scathing press, particularly the left-wing press. France was increasingly literate (newspapers had a circulation of 180,000 in Paris alone) and attacks on the crown and the government reached a wide audience. The cruel caricatures and satirical comment of a number of talented cartoonists who worked for the weekly *La Caricature* and daily *Le Charivari* were damaging. Most famous is the comparison made between Louis-Philippe and a pear (see page 136). Alienating the media was dangerous, and the various press laws introduced after 1830 (when Louis-Philippe had agreed to freedom of the press) did little to endear him to journalists or printworkers.

But Louis-Philippe was in a difficult situation from the start. He was a compromise candidate in some senses, foisted on the French people in July 1830 by a middle-class elite fearful of a republic. The true basis of his support was then very narrow. It was claimed he was king by 'will of the people', but there was no election – merely endorsement by an assembly representing less than 3 per cent of the population. The events of July 1830 raised expectations of a strong revolutionary nationalist foreign policy and of reform to bring social justice. These hopes were quickly dashed. Louis-Philippe's own inclinations and the interests of his supporters in the assembly dictated a different approach. The repressive policies pursued in the early years of the monarchy did much to alienate the growing working classes of the towns and to drive them into support of republicanism as the only political option that offered the prospect of a better life.

Foreign policy plays an important part in explaining the regime's lack of support. Whatever its merits in terms of allaying international fears of a revived expansionist and revolutionary France, its caution and its desire to stay on good terms with Britain cut little ice with the French people who yearned for a return of French greatness and leadership in Europe. The nationalist passions aroused over Belgium, Poland, Italy and the Mohammed Ali crisis were not confined to a few politicians but were the stuff of street politics born of France's revolutionary and Napoleonic past. Republicans and Bonapartists saw an active foreign policy as a sign of a great nation. All Louis-Philippe appeared to offer was safety and humiliation. 'France is bored,' commented the left-winger Lamartine.

Just as with Charles X, one problem facing Louis-Philippe was that there were ready political alternatives to constitutional monarchy and a revolutionary heritage that legitimised the violent overthrow of the existing regime. Republicanism was the most dangerous threat from the left; despite the repression of the 1830s it was not destroyed, merely driven underground for a time – to revive in times of economic and political crisis, as in 1840. On the right, although of less significance, was legitimism that sought a Bourbon

The regime revived **Bonapartism** by trying to buy some reflected glory through such measures as completing the Arc de Triomphe and interring Napoleon's remains at the Hôtel des Invalides.

restoration. And in the wings there was **Bonapartism**, which the regime inadvertently stimulated. Political opposition to Louis-Philippe was a constant feature of the regime, there from the start. It was found in the assembly, from those deputies sympathetic to more reform; on the streets; in the press; and amongst individual conspirators (there were a large number of assassination attempts – two in 1846).

Crucial to explaining the 1848 revolution is the economic crisis from 1846. Just as economic and social unrest formed the backdrop to the 1830 revolution, so it did to that of 1848. It was a short-term crisis, with a long-term aspect. Its effects have much to do with the social and economic developments within France over the first half of the nineteenth century (see pages 145–49). Although the government attempted to reflect the interests of the bourgeoisie in its economic policies, it signally failed to deal with the economic and social consequences of industrial change, population growth and urbanisation for the working classes. The liberal philosophy of laissez-faire (let it alone) meant that the government did not see it as part of its responsibility to become involved in such issues as industrial relations or wage rates. Also, it tended to deal with industrial unrest as a problem of disorder, reacting with repression. One criticism of Louis-Philippe's rule is that little social legislation was passed beyond an ineffective attempt to regulate child labour in 1841.

Compare the reasons for the downfall of Louis-Philippe with those for that of Charles X. How similar are they?

By 1848, the opposition **deputies** in the assembly were frustrated by the lack of government action, its manipulation of the electoral process and its failure even to consider reform. By 1848 businessmen and the bourgeoisie more generally blamed the government for their problems and were unwilling to come to its aid. In 1848 the workers and students of Paris took their economic, social and political frustration onto the streets. Louis-Philippe, aged 75 – old, tired and having buried his son and his much loved sister – did not have the stomach for a fight and in any case could not rely on the army. The regime fell because there was nothing left to support it.

What were the key social and economic developments?

This chapter has pointed to the intimate connection between the performance of the economy and the relative political stability of the governments of France. The two revolutions of 1830 and 1848, for instance, coincided with economic crises. The French economy was under development in this period, which – coupled with other changes such as population growth and urbanisation – created stresses and strains in French society that produced new political problems and new political ideas.

The changing economy

Throughout this period France remained a predominantly agricultural and rural country. However, there was industrial growth, when the expansion of railways did much to stimulate heavy industry and engineering. A more steady expansion occurred in the textile industry.

One way to demonstrate the growth of industry is to examine various **economic indicators**. Such figures indicate the trends in the economy but tell us little about the pattern or nature of industrial and agricultural **growth** across France. Generally, economic growth was irregular between 1815 and the late 1830s, but fast from then on. The basis of growth before 1840 was the expansion of the traditional agricultural and industrial systems; after 1840 this expansion continued but thereafter a further stimulus came from investment in railways.

With the coming of peace in 1815, agriculture recovered and expanded relatively quickly. The agricultural labour force increased, as did agricultural production. The main factors in producing this growth were the introduction of new methods such as crop rotation, which eliminated the need to leave land fallow, and the use of metal ploughs; and the expansion of the cultivated area. There was no revolution in farm organisation or the size of farms. Landholding and farming remained generally small scale, a feature of the French system reinforced by the **partage system** of inheritance. Such small-scale farming

Economic indicators include the following:

1810–50, pig iron production rose by over 400 per cent;

1810–40, coal consumption rose by over 300 per cent;

1830–40, consumption of raw cotton doubled;

by 1850, France had built about 2,000 km of railway lines.

Annual industrial **growth** averaged 2.5–3.0 per cent and annual agricultural production rose on average by 1.2 per cent.

The **partage system** divided property between the heirs rather than it going to the firstborn.

(80 per cent of farms occupied 20 per cent of agricultural land) inhibited change and improvement, which was much more evident on the farms of the larger landowners. Whatever the improvements and the increase in production, the coincident increase in population still meant that when the **harvest** was poor hunger and starvation threatened many.

In contrast to Britain, there was no large-scale transfer of population from rural areas to towns. Over 60 per cent of the labour force remained directly dependent on agriculture. This was not because agriculture was prosperous. The rural population had to supplement its income from various other sources such as spinning flax for linen, charcoal-smelting of iron and seasonal employment. Rural poverty remained a feature of many areas of France.

In industry France could not compete effectively with the mass-production techniques developed in Britain. French industry tended to concentrate on two main areas – the production of goods like candles and soap for local consumption, and **luxury goods**, whose production was labour-intensive. Units of production remained small – workshops employing a few skilled craftsmen rather than larger-scale factories were the norm.

French industry was protected by the state through tariff barriers and quotas against foreign competition. Arguably this held up the **development** of the French economy. On the other hand, this approach helped France develop its metallurgical and engineering industries. French economic development was arguably also hampered by the lack of an entrepreneurial culture. Those with financial resources preferred to invest in land, buildings or loans to government rather than riskier investment in industry.

These patterns began to change in the 1840s as industry, especially in textiles and railways, began to expand rapidly and to demand investment that offered high returns. The flood of investment into railways, however, brought its own dangers. The overspeculation in railway company shares contributed to the economic crisis that developed in 1846–47. The riskiness of industrial investment was also demonstrated by the textile industry. A collapse in domestic demand for cotton goods because of the rising cost of bread in 1846–47 is reflected in the sudden drop in the import of raw cotton. In 1846 France imported 64,000 tons of raw cotton. In 1847 this fell by 30 per cent, to 45,000 tons. Such figures demonstrate the sensitivity of industrial prosperity to performance in agriculture. When agriculture did well, harvests were good and food prices were low, so workers had more to spend on manufactured goods; when harvests were bad and food prices rose, the result was a fall in demand for manufactured goods with the attendant consequences of wage cuts and unemployment, which in turn exacerbated the situation.

Social changes

More generally, the changing nature of the French economy and, in particular, the growth of industry produced social and political consequences. Certain cities and **towns** where industry developed grew rapidly. Rapid urban population growth was not accompanied by parallel developments in housing and sanitation. The result was appalling living conditions, overcrowding and susceptibility to diseases like cholera and tuberculosis which reduced life expectancy and caused thousands of deaths in epidemics. In 1832, as a result of a major cholera epidemic, the death rate shot up to 34.1,000 from 27.1,000. In the poor areas of Paris it rose to 45:1,000. Poor living conditions and standards of health are brought out by the fact that in 1840 in manufacturing areas nine out of every ten men called up for military service were deemed physically unfit. Overcrowding was a major problem, with Paris surveys revealing in some areas 5-storey houses accommodating 60 people.

There was some attempt to respond to the problems of rapid urbanisation. After the 1832 cholera epidemic, for instance, major work was done to improve the sewerage system and to provide more fountains in Paris. Progress was hampered by the limited powers of local government and Paris remained more unhealthy in the 1830s than it had been in 1820. A steady number of Frenchmen sought a better life through **emigration** to the United States and to an extent in the 1840s to Algeria.

Whilst the poor, be they peasants or urban workers, formed the greater part of the population, it was the bourgeoisie that became the dominant class in this period. This is reflected in the description of the July Monarchy as the 'bourgeois monarchy'. Contemporaries and historians have found it difficult to give a precise definition of this group. The term 'bourgeoisie' seems to cover everyone from skilled craftsmen or small shopowners, through professionals like lawyers and doctors, to industrialists and wealthy financiers and bankers. To be bourgeois perhaps was more a state of mind than membership of a closely definable class. The bourgeois was politically literate and wealth oriented, enjoyed a certain prosperity and valued 'liberty'. Typically a bourgeois was neither a democratic republican nor a monarchist.

Some have distinguished between the higher bourgeoisie (*haute bourgeoisie*), who enjoyed considerable wealth and, through the vote, political influence, and the lesser (*petite*) bourgeoisie, who were jealous of the influence of the *haute bourgeoisie*, felt caught between the poverty of the poor and the closed doors of opportunity and political influence, and were threatened with ruin in times of economic crisis. The *petite bourgeoisie*, unable to influence politics directly because they did not qualify for the vote, felt increasingly alienated from the July Monarchy and in the late 1840s turned against it.

These included smaller **towns** like Roubaix (population 8,000 to 34,000 between 1831 and 1841) and St Etienne (16,000 to 54,000) as well as major cities like Paris and Lyons.

What problems did the growth of towns create?

On average there was **emigration** of 3,000–4,000 to the USA each year. This rose in years of hardship. In 1847, 20,000 emigrated.

Political consequences of social and economic change

The growth of towns and industrialisation along with the associated problems of overcrowding, disease, low wages and volatile patterns of employment provoked interest in and investigation into them. The result was the development of new ideas to deal with the problems and to reorganise society and politics. **Writers** like Victor Hugo and George Sand brought the problems and difficulties of ordinary Frenchmen to the notice of the middle classes in their novels. Their humanitarian concern helped make the condition of the workers a public issue. Other writers and thinkers began to suggest 'socialist' solutions. Henri de Saint-Simon advocated a society in which all should be given work according to their talents and rewarded correspondingly, whilst Charles Fourier promoted the idea of co-operative farming. **Louis Blanc** argued forcefully for the 'right to work' in his book *L'Organisation du travail* (1839). The existing system of business organisation should be replaced by a national economy in which the state ran industry and set up national workshops for the unemployed.

Others (such as the anarchist P. J. Proudhon, who coined the phrase 'all property is theft') were more extreme in their views. One of the features of European politics in the 1820s and 1830s was the existence of conspiratorial secret societies such as the Carbonari in Italy. France had its fair share of secret societies and conspiracies, many of them inspired by more or less 'socialist' desires to produce a France that benefited the ordinary Frenchman. Once the government made clear its opposition to the demands of workers, most notably in the suppression of the Lyons insurrection in 1831, such societies abounded and drew on the discontent of the workers and peasants. Particularly influential were the ideas of **Philippe Buonarotti**. Auguste Blanqui, influenced by him, organised a secret society – the Society of Families – in the aftermath of the suppressive legislation of 1834–35. By 1836 it had its own arms dumps and gunpowder factory and had infiltrated the Paris garrison. Blanqui, fearful of discovery, then reconstituted it as the Society of the Seasons and planned a rising for spring 1839. In May 1839 the society occupied the Hôtel de Ville in Paris and declared a republic but the mob did not rise in support, and with some bloodshed the rising was crushed.

Although such conspiracies and secret societies were unsuccessful, their existence reflected a deep disillusion amongst ordinary workers with the restoration and Orléanist monarchies. Republicans were able to draw on this and win support by absorbing 'socialist' ideas, promising, as the republican *Tribune* newspaper did, a 'social republic' in which the problem of economic inequalities would be addressed. In 1830 the workers of Paris had hoped for a republic that would improve their condition in life; in 1848 they were to seek

In England, **writers** such as Charles Dickens were concerned with similar issues.

Louis Blanc, as a member of the republican government immediately after the 1848 revolution, had the chance to experiment with such workshops, but the test was short-lived.

Philippe Buonarotti's *La conspiration pour l'égalité dite de Babeuf*, published in 1828, was a kind of handbook on revolution based on his assessment of the Babeuf conspiracy during the 1790s.

a republic once more. In February 1848 a republic was declared and the provisional government, including 'socialists' like Blanc, seemed to offer hope of a better future. It proved a forlorn one, as the brief experiment with socialist ideas was crushed with the radicals in the June Days that same year.

Summary questions

1 (a) Explain *two* main problems facing Louis-Philippe immediately after he became king in 1830.

   (b) To what extent was Charles X mainly responsible for his own downfall?

2 (a) Explain the nature and importance of the Charter of 1814.

   (b) Compare the importance of *three* main causes of the February Revolution of 1848.

6 Revolution and repression in Europe, 1815–49

Focus questions

◆ To what extent and why did nationalist and liberal movements develop between 1815 and 1848?

◆ How successful was Metternich in containing revolutionary forces in the period 1815–48?

◆ Why did revolutions break out across central Europe in 1848?

◆ Why did these revolutions fail by the summer of 1849?

Significant dates

1815	Vienna settlement redraws the map of Europe after Napoleon's defeat.
1817	Wartburg Festival in the German Confederation reveals early German nationalist and liberal feeling amongst students, academics and others.
1819	Karlsbad Decrees used to suppress liberals and nationalists in the German Confederation.
1820–21	Liberal revolutions in Italy suppressed by Austria.
1821	Troppau Protocol agreed between the Holy Alliance powers of Austria, Prussia and Russia against revolution.
1831	Liberal revolutions in central Italy suppressed by Austria.
1832	Hambach Festival – a liberal/nationalist celebration in the German Confederation. Six Articles introduce new measures of repression in the German Confederation.
1834	Prussia expands the customs union into the *Zollverein*. The Czech nationalist historian Palacky sets up 'Czech Mother' to promote Czech culture.
1840	Rhine crisis. Magyar (Hungarian) accepted as the official language of the Hungarian diet (assembly). Hungarian nationalist newspaper, *Pesti Hirlap*, begins.
1846	'Liberal' pope, Pius IX.
1848	Revolutions.
1849	Defeat of revolutions.

Overview

In 1815 it seemed as though the ***ancien régime*** had triumphed over the revolutionary forces that had led to Napoleon's dominance of the continent and 22 years of warfare. The Great Powers of Austria, Russia, Britain and Prussia (and even France) sat down in Vienna to redraw the map of Europe (see map on page 152). The politicians and rulers involved were all more or less conservative and had little sympathy for the new ideas of liberalism and nationalism spawned by the French Revolution. Their concerns were shaped by the desire to look after their own interests, restore a balance of power on the continent, contain and prevent a possible future French resurgence, and where practicable restore legitimate rulers (those who had ruled prior to the reorganisations imposed by revolutionary and Napoleonic France).

There was no wholesale return to 1789. The old, weak federation of over three hundred states, principalities and cities known as the Holy Roman Empire was not restored. In its place a German Confederation of 39 states was created. This was no concession to German nationalism, but a compromise designed to recognise the legitimacy of the more important rulers in 'Germany' and the need to contain France in the west (and arguably Russia in the east). Just as it had dominated the Holy Roman Empire, Austria was the president of the confederation, but Prussia gained extensive territories on the River Rhine on the borders with France, giving it a direct interest in containing French aggression.

In Italy, an extended Piedmont was returned to the house of Savoy, Austria was given Lombardy and Venetia, and the Bourbons were restored to the kingdom of Naples. In the north-west, Belgium – formerly Austrian territory – was united with Holland in the new kingdom of the Netherlands. These changes, along with those mentioned in the previous paragraph, were meant to hem in France behind a ***cordon sanitaire***. In the east, the main problem was what to do about Polish territories. Poland as an independent state had disappeared in a series of partitions in the late eighteenth century, divided up between Russia, Prussia and Austria. However, Napoleon had re-created a kind of Poland in the grand duchy of Warsaw, which Russia desired. At the peace conference at Vienna, Britain and Austria were concerned about Russian ambitions and conflict over the fate of Polish territories almost caused war. In the end a compromise was worked out whereby Prussia and Austria retained some Polish territory whilst the remainder became a semi-autonomous province of the Russian Empire referred to by historians as Congress Poland.

The rulers of the new and restored states determined at the Vienna Congress were all more or less absolute monarchs. There were few concessions to liberal ideas, except to a limited degree in France (see Chapter 5). Nor

The term ***ancien régime*** means 'old system of government' and is used to describe the society and government that existed prior to French revolutionary changes – a system based on absolute monarchy, privileged aristocracy and a powerful church.

A ***cordon sanitaire*** is a defensive curtain of states, strong enough to resist possible aggression.

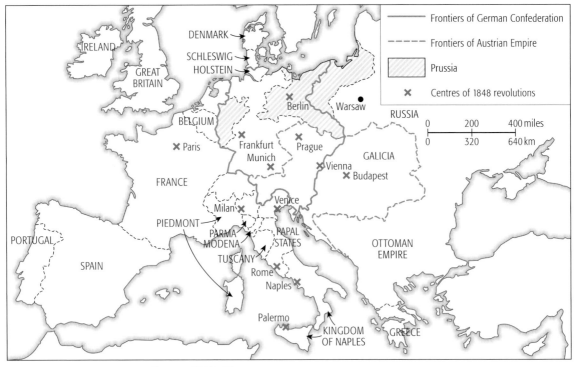

Europe, 1815–48.

Metternich said: 'Two words are enough to create evil; two words which because they are empty of any practical meaning delight the visionaries. The words are liberty and equality.'

were there any concessions to nationalism – nationality was not a criterion used for drawing up frontiers. Both sets of ideas were too closely associated in peacemakers' minds with the horrors of the French Revolution and the overthrow of the established order of kings and aristocracies. **Metternich**, the Austrian chancellor, had a typical view. In ideological terms liberalism and nationalism were to provide the greatest challenge to the order established in central Europe by the Vienna Congress. The challenge was to culminate in a series of revolutions across Europe in 1848 which, although they failed in the short term, were to shake the political foundations of Europe and would indirectly bring about political change in the second half of the century.

To what extent and why did nationalist and liberal movements develop between 1815 and 1848?

Liberalism

It is sometimes difficult to see the revolutionary implications of liberal ideas because they are now, at least in the western world, accepted as manifestly right. In the context of a society where privileged aristocracy and absolute monarchy were the rule, the implications of an ideology based on the equality of all individuals were revolutionary. To the established dominant classes the

French Revolution and especially the extremes of the Terror, when thousands were executed or killed, indicated that when traditional social and political structures were tampered with only violence and chaos could result. To them, freedom and equality meant bloodshed and war.

In the context of the early nineteenth century, three documents laid the foundations of liberalism: the American Declaration of Independence, the **Declaration of the Rights of Man and the Citizen**, and the Spanish Constitution of 1812. Indeed, it was in relation to the supporters of the last of these that the term 'liberal' was coined. 'Liberalism' refers to a body of ideas that can be grouped around five key terms: constitution, equality, individual freedom, property and reform.

A summary of the **Declaration of the Rights of Man and the Citizen** may be found on page 40.

Constitution

Metternich said of the period after 1815: 'There is scarcely any epoch which does not have a rallying cry to some particular faction. The cry since 1815 has been "Constitution".' This is perhaps the one word that distinguishes the demands of early nineteenth-century liberals. A **constitution** would guarantee the individual certain basic rights and also provide for the people, or a portion of them, to hold the government to account and limit its actions. Constraints on government would normally be achieved through some kind of elected assembly. At root, liberals believed in popular sovereignty – the idea that political power ultimately derives from the people. They also believed that the purpose of government was to serve the people and look after their best interests. This could be done only if the government had to answer to the people, either directly or through elected representatives.

A **constitution** is a set of principles specifying the various institutions of the state, the relationship between them and the powers of each. It also covers the rights of the individual.

Equality

Liberals argued that all men were equal in the sense that all possessed a range of natural rights. The American Declaration of Independence had described these as 'life, liberty and the pursuit of happiness'. The French Declaration of the Rights of Man included a range of 'liberties'. One fundamental equality was equality before the law. This refers to the idea that the law should apply to all and justice should be administered to all in the same way. It attacked the notion that churchmen should be tried in different courts and under different laws from ordinary citizens. Liberals were also concerned with equality in another sense. If all were equal, to distinguish between them on the basis of their birth, for instance, was irrational. Liberals, therefore, attacked all aspects of society based on privilege, most obviously the privileges of the aristocracy. They believed that social distinctions should be based on talent and hard work. They argued for 'careers open to talents' or 'meritocracy' – that offices should be given on the basis of the talents of the individual and not reserved, for instance, for members of the nobility.

Individual freedom

Liberty also means freedom. The basic philosophy was that individuals should be as free as possible to decide and do things for themselves. Individual rights should include, for instance, freedom of conscience (such as choice of religion), freedom of speech and the press, freedom of movement, freedom from arbitrary arrest and, as far as was consistent with others' freedom, freedom of action. The implication is that while it was important for governments to provide a framework of law and order so that all could feel safe, governments should not interfere unduly in the lives of citizens.

Property

One of the fundamental rights for a nineteenth-century liberal was the right to property and part of the purpose of the law was to protect property rights. Liberals talked of equality, but they did not mean material equality; there was to be no attack on the rich. Liberals revered property, seeing it as giving people a stake in society and bringing responsibility and respectability. That is why many liberals believed that the right to vote should be linked to some measure of wealth, such as a minimum level of liability to a property tax.

Reform

Make a list of the main principles of liberalism. In what ways do liberal ideas protect the interests of the middle classes?

Liberals generally believed in the reform of the state rather than revolution. They sought to wrest political concessions that would lead to constitutional limitations on absolute rule and the guarantee of certain rights to the people. They were also interested in reforms that would make the state more efficient and would help improve the economy and opportunities open to people, especially the educated ones.

Liberalism has been called a middle-class ideology, born out of middle-class frustrations in a society based on privilege. Certainly liberalism drew its support mainly from the middle classes or bourgeoisie. Students, academics, lawyers and professional men – more than businessmen – chafed at the lack of opportunities and the restrictions on their freedom. They believed they, and humanity in general, were being held back by the established elites whose position was based on birth and privilege. However, the bourgeoisie were afraid of the 'mob'. This was why many 'moderate' liberals preferred the notion of a property-based **franchise** or an indirect system of election that would effectively exclude the lower classes. Only radicals espoused the notion of universal manhood suffrage and democracy. For the moderate liberal the ideal was a constitutional monarchy with a law-making assembly elected by a limited franchise.

The **franchise** is the right to vote.

In this sense most liberals were middle class, caught between the privileged aristocracy who stood in the way of their ambitions and the lower classes whose violence threatened their property. The irony was that to achieve what they wanted they needed lower-class support, but the means could be violent and the result might be democracy or mob rule. If disorder threatened, the natural inclination of the bourgeoisie would be to look to the established forces of law and order.

Radicals, on the other hand, were much more ready to espouse revolution and the spread of political rights to all classes. They tended to support universal manhood suffrage and wanted constitutions that would severely limit the power of kings. Sometimes, like Mazzini (see page 162), they were republicans wanting to get rid of monarchy altogether.

How did radicals differ from liberals?

Nationalism

Liberalism is in some respects difficult to disentangle from nationalism in this period. Both drew their main support from the middle classes and both, in central Europe, were more or less opposed to the established order. And, according to the French model, the sovereignty of the people was the sovereignty of the nation. The term 'nationalism' defies simple definition. It broadly refers to the notion that the most important bond in society is that of nationality. What then matters is what defines the nation.

Any attempt to define the concept of the nation in more than the most general terms is open to criticism as the criteria we apply are unlikely to fit all nations. Benedict Anderson defines a nation as 'an imagined political community'. This refers to the belief that we have something in common that binds all together in a particular national community. It is a sense of belonging and mutual responsibility, of fraternity and, of course, difference from others. Historians have suggested that two concepts of the nation developed at the end of the eighteenth century: on the one hand, a basically political definition of the nation and, on the other, an essentially cultural definition.

The political nation

This concept relates to the ideas put forward by **Jean-Jacques Rousseau** in the eighteenth century and which were applied in 1789 in the French Revolution. In 1789, the people of France claimed to be the French nation (rather than merely the subjects of the king of France) and claimed that political power in the state ultimately rested with them. The French nation wrested political power from the monarchy and privileged elites. To be French after 1789 was simply to be a citizen of the French state. The idea of the political nation, then, focuses on a people's right to self-determination, its right to choose its own government and the responsibility of that government to respect and protect the people's rights. This idea of the nation is closely linked to the ideas of liberalism noted above.

In his book *The social contract*, **Jean-Jacques Rousseau** argued that political power (sovereignty) was possessed by the nation, that is, all the people of a particular political community or state.

The cultural nation

In central and eastern Europe a different concept of the nation developed which did not necessarily have any political overtones. A nation was defined by reference to a range of criteria such as a common history and culture, a common language and religion, and ties of blood and community derived from long settlement in a particular area. Such a list, of course, will not fit every case, nor is it meant to – to some nations (such as the Germans), history and culture were the defining elements; in others (such as the Poles), it was religion; and for yet others (such as the Italians), it was language. This concept allowed nations to define themselves without specific reference to an existing state. Some ardent German nationalists, therefore, could see themselves as German and wanted to encourage a sense of Germanness in others without necessarily desiring the creation of a German national state.

What characteristics would you say define British or French nationality today?

Whilst such a distinction is useful, the history of the nineteenth century demonstrates that in the end the two concepts are not mutually exclusive. As cultural nationalism developed in Europe it was quickly linked to political aspirations against existing regimes, and the notion of cultural nationhood lent legitimacy to claims for states to be organised on the basis of nations.

Definition of nationalism

This view of **nationalism** is expressed in the equation:
people = nation = state.

At the most basic level, **nationalism** refers to the belief that the state and the nation should coincide. Nationalists hold that the nation state is the highest, most desirable and even the only legitimate form of state. Additionally, the state in its constitution and actions should reflect the will of the nation. When nation and state did not coincide (as in a multi-national dynastic empire like that of the Habsburgs, the multi-state German Confederation or the multi-state Italian peninsula), the nationalists wanted to bring about the nation state or at least seek some political recognition of the nation, especially through some acceptance of national self-government and of the use of the national language.

It is difficult to generalise about nationalism in the period 1815–49. The nationalism of the Poles, the Germans, the Magyars, the Czechs and the Croats varied in character, partly in relation to individual historical contexts. There was no necessary agreement within nationalist movements about their aims. The German and Italian nationalist movements, for example, were not united in their aims or methods.

The development of liberal and nationalist ideas in the German Confederation

The German Confederation was set up by the Vienna settlement in 1815 (see map on page 152). It was dominated by Austria and Prussia. Both these states had territory inside and outside the confederation. It was a loose federation of independent states headed by a **diet** under the presidency of Austria. There was no federal law, foreign policy or currency; even agreements about a federal army were flawed. The confederation was not solely German; it contained also minorities of Czechs, Slovenes, Italians and Danes. However, the confederation did give Austria a major influence in German affairs, reflected in the policies pursued by Metternich (see page 167).

Liberal and nationalist movements in 'Germany' have their origin in the influence of French revolutionary ideas and in reaction to them and French depradations during the revolutionary and Napoleonic wars. In southern Germany, many bourgeois welcomed the liberal ideas that followed in the wake of French armies in the 1790s. It was in the southern states like Baden and Bavaria that French influence was felt longest and liberal ideas won much support. Elsewhere French revolutionary ideas were too closely linked with military defeat, French occupation and French exploitation to be attractive to others. To a degree German nationalism arose as a reaction against the French.

German intellectuals like **Fichte**, Arndt, Jahn and **Hegel** rejected political liberalism of the French variety and instead sought to identify and encourage a distinctive German sense of nationhood. They sought their inspiration not in the ideas of the revolution – which they viewed as alien – but in the culture, history and language of the ordinary German people, the *Volk*.

Liberalism did win some concessions in southern Germany after 1815. Baden, Bavaria, Württemberg and one or two other states granted very limited constitutions that guaranteed some rights and provided for the election (by a limited franchise) of assemblies (with very limited powers). Elsewhere (such as in Prussia), liberal aspirations were thwarted.

The first major manifestation of liberal and nationalist protest in the confederation occurred amongst students and academics. Students had begun to form patriotic societies (*Burschenschaften*) which called for liberal reforms and German unity. In 1817 students from across Germany assembled at Wartburg to celebrate the anniversary of the Battle of the Nations (1813), when Napoleon was defeated, and the tercentenary of the German Protestant Reformation begun by Martin Luther in **1517**. Nationalist speeches were made and reactionary books, along with effigies of Metternich, were burned. These early flames of German liberalism and nationalism were quickly extinguished by Metternich, who used the excuse of the murder by a student of a reactionary journalist (Kotzebue) to persuade the confederation diet to accept the **Karlsbad Decrees** in 1819. The measures were enough to stifle, but not kill, the liberal and national movement for a decade. Despite the decrees, liberal political groups continued to exist, as did a few organisations such as the Society of German Natural Scientists and the Exchange Association of German Book

The **diet** was not an elected assembly, but represented the rulers of the 39 states.

Fichte argued that Germans were the creative, original race in Europe whose distinctive *Volkgeist* (spirit of the people) needed to be protected.

Hegel argued for the creation of a strong, autocratic German state. There was little in the nationalism of either Hegel or Fichte that smacked of the French view of liberalism.

Before **1517** the Roman Catholic church headed by the pope in Rome was the only Christian church of central and western Europe. It had come under criticism and when Martin Luther put forward his different vision of Christianity he won support in Germany which led to a split in the religious unity of Europe. Christian opponents of Catholicism became known as Protestants.

The **Karlsbad Decrees** prohibited political meetings, censored the press, banned *Burschenschaften* and imposed controls on university teaching. See also pages 168–69.

Dealers. Their number was small and their membership confined to some members of the academic and professional classes.

Whilst political agitation was marginalised and pushed underground, other work was being done that would encourage German nationalism. Academics were researching 'German' history, especially the medieval period, and investigating 'German' folklore. The deeds of Frederick Barbarossa (literally 'red beard') and Grimms' fairy tales became accessible to an increasingly literate German public (adult literacy in Germany was about 30 per cent in this period).

In the **July Revolution** of 1830 the Bourbon king of France, Charles X, was overthrown and replaced with the more liberal Louis-Philippe (see Chapter 5).

In the 1830s agitation revived in the wake of the **July Revolution** in France. There were a few minor uprisings in the confederation and the rulers of Saxony, Hanover, Hesse and Brunswick granted constitutions. In 1832 an all-German festival held at Hambach brought together nationalist and liberal students, lawyers, professors, writers, burghers, artisans and peasants. The German tricolour of black, red and gold was raised and liberal and nationalist speeches were made. This first popular political assembly was met in the same way as the Wartburg Festival of 1817 – by repression. The confederation passed the Six Articles, which banned student societies and the wearing of black, red and gold symbols, and reinforced rigid control of the universities.

An engraving depicting the Hambach Festival in 1832. Note the numbers present, the women and children and the tricolour flag of black, red and gold of the German liberals and nationalists.

As a result of such repression the famous '**Göttingen Seven**' were expelled from their university posts for protesting at the abolition of the Hanoverian Constitution in 1837. As the abolition of this Constitution shows, liberals and nationalists had made little headway against the established authorities marshalled by Metternich.

The **Göttingen Seven** were a group of academics, including the Grimm brothers.

What were the key features of German nationalism and liberalism in the period 1815–40?

In the 1840s this was beginning to change. The new Prussian king, Frederick William IV, initially raised liberal hopes in 1840 by releasing political prisoners, relaxing press censorship and appointing some liberal ministers. However, the main catalyst for change was, as for the first stirrings of German nationalism, France. In 1840 the French press and politicians had begun to talk about recovering France's 'natural frontiers'. For Germany this meant a possible attack on the Rhine. The fears aroused by this 'Rhine crisis' led to a vociferous and widespread expression of German nationalism. The press put its weight behind the upsurge in national feeling, publishing such nationalist poems as Becher's 'They shall not have it, our German Rhine'. The **song** was so popular that Schumann put it to music. Although the crisis passed, German rulers felt they had to respond to growing mass nationalism. Rather than try to repress it, some began to try to appease it by dropping prohibitions on German organisations. Patriotic societies revived and new expressions of German national identity developed. In 1845, for instance, the first German choral festival was held.

Another of the popular **songs** of the time was 'Deutschland, Deutschland über alles' ('Germany, Germany over all'), which later became the German national anthem.

Whilst such cultural activities helped stimulate German nationalism, further encouragement came from economic developments. These have three aspects: the creation of a customs union covering much of the confederation, the growth in communications (roads, canals and railways), and the beginnings of significant industrialisation.

In 1818 Prussia decided to rationalise its customs arrangements. Trade was hindered by 67 different tariffs across its territories. It decided to abolish all duties on trade between its provinces and to simplify the tariffs imposed on foreign trade. Prussia thereby became a free-trade area. This stimulated economic development and encouraged other states to join it or copy it. However, Prussia's dominance of the major trade routes (especially the Rhine) compelled most German states to join the Prussian Union. By 1834 the *Zollverein* (customs union) had been formed from 17 out of the 39 German states. This represented two-thirds of the territorial area of the confederation and about the same proportion of its population. Crucially for the future of Germany, Austria was not a member. Economic union helped create ever closer links between the various states of the confederation. Some German **nationalists** quickly grasped its potential political implications: economic union could lead to political union.

The **nationalist** poet Fallersleben, for example, viewed the *Zollverein* as 'a bond around the German fatherland, and this bond had done much more than the confederation to bind our hearts together'.

In what ways did economic developments encourage the growth of nationalism?

As significant perhaps was the growth in communications after 1815. There

By 1828 about 4,500 km of new **roads** had been built.

was a rapid expansion of the **road** and canal network and in 1835 came the first German railway. By 1845 there were over 3,000 km of track. This, coupled with developments like the electric telegraph and the expansion of newspapers and journals, helped develop national consciousness and a sense of national community. One economist viewed railways as binding the limbs of Germany 'together into a forceful and powerful body'.

Finally, in the 1840s industrialisation began to take off in parts of Germany, with new industries feeding the demands of the railways for locomotives, carriages and rails. This new industrial activity and the growth of commerce as a result of the *Zollverein* meant the expansion of a commercial and industrial middle class. Many industrialists believed in the liberal economics of free trade and sought a national political structure that would recognise and respond to their concerns: they wanted a liberal and united Germany.

One should not get the impression that by the 1840s liberalism and nationalism were on the march and their victory was inevitable. On the contrary, some historians refer to these years before 1848 as the 'quiet years'. This emphasises the fact that, even in the 1840s, there was no coherent nationalist or liberal movement and certainly no movement that could deliver mass support. As elsewhere, rulers tended to overestimate the reality of the liberal and nationalist threat, if not its revolutionary potential. The above account illustrates the limitations; there were relatively few examples of liberal or nationalist agitation and no sustained pressure. A few festivals, some student and academic societies and a little anti-French xenophobia are hardly persuasive evidence of an extensive movement. Support for liberalism and nationalism was restricted to a proportion of the educated classes: students, some academics, some lawyers, some artisans and some members of the wider middle class. What is more, the vision of these supporters varied. Liberals were divided over the extent of liberal reforms desired and feared the radicalism of those who supported manhood suffrage. Nationalists were divided over the territorial extent and political structure of any potential 'united Germany'. These divisions were to become apparent in 1848. On the eve of the 1848 revolutions, the desire for liberal and nationalist reform was growing, and arguably in the 1840s it was beginning to grow faster, but it was still limited.

Liberal and nationalist ideas in Italy

The peacemakers at Vienna in 1815 were not concerned with liberal and nationalist aspirations when they decided on the future of the Italian peninsula. Whilst no confederation emerged on the German model, Austrian influence was still paramount and all the states were ruled by absolutist regimes. Austria directly ruled the northern provinces of Lombardy and Venetia, and – through members of the Austrian royal family – the central Italian duchies of

Modena, Parma and Tuscany. The pope ruled the Papal States and the Bourbons were restored to the kingdom of Naples. In the north-west Victor Emmanuel I ruled Piedmont (see map on page 152).

The potential for political unrest in the Italian peninsula was probably greater than in the German Confederation. Although the nationalist movement did not extend much beyond a few middle-class poets, writers and intellectuals in 1815, there was considerable resentment towards Austria and – amongst the middle class and some army officers – a strong desire for constitutional government. This was partly because Italy had experienced a greater and longer-lasting degree of reorganisation and relatively efficient government during the Napoleonic period; it also had, in the northern states, a larger middle class than Germany.

Before the 1830s unrest in Italy had more to do with liberalism than with nationalism. There was hatred of Austrian rule (especially in Lombardy and Venetia), but the main aim of political agitation was the cession of constitutions from existing rulers. The desire for a united Italy was little more than a vague aspiration linked to the overthrow of Austrian influence.

Before the 1830s the main agencies of change were conspiratorial secret societies, the most prominent of which were the **Carbonari**. Unrest until after 1830–31 was usually organised by such secret societies. The first uprising, in the Papal States in 1817, resulted from the purging of the administration of civilian officials and their replacement by priests. The plot was discovered and its ringleaders were imprisoned. More serious was the revolt that broke out in Naples in 1820. Carbonari, supported by some army officers, forced King Ferdinand I to grant a constitution modelled on the Spanish Constitution of 1812. Naively, perhaps, the conspirators then allowed the king to attend an international congress at Laibach to win the acceptance of the Great Powers to the constitutional changes. Instead of gaining international approval, the revolution was condemned and an Austrian army forcibly reversed it. Meanwhile, Carbonari had staged another uprising in Piedmont and similarly won a constitution, after the abdication of Victor Emmanuel I. However, the new king, Charles Felix, revoked the Constitution and the Austrian army crushed the revolt in 1821.

The July Revolution in France sparked another series of small Carbonari uprisings, this time in central Italy. The aim was to create a central Italian kingdom out of Modena, Parma and part of the Papal States. The uprising began in Modena in February 1831 and spread to Parma and Bologna in the Papal States. The existing rulers fled and a United Provinces of Central Italy was declared. The victory was short lived. Expected French help did not materialise and the pope called in the Austrian army, which quickly crushed the revolt. As in 1820–21, lack of agreement amongst the Carbonari leaders and lack of

The **Carbonari** were the secret 'charcoal-burners' society, formed in southern Italy (Calabria) in 1807. Such societies drew much of their organisation from the secret masonic societies.

What were the
weaknesses of liberal
and nationalist
movements in Italy in
the period 1815–40?

Giuseppe Mazzini
(1805–72) was an Italian
patriot with a romantic and
idealistic nationalist vision.
He founded the Young Italy
movement in 1831, having
become frustrated by the
efforts of secret societies
like the Carbonari which he
had joined in 1829. After
the abortive rising in Savoy
in 1834 he escaped and
settled in London. In 1848
he helped liberate Milan
from Austrian rule and
became a leading figure of
the short-lived Roman
Republic in 1849. After its
failure he continued to
agitate for Italian unity from
London. His vision of a
democratic Italian republic
was too extreme for
moderate nationalists, but
his passionate belief in
Italian unity inspired others
and he is often coupled
with Cavour and Garibaldi
as one of the three heroes
of the Risorgimento, which
brought about Italian
unification after 1859.

Mazzini said: 'The tree of
liberty does not bear fruit
unless it is planted by the
hands of citizens and
made fertile by the blood
of citizens and guarded by
the swords of citizens.'

Young Italy and Mazzini's
ideas spawned a number
of similar organisations
across Europe, such as
Young Ireland. There was
also a Young Europe

popular support made the job of the Austrian army easier. As in 1820–21, suppression of the revolt was followed by reprisals against the conspirators.

The risings of 1831 marked the end of Carbonari conspiracies and also led to a re-examination of aims. From this point onwards the concept of a united Italy as a means of achieving liberal or radical ends began to dominate. Initially the most important of those advocating a different strategy and aim was the radical nationalist **Giuseppe Mazzini**. Mazzini had joined the Carbonari in 1829 and had been frustrated by their failure in 1831. He was determined that the emphasis should be on all Italy rather than on a particular locality. His aim was a united Italian democratic republic. Mazzini believed that nations were created by God and that each individual needed to find a place in their own national community. He also believed that every nation had a purpose and that the Italian nation, which had already given the world the Roman Empire and Roman Catholicism, was now destined to lead the world into the era of nation states. In order to fulfil this destiny, the Italians must rise up and expel the Austrians. Importantly, they must achieve **liberty** themselves, without foreign help.

The secret society he founded in 1831, **Young Italy**, did involve conspiracy and uprisings, but it also aimed to educate the Italian people about the need for a united Italy. It published its own newspaper, which was smuggled through the peninsula. Mazzini was a romantic idealist who inspired many young middle-class intellectuals and others, like the guerrilla leader Garibaldi. By 1832 Young Italy had an estimated 60,000 members, in all major Italian towns. Metternich considered Mazzini to be one of the most dangerous men in Europe. He was, however, far from being a practical politician. Typical of his naive approach to politics was his 'invasion' (with a few hundred followers) of Piedmont from Switzerland in 1834. He believed it would spark a popular uprising leading first to the overthrow of the Piedmontese king, Charles Albert, and thence to popular risings throughout Italy that would expel the other rulers – crucially, Austria. The attempted invasion was a complete failure. Mazzini escaped to England, but many of his followers were captured and tortured, and in the eyes of many middle-class liberals and nationalists Young Italy was discredited. His idea of a democratic republic worried many moderates concerned at the prospect of mob rule.

Mazzini did succeed in putting the idea of a united Italy at the forefront of the political agenda. The revival of the idea of the Italian nation was helped by the works of poets, writers and composers like Manzoni, Niccolini, Rossini and Verdi. Their writing dwelt on themes of Italian heroism against foreigners – and their readers and audiences understood Austria to be the enemy. Political writers too began to explore alternative visions of a united Italy. Two writers stand out: Vincenzo Gioberti and Cesare Balbo. Both rejected revolutionary methods and the idea of a united democratic Italian **republic**. Instead, they advocated some kind of **federation** of existing states. In his book *Of the civil and moral primacy of the Italians*, published in 1843, Gioberti argued that the pope should become the head of a federation of existing Italian states. Balbo, in *Of the aspirations of Italians*, saw the expulsion of Austria as the priority. Piedmont was the only Italian state potentially capable of such a feat. On Austria's expulsion, therefore, an Italian federation should be set up under the leadership of Piedmont.

Other developments helped promote the idea of a united Italy. A number of 'national' academic societies were set up and began to meet in congresses. The first of a series of congresses of Italian scientists was held in 1839. Liberal economists, seeing the impact of the *Zollverein* in Germany, pressed for a similar customs union for Italy. In the 1840s the first railways began to bring the various parts of Italy closer together.

As in the German Confederation, the period up to the 1840s sees the growth, albeit limited and unsteady, of liberal and nationalist movements in Italy. The appeal of liberal and nationalist ideas was mainly to the educated middle classes and those in the towns. There was practically no support or interest from the peasantry. There was no united vision or aim and in the mid 1840s the reality was still that of a powerful Austria, conservative rulers and mass indifference.

Development of liberal and nationalist ideas in the Austrian Empire

The map on page 164 demonstrates the potential threat nationalism posed to the Austrian Empire, within which there was significant **ethnic diversity**. Recent changes had been introduced by the Treaty of Vienna. Broadly, the empire can be divided into five parts: the Italian provinces of Venetia and Lombardy, the lands of the Crown of St Stephen (including Hungary, Croatia, Ruthenia and Transylvania), Galicia (containing mainly Poles and Ukrainians), the lands of the Bohemian crown (Bohemia, Moravia and Silesia) and the hereditary lands (Upper and Lower Austria).

It was a vast, incoherent mass without natural unity beyond the common denominator of its ruling family. The lack of cohesion and the different traditions, privileges, cultures and geography of its constituent parts seemed to threaten imminent destruction. This is one reason why Emperor Francis I likened it to a 'worm-eaten house', liable to collapse at the slightest disturbance. It also helps to explain why Metternich, Francis I's chancellor, was determined to crush any threat to its existence and to the authority of the emperor.

The threat of liberalism and nationalism was more potential than real. However, in this period the foundations of Czech, Croat, Romanian and other

movement, begun in 1834 and sponsored by Mazzini, to support nationalist movements. Such movements, like Young Italy, had limited success.

What are the similarities and differences between Mazzini, Gioberti and Balbo in their vision of Italy?

A **republic** is a state without a monarch, ruled by representatives elected by the people. The head of state is usually an elected president.

A **federation** is a system of government in which a number of states join together for the purpose of administering common interests, such as foreign and economic policy, but retain their right to run their own internal affairs.

This **ethnic diversity** was the result of the way Austria's ruling family, the Habsburgs, had built up the empire over the centuries by inheritance, marriage, conquest and treaty. Within the boundaries of the empire were Germans, Magyars (Hungarians), Poles, Czechs, Slovaks, Ruthenes (Ukrainians), Slovenes, Croats, Serbs, Romanians and Italians.

What problems faced the Austrian emperor in ruling the empire?

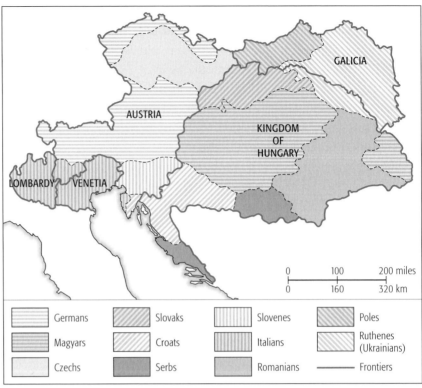

The nationalities of the Austrian Empire.

Count Istvan Szechenyi
campaigned for reform of
the economy,
improvement of
communications,
improvement in the lot of
the peasantry and the
revival of the Magyar
language.

Lajos Kossuth
(1802–94) was the
leading Hungarian
nationalist figure. A strong
believer in Hungarian
nationalism, his views led
to imprisonment between
1837 and 1840. His
newspaper, *Pesti Hirlap*,
was very influential in
promoting Hungarian
nationalism in the 1840s.
In 1848 he took the lead in
demanding and wresting
concessions from the
emperor, such as
agreement to the March
Laws which gave Hungary
self-government.
Proclaimed governor of
Hungary, he declared the
state independent in April
1849, but following
Hungarian defeat he fled
into exile.

nationalities were laid; whilst the Hungarians actively sought to establish some regional autonomy.

Hungary already had its own assembly or diet. This did not necessarily represent a challenge to Vienna; the upper house of the two-chamber assembly was dominated by the higher aristocracy and the Catholic bishops, all of whom were conservative in outlook and loyal to the emperor. The lesser nobility and gentry, based in the provinces, were less exposed to Vienna's influence. There were perhaps 500,000 of these. Often very poor, they were Protestant in religion, spoke Magyar, ran local government and acted as magistrates. Men from such ranks, frustrated at their exclusion from higher office (where the official language was Latin) and resentful at Vienna's interference in the 'historic rights' of the kingdom of Hungary, took the lead in the growing nationalist movement. At first the dominant voice was that of the moderate liberal aristocrat **Count Istvan Szechenyi**. He did not wish to see any breaking of the link with the monarchy; he tended to view such political demands as a diversion from the important issue of economic development.

A more radical leader emerged in **Lajos Kossuth**, who had been imprisoned in the 1830s for his activities. On his release, he rallied the Magyar gentry and lesser nobility to the nationalist cause and sought political independence for

Hungary. He publicised his views in his newspaper *Pesti Hirlap* in the 1840s. His aims included a mixture of liberal and nationalist ideas:

- Liberal measures such as freedom of the press and of religion and the abolition of feudalism (with compensation for landlords).
- Extension of the franchise.
- A separate Magyar government and parliament.
- The making of Magyar the only official language in Hungary.

Kossuth won widespread support amongst the Magyar gentry and Vienna was persuaded to concede his language demands in the early 1840s. The nationalists were not appeased and continued to demand a totally separate Magyar government and parliament.

Kossuth set out to unite all social classes in support of an independent Hungarian state based on the historic lands of the Crown of St Stephen (see map on page 164). He failed, despite the promise of basic civil rights for all and the abolition of feudalism. This was partly because many of those outside the nobility were not Magyar, but Romanian, Serb, Croat or Slovak. They viewed Magyars as foreigners trying to crush their own developing national identities.

This illustrates the problem facing nationalists in the Austrian Empire. Despite the apparent pattern shown on the map, in most areas there was a clash between at least two nationalities, with one nationality represented heavily in the ruling classes and one in the lower classes. In Hungary there was a

Lajos Kossuth addressing the people in 1848.

Why might Magyar nationalists find it hard to win mass support in the lands of the Crown of St Stephen?

largely Magyar nobility and – depending on area – a Romanian, Serb or Croat peasantry. In Bohemia the dominant class was German in a largely Czech population, and in Galicia a Polish nobility dominated a Ukrainian peasantry. Not surprisingly, Magyar attempts to improve their position in relation to Austrian rule were not greeted with enthusiasm by Croats or Serbs.

Hungarian nationalism experienced the strongest development in this period, but it was not the only national movement. In Bohemia Czech nationalism began to develop, partly in reaction to a German or 'Germanised' nobility loyal to Vienna. The roots of Czech nationalism took the form of an attempt to revive Czech and other Slav languages, culture and history. The leading figures in these developments tended to be academics, poets and writers, like the poet Jan Kollar and the historian **Frantisek Palacky**. This cultural nationalism had a political dimension. Czech nationalists wanted to revive the historic rights of the kingdom of Bohemia. In the 1840s the movement began to win support amongst the middle classes in the towns, and the tenor of the movement became increasingly anti-German. However, rather than seek independence from Vienna, many nationalists, like Palacky, sought a remodelling of the empire whereby the emperor would perform the role of protector and guarantor of rights of Czech and other Slav national groups. This idea is known as Austro-Slavism.

Elsewhere in the empire other national movements began to develop. These began, as with Czech nationalism, with the identification of a distinctive culture and language. The Croat nationalist Ljudevit Gaj did much to revive the Croat language. As in Bohemia there was a political overtone; Croats resented the dominance of the Magyars and the threat of a Magyar state that would include Croatia.

With regard to Austria itself, it is perhaps best to think in terms of liberalism rather than nationalism. The demand grew for more constitutional government by increasing the power of local assemblies and for the election of a national *Reichstag* (parliament). Again the clamour for political rights came from the professional classes – lawyers, office holders, academics and students – but also from some German nobility, such as Baron Andrian.

Nationalism and liberalism clearly threatened the nature of the Austrian Empire and the authority of its emperor. It is easy to overestimate the significance of this threat. Apart, arguably, from Hungary, national and liberal movements in the Austrian Empire were of limited appeal and had hardly any impact outside the major towns and universities. The bulk of the population, the peasantry, remained unmoved. The main support came from sections of the educated middle class and some elements of the nobility. Before 1848 there is little evidence of success.

Frantisek Palacky
(1798–1876) is regarded as the founder of the Czech revival in the first half of the nineteenth century. In 1834 he founded Czech Mother, an organisation to promote Czech publications, the development of the Czech language and the writing of Czech history. He produced the first volume of his own *History of Bohemia* in 1836, a history written in terms of conflict with the Germans. He chaired the Slavic Congress that met in Prague in 1848. A Czech nationalist, he sought protection from the Austrian emperor for Czech interests against German nationalists.

How successful was Metternich in containing revolutionary forces in the period 1815–48?

Prince **Klemens von Metternich** was made foreign minister in 1809 and became Austrian chancellor in 1821. He dominated the years 1815–48, so much so that this period has been called the 'Age of Metternich'. He was given one major task by Emperor Francis I – to maintain the authority of the emperor and the Austrian Empire. There was to be one major condition attached to this: there could be no reform.

In effect, what this task meant abroad was the maintenance of the Vienna settlement of 1815 and the preservation of hereditary monarchy against the threat and reality of revolution. What it meant at home was the crushing of any potential threat to the stability of the empire.

For Metternich the biggest threat came from liberalism and political nationalism, so any manifestations of these dangerous ideas had to be opposed and suppressed. His concern lay particularly with the middle classes, whom he viewed as the source of most trouble. Bureaucrats, lawyers, professors, financiers, students and journalists – among others – he saw as politically ambitious, wanting constitutional change in order to add political muscle to their increasing social and economic status. Such people were, in his view, 'presumptuous men', overconfident in their own wisdom and full of contempt for legitimate political authority that had been built up over centuries. Their success would result, he believed, in bloody revolution – as had occurred in France during the 1790s.

For allies in the fight against liberalism and nationalism, Metternich could look to fellow absolute monarchies abroad and to the aristocracy and the Catholic church in the empire.

The international aspect: the Holy Alliance and the suppression of revolution

Metternich was one of the principal architects of the Vienna settlement of 1815 and he, among other things, ensured that one of the guiding principles shaping decisions was that of legitimacy. Where appropriate and practicable, 'legitimate' monarchs were restored to their thrones and the preference everywhere was for absolute monarchy. Although France gained a constitution, this was granted by the restored king, Louis XVIII, not wrested from him by revolution. He was giving away powers to an elected body and theoretically could revoke them. Elsewhere one or two other princes granted constitutions, but Metternich used what pressure he could to have them revoked, or to persuade princes to minimise concessions. He managed to persuade the Prussian king Frederick William III against granting a constitution,

Prince Klemens von Metternich.

Klemens von Metternich (1773–1859), born in Koblenz in Germany, was the son of a diplomat in Habsburg service. After university he worked as an envoy of the Habsburg government and from 1806 to 1809 as ambassador in Paris. From 1809 to 1848 he was Austrian foreign minister and from 1821 chancellor. He was the dominant figure at the Congress of Vienna in 1815 and maintained Austrian influence in the German Confederation and Italy until his fall from power. In 1848 he fled to England, returning to Austria in 1851 where he died an influential elder statesman in 1859.

In what ways did liberals and nationalists represent a threat to the stability of the Austrian Empire?

but had less success in the more liberally minded south German states like Baden.

The Great Powers – Austria, Prussia, Russia and Britain – were committed to maintaining the territorial settlement established at Vienna. They were joined in the **Quadruple Alliance** (later Quintuple, when France joined in 1818). This at least meant there could be no reorganisation of frontiers; 'Italy' would remain divided into 9 states and 'Germany' into the 39 states of the confederation. Only in the case of the kingdom of the Netherlands was any revision allowed. Here the Belgians revolted against the Dutch in 1830 and a division was reluctantly agreed under pressure from Britain. Metternich was powerless to intervene.

The **Quadruple Alliance** was originally a military alliance set up in March 1814 by Britain, Russia, Austria and Prussia with the aim of defeating Napoleon. As part of the Vienna settlement it was agreed to continue the alliance to keep a watch on France and maintain the Vienna agreements.

Whilst the Quadruple Alliance committed its members to the maintenance of the territorial arrangements laid down in 1815, it was not clear that it committed them to maintaining the political arrangements within states. In 1820 it became apparent that Britain did not accept that this was the case. However, Metternich wanted the Great Powers to be able to intervene in the internal affairs of other states. In this he had the support of Prussia and Russia – which, with Austria, were members of the Holy Alliance set up by the Russian tsar Alexander I in 1815. At the time this was no more than a meaningless alliance of 'Christian rulers', but in 1820 Metternich gave the Holy Alliance a definite purpose. When Austria, Prussia and Russia met at an international congress at Troppau in 1820, they agreed the **Troppau Protocol**, despite British objections. The protocol was of immediate relevance because revolutions had occurred in Spain and Naples in 1820 and would happen in Piedmont in 1821. At a further congress at Laibach in 1821, the Holy Alliance gave backing to Austrian intervention to crush the revolution in Naples and Austria and felt able to use its forces to overturn the revolution in Piedmont as well. At Verona in 1822, the Holy Alliance powers sanctioned French intervention to overturn the Spanish revolution.

The **Troppau Protocol** effectively sanctioned action by members of the Holy Alliance to restore monarchs toppled by revolutions.

The Holy Alliance became an alliance of conservative powers committed to the maintenance of absolute monarchy in Europe. It was a key bond between Austria, Prussia and Russia that dominated central and eastern European affairs until the Crimean War tore it apart in the 1850s. This co-operation amongst conservative powers against the threat of liberal and nationalist ideas was also reflected in the co-operation between Prussia and Austria in the German Confederation. That ensured the passage of the Karlsbad Decrees in 1819 in the aftermath of the Wartburg Festival of 1817 and the murder of the anti-liberal writer Kotzebue. Metternich was worried at the spread of liberal and nationalist ideas; the murder of Kotzebue seemed to demonstrate their subversive nature. With Prussian support, he was able to persuade the confederation to pass the Karlsbad Decrees. These provided for co-operation between the German states for the suppression of revolutionary activity, the prohibition of political meetings and student societies, strict press censorship, supervision of university teaching and expulsion of liberal or nationalist teachers and students.

The decrees were enforced in all German states. A central commission based in Mainz co-ordinated action – including the use of spies and informers, and the imprisonment or exile or 'revolutionaries'. The decrees were supplemented in 1820 by the Final Act, which gave the confederation diet the right to intervene in the affairs of member states to suppress revolts. These severe measures were successful. Although liberalism and nationalism were not extinguished, they were suppressed and, apart from some minor problems like the Hambach Festival in 1832 (which resulted in a strengthening of the Karlsbad Decrees in the Six Articles), there was little open liberal or nationalist agitation until the 1840s.

The Austrian Empire: the repression and 'divide and rule'

In trying to maintain the ramshackle Austrian Empire and the authority of its emperor, Metternich was operating under a number of constraints that limited his freedom of action:

- In Francis I he had a master who, although he thought extremely highly of Metternich, would not countenance any of his (albeit limited) plans for reform. This attitude of the emperor was reinforced by the conservatism of the governing classes. For example, one possible way of helping to appease unrest might have been state encouragement of economic progress by investment in railways. Francis I quashed any talk of railways as he believed them to be the means by which revolution could come into the country. Others argued that the masses could only be ruled effectively if they remained poor.
- Metternich had rivals at court, especially after the death of Francis I in 1835. Principal amongst these was **Count Kolowrat**. Francis I was succeeded by the half-wit **Ferdinand I**. From 1835 Austria was ruled by a council of state in which Metternich had to struggle for support against Kolowrat.
- The vast and complex administration of the empire was inefficient and dogged by financial problems (on average about a third of its annual income went on interest payments on loans).
- German had become the language of government and administration and most of the higher officials in government and the Catholic church were German. This German dominance caused resentment, as we have seen, in Bohemia and Hungary and helped feed nationalist support.

Count Kolowrat became minister of the interior in 1826. He had great financial ability and was more sympathetic to liberal ideas than Metternich.

Ferdinand I reportedly said: 'To govern is easy, but to sign one's name is difficult' and 'I am emperor and I will have dumplings!'

All major post offices had special departments, called *Logen*, where the **private mail** of people listed by the police as potentially subversive was opened, copied and resealed before being sent on.

One contemporary characterised the nature of the Austrian **government** as 'absolutism tempered by slovenliness'.

How effective was Metternich's attempt to police public opinion in the Austrian Empire?

For example, he initially gave some encouragement to the Czech and Croat **revival** of interest in their languages and culture.

Such constraints left Metternich with few options for dealing with potentially revolutionary forces. One was straightforward: repression. Superficially the nature of the repression was impressive. Metternich used all the means associated with a police state: secret police, spies, informers, surveillance, strict censorship, restrictions on freedom of movement and imprisonment for political crimes (Kossuth was imprisoned in the 1830s). In theory, the secret police involved themselves in all aspects of public life. They even monitored **private mail**.

The effectiveness of such measures as these is open to question. This was no twentieth-century police state. The Austrian Empire was too vast, the machinery of **government** too complex, the local variations in efficiency too great for this to be true. Censorship failed to prevent the circulation of liberal literature from abroad, even in Vienna, where the university became a centre of radical and liberal activity. Restrictions on political discussion also failed; liberal clubs and societies were able to advertise more or less openly and nationalist leaders like Kossuth were able to publish their newspapers.

One weapon Metternich had to hand was the traditional Habsburg policy of divide and rule. We have already seen the mutual hostility apparent between Germans and Czechs, Magyars and Croats. To a degree such antagonisms were played on by the government. This can be seen in military policy. Units of different nationalities were used to garrison the provinces because they would have little sympathy with local people. For example, Austrian units in Lombardy and Venetia would not be Italian.

Another method used to encourage regional difference and, Metternich hoped, local contentment (at least amongst the landowners) was the acceptance of local diets, to give the appearance of regional involvement in imperial affairs. He did not expect them to do more than in the past – to endorse the taxes and laws requested by Vienna. He certainly did not intend them to become centres for the expression of liberal and nationalist ideas. Metternich also encouraged cultural nationalism, and the **revival** of local traditions and languages, in the hope that this would contribute to continued loyalty to the emperor.

Metternich believed such policies worked. Asked about the prospect of revolution in the Austrian Empire in the wake of the French revolution of 1830, he appeared complacent: 'If the Hungarian revolts we should immediately set the Bohemian against him, for they hate each other; and after him the Pole, or the German, or the Italian.'

With the benefit of hindsight, it is easy to condemn Metternich's regional policies as naive. Local diets became the assemblies where national grievances and demands could be expressed. It was a short step from cultural nationalism to political demands for national rights and recognition. In this respect

Metternich's policies seem misguided. However, there was some validity to Metternich's and Francis I's belief that they could play off one nationality against another. One important reason why the 1848 revolutions failed in the Austrian Empire was that national movements did not co-operate. In fact, the Austrians connived at the defeat of the Czechs, and the Croats fought against the Hungarians.

Overall, Metternich's policies must be deemed a success – at least in the short term. Perhaps he overestimated the degree of immediate threat posed by liberal and nationalist movements, but he certainly gave them as little opportunity as possible to expand and develop before the 1840s. For over 20 years after the upheavals of the French Revolution and Napoleonic wars there was no significant threat to the empire or the authority of the emperor. In that sense repression (at the heart of his policy) worked. In the longer term, it can be argued that repression stoked up increasing resentment and opposition. Perhaps this helps to explain the nature and extent of the revolutions of 1848.

What do you understand by the policy of divide and rule? Is such a policy a sign of weakness or of strength?

Did Metternich have a 'system'? If so, what were its main features?

Why did revolutions break out across central Europe in 1848?

Contemporary Germans referred to the revolutions of 1848 as the 'springtime of the peoples', and in relation to central Europe this was how they appeared. From January 1848, when Sicilians revolted against their masters in Naples, unrest and revolution rocked central Europe. Revolutions occurred throughout Germany, from Bavaria to Prussia, throughout Italy (including Lombardy and Venetia) and in Hungary (Budapest), Austria (Vienna) and Bohemia (Prague). What causes revolution? This question has exercised historians for many years. Whilst there are differences of view, examination of the revolutions of 1789, 1830 and 1848 suggests that a combination of three main features made revolution possible. These were social and economic crisis, pressure for political change, and weak, divided or indecisive leadership by governments. Revolutions do not come out of the blue, even though those of 1848 in some ways seemed to, as apparently firm governments suddenly gave way in the aftermath of the French revolution of February. Revolutions are the product of longer-term developments, short-term causes and triggering events. Longer-term developments and changes in politics, society and economics made revolution seem increasingly possible. Short-term causes (principally the increase in liberal and nationalist activity in the 1840s coupled with a deep economic crisis) made revolution seem increasingly probable. Finally, triggers such as the overthrow of the French monarchy in February 1848 brought about **revolution**.

In this context the **revolution** is a political one. By this is meant an overthrow of the existing system of government and its replacement by another based on different principles.

Longer-term developments

Europe in the period 1815–48 was dominated by more or less absolute monarchies, supported by a privileged landowning aristocracy and the Catholic church. The bulk of the population was a rural peasantry, illiterate and mainly concerned with the day-to-day issues of survival. These forces proved the major obstacles to change.

There was a range of increasingly powerful forces that made change and revolution more likely. Two of these we have already considered – the growth of liberalism and of nationalism. These ideas proposed a new way of ordering government and society that threatened to overturn the power of kings and reduce the influence of privileged aristocracies and the church. There was also the precedent of the American and the French revolutions. Liberals and nationalists might consider the forcible overthrow of the established system (revolution) as legitimate, justified as necessary to establish governments answerable to the people. Deep fear and pessimism were provoked in the minds of kings across Europe. Governments, like Metternich's, were preoccupied with a fear of revolution. As time passed, this was coupled with a growing pessimism that revolution and change were inevitable. In October 1847 Metternich expressed this pessimism: 'I am an old doctor; I can distinguish a passing illness from a mortal ailment – we are in the throes of the latter.'

Ideas alone, especially when limited to a relatively small proportion of the population, do not bring about revolutions. Other changes were making some kind of challenge to the 'old order' more and more likely. One of these was change in the **demography** of Europe. Much of the population growth was absorbed by the growth of towns (urbanisation). The figures for **cities** reflect the rapid growth of urban centres more generally. Urban populations were growing fast, but it is worth noting that the vast majority of the population was still rural. It is estimated that about 75 per cent of the population in the Austrian Empire relied on agricultural occupation in 1845.

Expanding populations brought with them problems of increased pressure on the land and – in the towns – overcrowding, disease and poverty. The growing pressure on the land was reflected in the subdivision of land holdings. By the mid 1840s in Moravia–Silesia, for example, about 65 per cent of peasant farms were less than a quarter of a full-size holding. Thousands of peasant families were entirely landless. Pressure on the land resulted in a movement of people to the towns. Much of the urban workforce was unskilled and subject to the vagaries of the economy. Urban development could not keep pace with the swelling masses. In Vienna, for example, population grew by 45 per cent between 1827 and 1847, but housing increased by only a little over 10 per cent. Landlords were able to increase rents, while labouring families were often forced to live in overcrowded and insanitary conditions (in

The **demography** (the size and distribution of population) of Europe was changing rapidly. In the Austrian Empire, the population grew from 19 million to 31 million between 1815 and 1848; in the German states growth was from 23 to 35 million; and in those of the Italian peninsula it was from 17 to 24 million.

Specific **cities** include Vienna, which had a population of 247,000 in 1800. By 1850 this had grown to 444,000. Berlin's population more than doubled from 172,000 to 419,000 and Budapest's nearly trebled from 54,000 to 156,000.

> Did the growth of population and of towns necessarily mean a political revolution was possible?

towns diseases like tuberculosis and cholera were endemic and periodically epidemic). Some workers even slept by their machines in the factories. The unskilled nature of much of the work and the ready supply of labour meant that wages were low and hours long. Much of the work in cotton and paper factories did not require strength; here, over half the labour force was made up of women and children.

Identify the main problems arising from the growth of towns.

Another feature of the beginnings of industrialisation in the Austrian Empire and the German Confederation was the mechanisation of previously skilled operations like weaving. The result was protest from displaced skilled workers and craftsmen, often taking the form of machine breaking. However, factory production was not the dominant mode before 1848. More typical was the small workshop employing a small number of workers.

While industrialisation was beginning, the urban economy was still intimately bound up with the fortunes of agriculture. Although agricultural production grew, it did not grow as quickly as the population. In such a situation poor harvests could lead to severe social and economic problems, pushing up bread prices, which in turn reduced the resources available for the purchase of manufactured goods. Poor harvests, therefore, could lead to industrial depression and unemployment.

What is the connection between fluctuations in agricultural production and the economy more generally?

Industrial depression not only affected the workers, but also their employers. Another feature of industrialisation was the growth of a middle class of traders and manufacturers. Whilst there were some wealthy **industrialists**, many were small shop and workshop owners whose lives were intimately bound up with those of the working classes and who were directly affected by the forces that brought unemployment and privation to the poor.

One of the **industrialists** was Krupp, whose steelworks in Essen began to boom in this period.

However, industrialisation was beginning to change economic life. Industries like **textiles** began to expand rapidly. Meanwhile communications were slowly improving and by 1848 Austria could boast 1,400 km of railway. These figures need to be put in perspective. Industrialisation and the growth of railways in the Austrian Empire were limited in this period and concentrated in the western half (Bohemia–Moravia and Austria itself). The figures for some of the states of the **German Confederation** were far more impressive. Economic development was also encouraged by the expansion of the Prussian customs union into the *Zollverein* to which, by 1848, most German states belonged. Austria had not joined because it wanted to protect its industry from foreign competition.

The growth in the manufacture of cotton is an example of developments in **textiles**. Between 1829 and 1847 the number of cotton mills in the Austrian Empire doubled and the imports of cotton yarn to feed these mills increased by 800 per cent in just seven years after 1835.

By 1845 there were over 3,200 km of railway in the **German Confederation**.

Many of the middle class, from the small shop owner to the wealthy industrialist, were attracted to liberal and nationalist ideas that offered the prospect of giving them the political influence and power that their growing economic power seemed to justify. The main section of the middle class attracted to such ideas was the professionals and academics, expanding and often frustrated by the lack of opportunity for advancement. Yet the existing social and political systems were dominated by a land-owning aristocracy and a relatively small governing elite whose fear of change and revolution meant that calls for reform were largely rejected. Repression rather than reform was the rule.

Short-term causes

Some long-term developments threatened to destabilise the existing social and political order. There was the growth, albeit limited and unsteady, of support for liberal and nationalist ideas and for the legitimacy of revolution if peaceful reform could not be achieved. Some radicals, as we have seen, openly espoused the idea of revolution as the only means of achieving change. At the same time, economic and social developments were creating new strains and stresses in society. As the French revolutions of 1789 and 1830 had shown, the coincidence of political unrest with economic and social crisis coupled with a lack of united and decisive leadership by government could produce revolution. Such a combination of circumstances developed in the mid 1840s.

Economic crisis

A severe economic crisis hit Europe between 1845 and 1848. It was a result of a combination of a traditional subsistence crisis, caused by bad harvests; and a newer economic crisis more typical of industrialised countries, caused by overproduction and underconsumption. The two elements were related. The high food prices following bad harvests helped provoke the industrial crisis as consumers had fewer resources with which to buy manufactured products.

In 1845 **potato blight** struck the crop across Europe, causing hunger and starvation for millions. The potato formed a major part of the basic diet of the peasant population in Europe from Ireland (where it was the staple) through the Low Countries and Germany to Poland. The effects of the blight continued into 1846, when the plight of the poor was compounded by a disastrous grain harvest. There were steep **price rises**. In normal circumstances, perhaps up to 70 per cent of a family's income went on food, and the impact of such increases could be disastrous. In Vienna in 1847, a factory worker might earn 40 kr. a day; one egg might cost 7.5 kr. and a pound of butter 66 kr. Often the effects of poor harvests were compounded by poor transport systems, the inability to find alternative means of supply, panic and speculation. In some places the effects were mitigated by relief measures, but the general situation across large areas of central Europe was dire. Hunger and desperation led to violence and protest; rural unrest and urban **riots** broke out in many areas. In rural areas, especially in the Austrian Empire, unrest might be directed against feudal **dues** such as the tithe paid to the lord and the compulsory labour

The effects of **potato blight** were particularly severe in Ireland, where the Irish potato famine led to the deaths of hundreds of thousands and large-scale emigration, especially to the USA ('a million dead, a million fled'). The disaster and the apparent poor response of the British government led to deep-seated resentment that has echoed down to the present day.

In Hamburg the price of wheat rose 60 per cent between 1845 and 1847. Elsewhere the **price rises** were often steeper – in some parts of Germany the price of potatoes rose 135 per cent in a year.

There was a potato riot in Berlin in 1847, with bread **riots** in Stettin, Stuttgart and Ulm.

It has been estimated that in normal circumstances perhaps 70 per cent of a peasant's income went on such **dues**, leaving only 30 per cent for the purchase of food and other items.

service (*robot*). In 1846 Galician peasants took out their anger on their land-lords, slaughtering hundreds.

The agricultural crisis and the shortages and inflation it produced contributed to the coincident industrial slump. The slump of 1845–47 was the most severe of the periodic industrial crises in the first half of the nineteenth century. The connection between industry and agriculture has already been stressed; certainly a major cause of the industrial slump of these years was the result of the contraction of demand because of the increased proportion of income being spent on food. It was also due in part to a contraction in investment as government and bankers' funds were redirected to the purchase of grain. Another cause was overproduction as available markets had been swamped. The combined effect of these factors was reduced production (cotton exports from the *Zollverein*, for instance, fell by 40 per cent between 1844 and 1847). There were also numerous bankruptcies and factory closures (times were so bad by 1848 that Alfred Krupp had to melt down the family silver to pay his steelworkers). For **workers**, the crisis meant reduced wages, short-time working or unemployment. Unemployed craftsmen and skilled workers, who had seen their skills replaced increasingly by machines, vented their anger by attacks on factories and by machine breaking (as in Düsseldorf and Chemnitz in 1848). For the middle classes too, times were hard. Some faced bankruptcy, others were heavily in debt or suffered severe losses from the fall in share prices. Many workshop owners, already hard pressed by factory competition, were forced out of business.

In 1847, 10,000 factory **workers** lost their jobs in Vienna alone.

Why might economic problems result in demands for political change?

This social and economic crisis formed the backdrop to an increase in liberal and nationalist activity in the 1840s. We have seen in the first half of this chapter that there was relatively little liberal or nationalist activity or success until the 1840s. However, the 1840s do seem to mark some stepping-up of interest and support. In Hungary, for example, Lajos Kossuth was winning support and a readership for his nationalist newspaper; in Italy middle-class intellectuals, liberals and nationalists were publishing ideas; and in Germany, in the wake of the Rhine crisis of 1840, there was some relaxation of the measures against liberal and nationalist activity. In the two or three years before 1848 this activity appears to have increased.

Italy

In Italy the stimulus to increased activity was the election in 1846 of an apparently liberal pope, Pius IX. Until this point Italian nationalism and liberalism had been largely confined to discredited radicals like Mazzini and moderate intellectuals happy to discuss some possible future 'Italy' without Austria. The actions of Pius IX seemed to indicate that that future might be close. Once elected, he released political prisoners, admitted laymen into government, relaxed press censorship, reduced taxes, instituted an advisory council with representatives from the various Papal States and suggested a customs union modelled on the German *Zollverein*. These moves encouraged liberals and nationalists throughout Italy. Mazzini even wrote to Pius IX suggesting he lead a movement for Italian rights. Pius IX's actions encouraged other rulers to introduce liberal reforms. Charles Albert of Piedmont, for example, relaxed censorship, leading to a wave of liberal journals including Cavour's *Il Risorgimento*. He also allowed elected local councils and freedom of association. Meanwhile, in Switzerland a civil war broke out, the result of which was the creation of a liberal federal regime espousing guaranteed civil rights and popular sovereignty.

Austrian supremacy seemed threatened even in Lombardy and Venetia. The new archbishop of Milan, for instance, had some sympathy with 'Italian' aspirations. Milanese liberals petitioned for civil liberties and self-government, but gained no response until they tried an unusual form of direct action in January 1848. Austria depended heavily on the taxes raised from the sale of tobacco and from gambling. In January the Milanese began to protest by not smoking or gambling. Support grew and tension rose. Six were killed by Austrian troops in disturbances, and in February the Austrians declared **martial law** in both Lombardy and Venetia (whence the protest had spread).

In Naples, protest in Sicily led Ferdinand II to grant a limited constitution in January 1848, but the Sicilians wanted autonomy and set up their own provisional government headed by liberal aristocrats.

Germany
Although the Rhine crisis was short lived, it revealed the extent to which a sense of 'Germanness' had extended into the wider population. This may not have constituted a desire for a united German state, but it did make German rulers pay attention. In response they relaxed restrictions on 'German' organisations. There was a revival of nationalist clubs such as gymnastics societies and choral societies. Liberals took note, seeing in the prospect of a united Germany a means of ensuring their aims were achieved. The appeal of German nationalism was revealed once more in 1846 when the king of Denmark attempted to incorporate Schleswig–Holstein more fully into his kingdom. The issue aroused German anger because Holstein was inside the German Confederation and both Schleswig and Holstein had large German populations. The issue died away, to return in 1848 when Denmark repeated its attempt. Meanwhile liberal and nationalist activity increased. In 1846 there was a meeting of German professors at Frankfurt – dubbed the 'Intellectual Diet of the German people' – and in 1847 Frederick William IV of Prussia appeared to make a liberal move when he summoned a united diet in Prussia.

Martial law is a situation in which the normal regime of law is suspended and replaced by military rule.

He had also relaxed press censorship. However, he was no liberal. He expected co-operation from the diet and a loan to fund railway building. When liberal views were expressed, the diet was dissolved, a move that contributed to increased discontent.

Austrian Empire

Here, too, there was increased liberal and nationalist activity in the 1840s. Kossuth won support in Hungary and Austrian liberals were beginning to make themselves heard, despite official repression. Liberal critics of the regime attacked its inefficient bureaucracy, censorship, taxation system, centralised decision making and favouritism towards the nobility. They pointed the finger in particular at Metternich. Liberal discussion **clubs** and societies were able to meet almost openly in the 1840s, even under the noses of the administration in Vienna. Meanwhile pressure was mounted in the diet of Lower Austria for the relaxation of the remaining feudal burdens.

Such **clubs** as the Legal-Political Reading Club and the Lower Austrian Manufacturers Association met in joint sessions to discuss constitutional change.

In conclusion, it could be said that 1845–48 brought economic and social discontent together with political pressure for change. The economic crisis brought despair and unrest over a wide spectrum of society and governments were unable to cope. At the same time, liberals and nationalists were more vocal in arguing for political change that had some relevance to those who were suffering. Liberalism offered an end to feudalism and representative government might be a mechanism for protecting artisans and skilled workers from the new competition from powered machinery. It would certainly provide for government that was more responsive to middle-class concerns. Nationalism provided a unifying emotional focus for such aspirations in Germany, Italy and the Austrian Empire. However, there was no revolution in 1847 when, arguably, poor economic conditions peaked. During the period of recovery revolutions broke out, albeit on top of three years of hardship.

Is there a straightforward relationship between economic hardship and political unrest?

Triggers

There was one main trigger to revolutions across Europe in 1848: the February Revolution in Paris, resulting in the overthrow of Louis-Philippe and the declaration of a republic. News of the event had two main effects. It encouraged liberals and nationalists to step up their activities and to demand immediate change. It also seemed to break the nerve of European rulers, whose will to stand up to liberal and nationalist demands appeared to crumble. There was a domino effect, also stimulated by the fall of Europe's 'policeman' Klemens von Metternich, in Vienna. In the extraordinary days of March and subsequent months, liberal and nationalist protesters seemed to carry all before them. Rulers bent over backwards to grant constitutions and agree to elected assemblies. German and Italian unification and Hungarian independence seemed a real possibility in that spring. The collective loss of will by the monarchs left governments temporarily paralysed and unable to resist demands for change.

Austrian Empire

News of revolution in France was the spark that stimulated revolt in Vienna where, in the first weeks of March 1848, middle-class liberals, students and workers joined in street demonstrations and presented petitions to the emperor. Clashes with troops led to loss of life and consequent anger. Although Metternich urged resolution, a combination of fear, loss of nerve and ministerial rivalry (he had personal enemies at court) persuaded the emperor that he should be sacrificed to appease popular opinion. On 13 March Metternich resigned. He managed to escape from Vienna in a laundry van and made his way to England.

Popular pressure remained, however, and in April the government granted freedom of the press and permission for a constitution for the western part of the Austrian Empire. In May the emperor promised the free election by universal suffrage of an assembly whose task would be the drawing-up of a constitution. He also accepted the setting-up of a citizen militia or the National Guard in Vienna.

Meanwhile, the emperor's hand had also been forced over Hungary. On 3 March, in the Hungarian diet, Lajos Kossuth had demanded self-government for Hungary. The diet proceeded to draw up the March Laws, which combined a series of liberal **demands** with nationalist ones such as the removal of all non-Hungarian troops from Hungary and the effective independence of the lands of the **Crown of St Stephen**. On 11 April the emperor conceded all these demands.

In Prague, the Czech nationalist Palacky organised a Pan-Slav Congress which assembled on 2 June. Palacky demanded acceptance of the Czech language alongside German, recognition of Czech nationality and abolition of the *robot* (see page 184), but did not demand independence. Rather he argued for Austro-Slavism – a reformed Empire in which the emperor would act as the protector of the various Slav nations (Czechs, Slovaks, Serbs and so on) against German or Russian domination. Czech nationalism was much weaker than Hungarian and the emperor was much less willing to give way here. It was in Prague that he was to achieve the first turn around in his fortunes.

In the Austrian Empire's Italian possessions of Lombardy and Venetia revolution had also broken out. We have already seen evidence of unrest in the peninsula, with the revolt of Sicily and the 'tobacco riots' in Milan in January. In February the king of Naples granted a constitution, as did the duke of

The **demands** were freedom of the press, equality before the law, freedom of religion, and the abolition of serfdom and the *robot*.

The lands of the **Crown of St Stephen** were not only Hungary but also Transylvania, Croatia and Ruthenia.

Tuscany. In March Charles Albert of Piedmont and Pope Pius IX also granted liberal constitutions. In Venice the revolutionary leader Daniele Manin proclaimed a republic, and an uprising in Milan forced the Austrian army – led by the aged Marshal Radetzky – to withdraw. Across the peninsula the Italian tricolour of green, white and red was flown. Great hopes were placed in the 'liberal' pope, Pius IX, and Charles Albert sought his support when he answered the cry of his 'Italian brothers' in Milan and Venice and ordered his forces into Lombardy. Here, as elsewhere across the empire, the authority of the emperor was temporarily paralysed.

Germany

A similar pattern emerged in the states of the German Confederation. Hunger had already stimulated unrest, with riots against grain merchants and tax collectors. Radicals and liberals – through their newspapers, political clubs and gymnastic and rifle associations – were demanding reforms. Both could agree on demands for the abolition of the remaining feudal obligations on the peasantry, for the end of censorship, political repression and for a constitution. Where radicals departed from liberals was in the demand for universal manhood suffrage. Liberals wanted a more modest extension of the franchise that would place political influence in the hands of the middle class.

The initial impetus here came in the states closest to France, where liberal and nationalist sentiment was strongest. News of the French February

An example of the violent unrest in many capitals. Revolutionaries have thrown up a barricade in a main Berlin street. The fighting depicted here took place on 19 March 1848.

Revolution triggered political confrontation. In Bavaria, students and others had already begun protesting, building barricades and demanding a republic. King Ludwig I at first tried concessions such as allowing freedom of the press. When these failed to appease the demonstrators, he abdicated in favour of his son, Maximilian II, who granted a constitution (9 March). Other rulers in Germany were also panicked into granting **concessions** and in Hanover, Württemberg and Saxony liberals were given ministerial positions.

The crucial developments occurred in Prussia. In response to liberal demands for political reform and nationalist agitation for a united Germany, Frederick William IV, like other sovereigns, made concessions. He called a united diet (a Prussian assembly) and, demoralised by news of the fall of Metternich, on 18 March appointed a more liberal cabinet, promising to end press censorship, grant a constitution for Prussia and press for a constitution for Germany. However, as troops moved in to disperse the crowds, shots were fired, leading to the raising of barricades, violent clashes with troops and the deaths of around 250 people. With the situation descending into chaos, the king appealed for calm and ordered the soldiers out of Berlin. He met with popular leaders and agreed to the formation of a civic guard and the release of political prisoners. He also announced: 'Prussia is henceforth merged with Germany.' It seemed as though liberal and nationalist hopes were about to be realised.

These **concessions** included the abolition in Baden of the feudal obligations on the peasantry (10 March).

How similar was the sequence of events in the various revolutions in the Austrian Empire and German Confederation?

Drawing of the entrance of the members of the *Vorparlament* into St Paul's church in Frankfurt on 30 March 1848. Notice the flags. These were in the German liberal colours of black, red and gold.

Most remarkably, Frederick William IV – along with other German princes – agreed to the organisation of a German national parliament. Preparations for this had begun when nationalists, mainly from the southern states, had met in Heidelberg on 5 March to summon a pre-parliament (*Vorparlament*) to supervise elections to an all-German national assembly. Elections would be by universal manhood suffrage and the assembly would gather in St Paul's church in Frankfurt in May. A united Germany seemed in the making.

Why did these revolutions fail by the summer of 1849?

In those heady spring days it seemed that a new Europe of liberal governments and national states might emerge. Germans talked of a 'springtime of the peoples', but there was to be only the briefest of summers before the dreams of liberals and nationalists across central Europe were shattered by the wintry winds of reaction.

The pattern of events

Germany

Elections to the German national parliament went ahead and the new assembly gathered in Frankfurt in May. Those elected as **members** were predominantly liberal (rather than radical), drawn from the educated and professional middle classes. Great hopes were placed in this assembly, but it had no settled programme or plan of action.

One of the first questions it needed to settle was the nature of the new Germany. Should it be a republic or a federation? If the latter, what should the nature of the federation be? Which monarch should be its head of state? What should be the relationship between the parliament and the various states? Most members, cautious and moderate in their approach, rejected the republican option because of its association in their minds with radical politics, democracy and mob rule. Other questions were less easily resolved and, though debate was heated, decisions were slow in coming.

In June it was finally decided that the Frankfurt parliament should claim supreme executive authority in Germany, thereby placing it above that of any state. It was also decided to offer the leadership of Germany to Archduke John, a member of the Habsburg family. This decision seemed to provide an answer to another question that caused great debate: the territorial extent of the new Germany. Should it be a *Grossdeutschland* or a *Kleindeutschland*? It seemed the assembly had decided on the former, but events were to make this impossible.

Meanwhile, another crucial question had arisen. What should be the attitude of the parliament towards non-German national movements? This question was of immediate relevance because the old German Confederation

Of the **members** 275 were state officials, 66 were lawyers, 50 were university professors and another 50 were teachers. Only one peasant and four artisans were elected.

Grossdeutschland (Big Germany) would encompass the areas of the Austrian Empire inside the German Confederation. *Kleindeutschland* (Little Germany) would exclude the Austrian Empire.

contained Polish, Danish and Czech areas. In March 1848 Danish troops had occupied the duchies of Schleswig and Holstein; the Czech nationalist Palacky claimed Bohemia for the Czech nation and was organising a Slavic Congress in Prague; and Polish nationalists had risen in Prussian Posen. Initial sympathy for other national movements evaporated in the light of these challenges to what most delegates believed to be integral parts of the German Fatherland. However, the actions of the Danes and others highlighted the impotence of the Frankfurt parliament. It could claim power but had no means of enforcing its decisions. The members were therefore forced to applaud the actions of the monarchs whose power and authority they, as liberals and nationalists, had so recently challenged. The victory of the Austrian forces in Prague and the suppression of the Polish rising by the Prussian army were praised, as was Prussian action against Denmark over Schleswig and Holstein.

As we have seen, the Frankfurt parliament was an essentially liberal and middle-class body. Yet many of those who had manned the barricades and protested in March were workers and artisans with their own demands. The assembly was unsympathetic to their mainly economic and radical demands and so separate workers' assemblies met in Hamburg and Frankfurt. The anxiety of skilled workers and craftsmen threatened by the deskilling effects of industrialisation was reflected in demands for protection against competition from mechanisation and the maintenance of the privileges of craft guilds. The Frankfurt parliament, busily debating the drawing-up of a constitution for the new Germany, rejected their demands as incompatible with **economic liberalism**, provoking unrest and demonstrations in several German states in September. As the barricades went up once more, the parliament, itself invaded by desperate workers but helpless to act, relied on Prussian and Austrian forces to suppress the unrest.

By this time it was clear that the Austrian Empire was opposed to the German project – a fact that the Frankfurt parliament seemed to accept when in October it declared that any German state could join the new Germany, provided it did not bring with it non-German lands. This solution implied that if Austria wished to join it would mean the break-up of the Austrian Empire, which the Austrian emperor was presently fighting to avoid. The talking continued in Frankfurt and in December it finally agreed the **Basic Rights** of the German People, a German version of the French Declaration of the Rights of Man and the Citizen. It then proceeded to work on a detailed constitution for the new Germany, which it finally published in April 1849. This included the creation of a hereditary 'emperor of the Germans' to head the new state, a position the parliament offered to the king of Prussia.

By this time there was little chance of the German project succeeding. The Austrian Empire was well on the way to crushing all challenges to its authority

Economic liberalism demanded free trade and non-interference by governments in economic affairs. To middle-class liberals, the demands of the artisans would, if met, have retarded economic progress and required state intervention.

The **Basic Rights** proclaimed the principles of equality before the law; freedom of speech, assembly and religion; the end of feudal privileges; and the right to private property.

and Frederick William IV had recovered his power in Prussia. He rejected the offer of the **crown** out of hand.

The Prussian king had recovered his nerve and thence his authority in autumn 1848. The United Diet had met in May 1848 to draw up a Prussian constitution. It proposed to make the civic guard permanent, ban noble titles and end feudal privileges – all moves that alienated the **Junker** nobility and encouraged them to support the king. He had never lost the support of the army and, encouraged by the successful reaction against radical republicanism in France during the June Days, he dismissed his liberal ministers, sent the army back to Berlin, dissolved the United Diet (December) and disbanded the civic guard. All resistance was crushed by Prussian troops.

Frederick William IV's rejection of the German crown marked the effective end of the Frankfurt parliament. It lacked support from Austria, and other princes were recovering their authority. Delegates began to disperse. Some more radical delegates gathered briefly in Stuttgart, but they were dispersed by force in June. The attempt to create a liberal and united Germany had failed.

This was not quite the end of the story. The king of Prussia, now that the revolutions had been effectively crushed, saw an opportunity to extend Prussian influence in Germany. He suggested a Prussian union that would effectively reduce Austrian influence. Austria reacted by unilaterally announcing the revival of the old German Confederation in September 1849. Few states were willing to support the Prussian position and in the end Prussia was unwilling to use force. It finally gave way in November 1850, signing the so-called 'humiliation of Olmütz' which effectively accepted the revived German Confederation.

Austrian Empire

Between March and May 1848 it seemed that the liberal, radical and national movements carried all before them. The emperor had agreed to the drawing-up of a national constitution and allowed the creation of a basically independent Hungarian government. In Prague Slav nationalists were gathering for the Pan-Slav Congress; and in Italy the emperor was faced with not only revolution in Milan and Venice, but a war of 'national liberation' led by Piedmont. Everywhere, at first, it appeared that the loose-knit multi-national empire was unravelling. However, the success of these movements was short lived. The paralysis of imperial authority was to be temporary. Concessions were made in the hysteria of revolutionary fervour, but the Austrian emperor remained on his throne and, crucially, his armed forces remained loyal.

In March the emperor had agreed to liberal demands such as the formation of the National Guard in Vienna, a constitution, freedom of the press and

The king of Prussia contemptuously dismissed this '**crown** from the gutter' offered 'by bakers, and butchers, and reeking with the stench of revolution'.

The **Junker** nobility were the landowning aristocracy of Prussia, naturally conservative and historically loyal to the monarch.

Find evidence of how the following contributed to the failure of revolution in Germany: divisions amongst revolutionaries; the revival of royal power; the loyalty of the armies to their princes.

widening of the franchise. He also agreed to the setting-up of workshops in the capital to provide temporary work for the unemployed. The franchise was widened, but it would only extend to taxpayers. This led to renewed protest and further concessions accepting universal manhood suffrage and a single-chamber elected assembly. No primacy was given to Germans, so in this assembly the monarchy's ethnic minorities would dominate.

The new parliament assembled in July to draw up a new constitution based on universal suffrage. In September the emperor, still uncertain of his position and wanting to avoid rural rebellion, agreed to the parliament's abolition of all feudal obligations on the peasantry, including the much hated **robot**, or labour service. In this way the peasantry were bought off and the chances of their supporting the revolutionary leaders in Vienna were diminished. Mean-while, the splits between the aims of middle-class liberals and the more radical demands of the workers had become apparent. When in August Ferdinand had closed down the workshops for the unemployed, the resulting unrest had been put down by the middle-class National Guard. In October the workers rebelled again, partly in support of the Hungarian rebels against whom the emperor had just declared war. Unrest persuaded Ferdinand and the parlia-ment to leave Vienna for Kremsier, but the rebels in the capital were in a difficult position and Austrian forces, supported by General Jellačic's Croatians, bombarded and invaded the city, killing over three thousand people. This was the opportunity the emperor had been waiting for. The revolt crushed, he proceeded to impose martial law, closed down political clubs, dissolved the National Guard and re-established censorship. Arrests, trials and executions followed. He also appointed an able new chief minister, Count Schwarzen-berg, who persuaded Ferdinand to abdicate in favour of his nephew Franz Josef. Meanwhile, another new minister, Alexander Bach, had begun to implement a new system of surveillance and policing designed to prevent any further uprising in Vienna.

The parliament still existed, and from its base in Kremsier it drafted a new constitution that approved the abolition of feudalism and aimed to create a decentralised multi-national state under a constitutional monarchy. Ministers would be answerable to a parliament elected by universal manhood suffrage. This liberal constitution was not implemented, because the government dissolved the parliament in March 1849 and arrested some of its leaders. A limited constitution was proposed by the government to appease moderate opinion, but never took effect. The emperor was back in charge in Austria and, although martial law was to continue until 1851, the revolutionary crisis in Vienna was over.

Robot, or labour service, was required of peasants. It meant that peasants could be required to work for a certain number of days on their lord's land.

How important was the loyalty of the armed forces in helping the Austrian emperor to restore his authority?

Czechs

Initially there had been some co-operation between German and Czech liberals and nationalists when unrest broke out in March 1848, and both were represented on the 'national committee' set up in Prague. By May the growing demands by Czech nationalists for political rights alienated German liberals, who withdrew from the committee. Later the Germans were to welcome the violent suppression of the Slavic Congress in June.

The friction between German and Czech arose partly from Czech resentment at German domination in Bohemia, and was exacerbated by the resistance of the Frankfurt parliament to the idea of Czech self-government. At Frankfurt, the *grossdeutsch* idea then dominated debate and this viewed Bohemia as part of the German Fatherland. This partly explains why the Czech leader Palacky sought the protection of Czech and other Slav nationalities through his concept of Austro-Slavism. The idea was that the Austrian Empire should be reorganised on federal lines, equal status being given to all nationalities within it. The Austrian emperor would act as protector of Slav nationalities against the threat of domination by German (in Bohemia) and Magyar (in the lands of the Hungarian crown). Palacky was referring to this idea when he famously declared: 'If the Austrian Empire did not exist, it would be necessary for us to create it.'

Palacky's ideas, which fell short of national independence, did not meet universal approval at the Slavic Congress. The Poles, for instance, wanted full independence and other Slavs urged that Russia, not Austria, might be the best protector of national interests. These divisions threatened the collapse of the congress. Frustrated Czech nationalists, impatient with Palacky's solution, tried to set up an independent republic. This was the excuse for which the Austrian army under General Windischgrätz had been waiting, and the shooting of the general's wife added a personal element to the decision to crush the attempted republic. In June the army attacked Prague. Palacky's ideas were to prove academic – Austrian cannon saw to that. After a week's fighting it was all over and Austrian authority was restored.

> In what ways did divisions amongst the revolutionaries contribute to the failure of the Prague revolution?

Hungary

The chances of Austrian recovery in Hungary seemed far less probable. In March and April the emperor had agreed to all Hungarian demands. A national assembly had been elected and set about reorganising the state and recruiting an army. This latter move helps explain why the Hungarian revolt lasted longer than other revolutions.

In spring and summer 1848 the Austrian emperor was preoccupied with events in Bohemia, Vienna and northern Italy. By autumn his position had dramatically improved. He had crushed unrest in Prague, defeated Piedmont in northern Italy and overcome, by October, revolution in Vienna. He could now give some attention to Hungary. He was not without help from within the new Hungarian state. The Magyar view that other national groups within its frontiers should accept Magyar domination was deeply resented, especially by the Croats. Croatia rejected absorption within Hungary and, with the emperor's approval, the Croat governor General Jellačic led an army of 40,000 into Hungary. So began what was called the Hungarian War of Independence. It began well for the Hungarians; Jellačic was defeated. A second Austrian offensive in December forced the Hungarian government out of Budapest, but was unable to crush the Hungarians. This became apparent in spring 1849, when a revived Hungarian army pushed the Austrians back, and in April the national assembly declared full independence.

It was to be a short-lived victory. Tsar Nicholas I responded to the new **Austrian emperor**'s appeal by sending an army of 200,000 men in June. This force, alongside renewed Austrian and Croat attacks, sealed Hungary's fate. In August Hungarian leaders accepted defeat and the Austrian army exacted revenge, executing many. Lajos Kossuth managed to escape to England.

The **Austrian emperor** Ferdinand had abdicated in favour of the young Franz Josef in December.

Italy

Almost as soon as the war of 'national liberation' had been declared by Piedmont, the superficial unity of the movement began to crack. By the time the Piedmontese army fought the Austrians under General Radetzky at Custoza in August 1848, Pius IX had withdrawn his forces and declared against revolution. The king of Naples, too, had withdrawn his forces. This was not the end of the matter. Under the terms of the armistice between the Austrians and Piedmont, Venetia and Lombardy were evacuated, but Venice remained in revolutionary hands under the republican leadership of Daniele Manin. In February 1849, after Pius IX had fled Rome, a Roman Republic was set up. In March 1849 Piedmont again attempted a military solution to Austrian dominance in Italy and was once again defeated, at Novara in March 1849. This second defeat of the Piedmontese army ended its efforts to remove the Austrians and led to the abdication of Charles Albert in favour of his son Victor Emmanuel. The Roman Republic was eventually bludgeoned into defeat by French forces in July and, after a long siege, Austrian bombardment and decimation by starvation and cholera, Manin's Venetian Republic surrendered in August.

Analysis

All the revolutionary activity of 1848–49 had failed. There was no break-up of the Austrian Empire, no united Germany and no united Italy. Why had they failed? The particular circumstances in each of the revolutionary centres were very different, but some general observations about the factors involved in the failure of the revolutions can be made. The importance of the various factors varied, but all help to explain the failure of the revolutions. The factors include:

- divisions amongst the revolutionaries / uncertainty of aims;
- lack of military strength;
- recovery of nerve by rulers and loyalty of armed forces to their rulers;
- lack of popular support.

Divisions and uncertainties

Almost everywhere the revolutionaries were divided amongst themselves about aims and methods. There was a basic division between moderate liberals and radicals, for example. Moderate liberals, generally middle class, wanted constitutional government, press freedom and an end to feudalism. They were fearful of universal suffrage, republicanism and measures designed to help workers. For instance, the middle-class delegates to the Frankfurt parliament ignored or rejected the demands of the workers, even when the protests happened under their noses in Frankfurt. The divisions were real and serious. Whilst much of the early success of the revolutions had been due to the actions of workers and craftsmen who had manned the barricades, these were to gain little from their actions. Moderate liberals dominated the elected assemblies and they feared the mob and radical social and economic measures even more than they hated absolutism and privilege.

There were divisions, too, between and within national movements. In Germany, for instance, there was division between the supporters of the *grossdeutsch* and the *kleindeutsch* solutions. The former was more attractive to the nationalists of the Catholic south and west of Germany, who saw advantage in the inclusion of Catholic Austria. The latter was more attractive to nationalists from the Protestant north, who looked to Prussian leadership. Nationalists, too, were often not nationalists first. They were deeply concerned about the form any new nation state would take. In Germany there was debate over a republican or a federal Germany, and if the latter the exact relationship between federal authority and individual states. In Italy even Mazzini, the most ardent of nationalists, wanted not a federal Italy but a unitary republic.

Mazzini had written of a Europe of nation states working in harmony. However, there was little love lost between different national movements, which goes some way to explaining the failure of them all in 1848–49. German nationalists had little time for the aspirations of Danish, Polish or Czech nationalists in areas considered 'German'. They welcomed the crushing of these movements by the 'reactionary' forces of Austria and Prussia. Within the Austrian Empire national divisions were, ironically, to work in favour of the survival of the empire. Metternich's policy of divide and rule reaped dividends in the aftermath of the 1848 revolutions. In Bohemia, the rivalry between German and Czech made Austria's task easier in June 1848. Germans in Prague welcomed the Austrian army's suppression of the Slavic Congress. In Hungary, the arrogant attitude of Hungarian nationalists towards Croats, Romanians and other national minorities within the lands of the Crown of St Stephen hindered their success. The Croats especially were to prefer loyalty to Vienna to dominance by Budapest and, under Jellačic, were to play a prominent role in the defeat of Hungary. Many Austrian Germans had little sympathy with the aspirations of Czechs, Magyars or Italians and applauded the victories of the imperial forces.

One other feature deserves mention. The revolutionaries in 1848 had no clear idea of what they wanted to achieve or how to achieve it. Once revolution had occurred, they had to put ideas into practice. This inevitably took time as different revolutionaries had very different ideas. It took the Austrian assembly eight months to draw up a constitution. The Frankfurt parliament had only agreed on a set of principles after eight months; it took another three to agree a constitution. Only the Hungarians seemed better organised and rapidly set about organising their state after March 1848. In a way, talk and debate took precedence over action at a time when action was essential if the revolutions were to have any chance of success. By the time liberal parliaments had finished their deliberations, their conclusions were already irrelevant as the forces of reaction had already succeeded.

Lack of military strength

Any government needs to be able to enforce its decisions. Armed forces are necessary to enforce laws passed and defend the new regime. One major reason why the Frankfurt and the Austrian experiments failed was that they had no independent means of making their decisions stick. The situation became quickly obvious in Germany. The Frankfurt parliament might condemn the attempted annexation of Schleswig and Holstein by the Danes, the Polish rising in Posen and the Czech in Prague, but the only forces available to deal with these challenges were the royal armies of Prussia and Austria. The Viennese National Guard might be strong enough to deal with radical unrest in the city and to give the emperor pause, but was no match for regular forces.

Armed force was no guarantee of success, but it certainly helped. The Piedmontese army gave Italian nationalists a chance in 1848 and again in 1849. More significantly, the Hungarians managed to raise their own army that was able to take on and win victories against Austrian and Croat forces. This was a major reason why the Hungarian revolt lasted longer than others. Austria was forced to call on the help of Russia to assist in the crushing of Hungarian independence.

Recovery of nerve and loyalty

Whilst revolutionaries were militarily weak, the armies of the monarchies remained loyal. Princes had learned from the French revolutionary and Napoleonic periods the importance of avoiding the possibility of revolutionary contagion spreading from people to army. Since 1815 states had been careful to keep armed forces away from the people and to ensure they remained professional and loyal. The Austrian policy, for example, of ensuring that units serving in different areas of the empire did not originate from that area was to pay dividends after the revolutions of 1848. In northern Italy Radetzky's forces did not go over to the rebels. The Austrian forces available to General Windischgrätz in Bohemia remained loyal and were used effectively in June 1848 to crush the nascent Czech Republic; and General Jellačic had no problem using his forces against the Hungarians and against the Viennese (in October 1848). In Galicia Austrian forces crushed an attempted Polish rising. In Germany the armed forces of Prussia remained loyal to Frederick William IV, whether used offensively against Denmark or in suppressing revolutionary activity in Prussia, Posen or elsewhere.

Such forces can only be used if ordered to do so by their royal commanders. At the time of the revolutions in March and April 1848, sovereigns had lost their nerve and will to resist the demands of the rebels. Frederick William IV ordered his armed forces out of Berlin rather than risk further bloodshed in the city. Emperor Ferdinand surrendered Metternich and granted concessions

A French satirical cartoon drawn following the defeat of the 1848 revolutions in the Austrian Empire. It shows the three generals whose forces crushed the revolutions in Bohemia, Vienna, Hungary and Italy in 1848–49. From left to right: Generals Jellačic, Radetzky and Windischgrätz.

rather than resist. Once these monarchs realised that their armed forces remained loyal, they began to recover their nerve. A crucial event that helped the Austrian government recover was its decision to leave Vienna for Innsbruck in May 1848. Foolishly, perhaps, the revolutionary committee in Vienna did not prevent the departure. Outside Vienna the emperor regained some freedom of action. News of victories in Lombardy by Radetzky and at Prague by Windischgrätz undermined the view that the success of the revolutionaries was inevitable. Meanwhile, in Prussia Frederick William IV realised that he could rely on his forces to help restore his authority in Berlin. The monarchs were also encouraged by the successful reaction against radical republicanism in France when more conservative elements there asserted their control in the June Days.

Lack of popular support

Also working against the revolutions was the lack of widespread popular support. In particular, the peasants failed to rise in support of liberal or nationalist ideas. One reason for this might be that by 1848 there had been an improvement in economic conditions. The real year of hardship had been 1847, and thereafter harvests improved. Another was that the only other direct reason for rural unrest was the existence of **feudal** burdens on the peasantry. These, with the agreement of the monarchs and even the nobility in the main, had been abolished early in the revolutions.

The emperor of Austria, for example, correctly judged that the abolition of serfdom and the *robot* in September 1848 would render any rural unrest unlikely. **Feudal** obligations had also been abolished in the states of the German Confederation.

Popular support for liberal assemblies was also conditional. The Frankfurt parliament – dominated by moderate, middle-class liberals – rejected the kind of social and political programme that would have won the support of urban workers and artisans. When there was a choice between the disorder threatened by radicals and urban workers, liberals tended to come down on the side of the traditional forces of order. The antipathy of the Frankfurt parliament towards petitions for social reform and the agitation of radicals led to serious unrest in September 1848. The middle-class delegates in Frankfurt relied on the bayonets of the Hessian and Prussian soldiers to preserve them from the anger of the mob. Even so, bitter street fighting led to the deaths of two members and was only crushed by the use of artillery. Such events confirmed liberal fears. In Vienna, too, there was a clash between the interests of the workers and radical students and the more moderate middle-class liberals. A rising by workers in August 1848 in protest at the closure of workshops and reductions in wages was suppressed by the middle-class National Guard.

The determination of the liberals to persist in their revolutions was perhaps undermined by their fear of the mob and more radical politics. Whilst the revolutions had been initially successful because of the popular unrest and the lack of will amongst the princes, arguably one element in the explanation for the failure of the revolutions was the loss of will amongst liberal leaders. Certainly, when the king of Prussia rejected the German crown in 1849 and constitutions were revoked by one German prince after another, there was, it appeared, meek acceptance by liberals. Moderate delegates at the Frankfurt parliament went home, leaving only a radical rump that had to be forcibly dispersed by troops when they assembled in Stuttgart. Similarly, when the Kremsier Constitution was rejected by the Austrian emperor and the assembly was dissolved by Schwarzenberg in March 1849 there was no resistance.

Conclusion

It has been suggested that in 1848 European history reached its turning point and failed to turn. Certainly it seemed in 1850 that the *ancien régime* was still supreme and that liberalism and nationalism had failed. This idea can be overemphasised. One lasting legacy of 1848 was the removal of feudal burdens on the peasantry. In places there remained limited constitutions, albeit granted by kings. In Piedmont Victor Emmanuel retained the *Statuto*, which provided for an assembly elected by a very limited franchise. When the dust settled, Prussia too had a constitution, even though the powers of the elected assembly were weak.

Other changes were perhaps less tangible. The revolutions had involved large numbers of people directly in politics for the first time and – although nationalist, liberal and radical movements had failed – the ideas remained and politics could never be quite the same again. In a little over 10 years Italy would become a united state with a liberal constitution, in under 20 the Austrian Empire would be drastically reformed to create the dual monarchy of Austria-Hungary, and in under 25 a *kleindeutsch* German empire would be created.

Summary questions

1 Explain *two* reasons why the Hungarians failed to achieve independence in 1848–49.

2 Compare the importance of *three* causes of the 1848 revolutions in the Austrian Empire.

Document study
The origins of the French Revolution, 1774–92

Focus questions

- ◆ What were the economic and social causes of the French Revolution?
- ◆ What were the political causes of the revolution?
- ◆ What was the nature of the revolution during 1789–92?
- ◆ How important were religious divisions in creating unrest in France?

This document study provides extra insight into the period presented in Chapter 1. Historians work from the sources available to them. The sources that survive do not provide a complete or necessarily coherent picture of the topics being investigated. Often they will not be able to answer the questions the historian asks of them directly. That is why the historian has to sift the evidence carefully – to evaluate its utility and reliability, and to assess how far it confirms or refutes evidence from other sources. AS source questions seek to introduce you to some of the techniques that become part of the historian's approach.

At AS level you will be asked questions that will seek to test your understanding of the topic area and the relevance of key ideas, your ability to evaluate the reliability and usefulness of sources for particular purposes, your ability to compare and evaluate sources, and your ability to use given sources to test a particular argument or hypothesis.

One useful tool historians have in their armoury is what they know already. No historian comes to the primary source material without some prior knowledge of the subject. Historians can use that knowledge to inform their understanding of the sources and to judge their reliability and utility. AS questions assume you come to the subject with some knowledge. That is why, for example, the first question seeks to test your basic knowledge and understanding directly by asking you to explain a key reference or term. This requires more than a brief definition; rather it requires you both to define and to explain its significance in the context of the source and topic. So, for example, in question 1 for Document Study 3 it would not be enough to identify the 'privileged order' as the nobility (in this context it may refer to both the nobility and the clergy). It would also be necessary to explain that French society was divided into three orders and why the privileges of the first two had become a major issue by the spring of 1789.

Question 2 asks you to assess the reliability or utility of particular sources for a particular purpose. It is very important that you assess the reliability/utility of the source for the particular purpose highlighted. Remember that reliability and utility are not the same thing. Reliability refers to the accuracy, typicality or validity of a source for a particular purpose; whereas utility is concerned with the degree to which the historian can make use of the source and its contents for a particular purpose. A source may therefore be reliable but not particularly useful and vice versa.

The answers to various questions will help you to evaluate the sources. These questions are concerned with the following issues:

- The content of the source. (What does the source say? What can you tell from the language and tone of the source?) For example, Source 3.3 at first glance appears to give a fairly factual breakdown of the groupings in the First Estate, but the words used to describe the first two groups of the nobility give a clear indication of the view of the writer.
- The nature of the source. (What kind of source is it? Was the author in a position to know/comment on the relevant issue? Who is the author? Does that prejudice how far you can believe what they say? What of their intended audience? Does that affect how believable the piece is?) For example, the writer of Source 1.2 was clearly in a position to comment about the clergy (he was an abbé), but the title of his book suggests that his view was coloured by his hopes for France.
- The historical context. (How far does what is said fit in with what you already know? How typical is it? Is what is said corroborated by other sources?) For example, Source 4.3 gives a royalist view of the split in the Catholic church over the constitutional oath in 1791, and the views expressed about the nature of the two sides can be said to be typical of royalists. However, the numbers quoted (50,000 priests: 7,000–8,000) do not square with the idea that the clergy were split about 50:50 over the oath.

Source comparison (question 3) requires you not simply to compare the content of each source (where they agree or disagree) but also to compare them as evidence. (Is one source more reliable/useful than the other for the purpose given in the question? How typical are they? Can you explain the differences and similarities?) For example, in question 2.3, Sources 2.2 and 2.3 are both by outside observers of the situation in France and both agree that the key problem facing the monarchy was that of financial bankruptcy. However, whilst 2.2 attributes this to the consequences of a mistaken intervention in the American War of Independence, 2.3, from an American, sees it as evidence of the failure of the monarchical system – one man cannot effectively govern a large nation.

Finally, question 4 requires you to test the sources against a hypothesis outlined in the question. You are explicitly required to set the sources in the context of your own knowledge. Try to evaluate the sources both individually and as a set. Whatever the balance of evidence in the sources, this may or may not conflict with your wider knowledge and understanding of the topic. There may be, for instance, good reasons for rejecting the evidence in the source(s) or for accepting the evidence even though the source(s) may be flawed in one way or another.

Document study: What were the economic and social causes of the French Revolution?

1 The nature of society before the revolution

Study these four sources on the nature of French society before the French Revolution and answer the questions that follow.

1.1 An extract from the *cahier des doléances* of the village of Collan in Champagne, drawn up in early 1789

The said inhabitants affirm and declare:
That most of the land is owned by outsiders from neighbouring areas and by bourgeois;
That they are nothing but farm labourers on other people's land;
That they pay a general tithe of one in twenty-one on their crops to the seigneur;
That they also pay the same lord a fee by property owned and by household, as well as one hen or ten sous;
That their parish priest has only the basic stipend and is therefore in much distress that he cannot relieve their property as he would wish.

Source: R. Cobb and C. Jones, *The French Revolution* (1988)

1.2 Some observations on the situation of the lower clergy in the period before the revolution by an abbé, written before the revolution broke out

None are so wretched and so oppressed as the lower clergy. While the bishop plays the great nobleman and spends scandalous sums on hounds, horses, furniture, servants, food and carriages, the parish priest has not the wherewithal to buy himself a new cassock. The burden of collecting the tithe falls on him, but the bishops, not he, pocket it.

Source: Abbé Michel Lavassor, 'The groans of enslaved France, which hopes for freedom'; quoted in L. W. Cowie, *The French Revolution* (1988)

1.3 A contemporary writer comments on the position of the nobility of France in the eighteenth century, written before the revolution

The castles, which bristle in our provinces and swallow up large estates, possess misused rights of hunting, fishing and cutting wood; and these castles still conceal those haughty gentlemen who separate themselves effectively from the human race, who add their own taxes to those of the monarch, and who oppress all too easily the poor, despondent peasant, even if they have lost the privilege of killing him.

The rest of the nobility surround the throne, their hands continually open to beg eternally for pensions and places. They want everything for themselves – dignities, employments; they will not allow the common people to have either promotion or reward, whatever their ability or their services.

Source: L. S. Mercier, *Description of Paris* (12 volumes written 1783-89), VIII; adapted from passage quoted in Cowie, *The French Revolution* (1988)

1.4 A group of lawyers give their views on the question of noble privileges

The privileges of the nobility are truly their property. We will respect them all the more because we are not excluded from them and because we can acquire them: great actions, gallantry, courage, personal merits, offices, fortune even, all these are paths that lead us to them. Why, then, suppose that we might think of destroying the source of emulation which guides our labours?

Source: letter by the lawyers of Nuits in Burgundy, 31 December 1788; quoted in Cowie, *The French Revolution* (1988)

Document-study questions

1 Study 1.4. Using this source and your own knowledge, explain the reference to noble 'privileges' in line 1.
2 Study 1.2. How reliable is this source as evidence of the state of the clergy in the 1780s?
3 Study 1.3 and 1.4. Explain why these sources differ in their view of the opportunities for advancement open to non-nobles.
4 Study all the sources. Using these and your own knowledge, explain how far you agree with the view that the essential differences in French society were between rich and poor rather than between the privileged orders and the Third Estate.

Document study: What were the political causes of the revolution?

2 The monarchy and its problems

Study these four sources on how far Louis XVI was responsible for the problems he faced and answer the questions that follow.

2.1 An educated Englishman travelling in France comments on a dinner party with French hosts attended in Paris on 17 October 1787

One opinion pervaded the whole company, that they are on the eve of some great revolution in the government; that everything points to it; the confusion in the finances great; with a deficit impossible to provide for without the Estates General of the kingdom, yet no ideas of what would be the consequence of their meeting; no talented ministers; a prince on the throne with excellent intentions, but without the resources of a mind that could govern in such a moment without [able] ministers; a court buried in pleasure and dissipation . . .

Source: Arthur Young, *Travels in France during the years 1787, 1788 and 1789*; adapted from Cowie, *The French Revolution* (1988)

2.2 The Russian envoy comments on the problems facing the monarchy in a report to the tsar

By succeeding in rendering America free, France has so exhausted herself that in her triumph, having sought to humiliate English pride, she has ruined herself and now sees her finances exhausted, her credit diminished, the Ministry divided and the whole Kingdom in faction.

Source: report of J. F. H. Oldencop, Russian consul in Amsterdam, 1788; quoted in P. Vansittart, *Voices of the revolution* (1989)

2.3 An American in Paris comments on 20 August 1788 on the declaration of bankruptcy by the French government

The lack of money has in fact overborne all their resources, and the day before yesterday the government published a decree suspending repayments of capital and reduced interest on loans. The consternation is as yet too great to let us judge of the issue. It will probably open the public mind to the necessity of a change in their constitution. It is a remarkable proof of the total incompetency of a single head to govern a nation well, when with a revenue of 600 millions they are led to a declared bankruptcy, and to stop the whole of government for lack of money.

Source: Thomas Jefferson, *The papers of Thomas Jefferson*, ed. J. P. Boyd, XIII (1950-83); adapted from Cowie, *The French Revolution* (1988)

Louis XVI was exempt from the vices which spring from strong emotions, but he also lacked the energy to which they give birth. Nature, having given him the amiability and the virtues pleasing in a private individual, denied him the qualities needed by one destined to command. Timidity and mistrust of himself were at the centre of his character; and it was soon recognised that, if he were not to be guided by his own inclinations, others could succeed by skill and perseverance in influencing his decisions.

Source: Guy-Marie Sallier, *Annales françaises depuis le commencement du règne de Louis XVI jusqu'aux Etats Généraux de 1774 à 1789* (1813); adapted from Cowie, *The French Revolution* (1988)

Document-study questions

1   Study 2.1. Using this source and your own knowledge, explain the reference to 'confusion in the finances' (lines 2–3).
2   Study 2.4. How reliable is this source as evidence of Louis XVI's character?
3   Study 2.2 and 2.3. Compare these two sources as evidence for the problems facing France in the years before 1789.
4   Study all the sources. Using these and your own knowledge, explain how far these sources prove that Louis XVI was mainly responsible for the difficulties facing his monarchy.

Document study: What was the nature of the revolution during 1789–92?

3   The Estates-General in the spring of 1789

Study these four sources on the nature of the Estates-General and answer all the questions that follow.

3.1   An extract from a pamphlet widely circulated in the run-up to the elections to the Estates-General in January 1789

What is the Third Estate? EVERYTHING.
What has it been in the political order until now? NOTHING.
What is it asking for? To become SOMETHING.
Who would dare to say that the Third Estate does not have in itself all that is needed to form a complete nation? It is a man who is strong and robust but still has one arm in chains. Take away the privileged order, and the nation would be not less, but more.

And so what is the Third Estate? It is EVERYTHING but an EVERYTHING shackled and oppressed. Without the privileged order, what would it be? EVERYTHING, an EVERYTHING flourishing and free. Nothing can go well without it; everything would go infinitely better without the others.

Source: Abbé Sieyès, *Qu'est-ce que le Tiers Etat?* (January 1789); adapted from Cobb and Jones, *The French Revolution* (1988)

3.2 A Third Estate deputy comments on Necker's speech to the Estates-General in the opening session on 5 May 1789

Next came M. Necker; he was clapped the moment he rose, and spoke for at least three hours. By no means everyone can have been pleased with his speech: he praised the king every line; no new ideas in administration or finance, but the worst was this: a clear statement that the Estates have only been convoked to re-establish the finances.

He was taking it for granted that the Estates are only a consultative assembly, arguing that taxes must be left as they are at present. He took over three quarters of an hour to prove that the French nation must avoid bankruptcy.

Necker also explained himself loftily on the question of voting by head or by order and demonstrated with determination that the court intends voting to be by order; everlastingly repeating that the king did not summon the Estates because he needed them, but out of his own good pleasure.

In a word, it all seemed prejudiced in favour of the king and the first two orders. I thought a third of the assembly was very displeased: no applause, often a chilly silence.

And so the battle is joined!

Source: *The journal of Adrien Duquesnoy*, ed. R. de Crèvecoeur, 2 vols., I (1894); adapted from Cobb and Jones, *The French Revolution* (1988)

3.3 In a private letter a Third Estate deputy describes the make-up of the First Estate order at Versailles in May 1789

The nobility is divided into three parties, the parlementaire party, which would immolate the whole human race to preserve the power of the parlements; the party of grand seigneurs of the court who combine all the sentiments conjured up by the pride of aristocrats with the servile baseness of courtiers; and that of reasonable men which is small in number and not all of whom are exempt from the prejudices of the nobility. Numbered among this party are M. de la Fayette and the duc d'Orléans.

Source: Robespierre to Buissart, 24 May 1789, *Oeuvres*, III; adapted from J. Hardman, *The French Revolution sourcebook* (1999)

3.4 Extract from a letter from one of the Polignac circle giving an account of a meeting between the queen and the king in the aftermath of the Tennis Court Oath

Then the queen, unable to contain herself, depicted the throne overturned by the men of faction and the formation of a flagrant conspiracy aimed at changing the order of succession, to aid a guilty prince, the duc d'Orléans, in seizing the crown.

Just when this princess was at her most impassioned, a secret deputation from the *parlement* of Paris was announced. It had come to beg the king to dissolve the Estates-General, whose existence was compromising the existence of the monarchy; at the same time it gave assurances that the *parlement*, to stop the tempest, would not hesitate to register such tax decrees as might be sent before it and would furthermore promise in advance to do anything which His Majesty wanted.

Source: letter from the chevalier de Coigny to the bishop of Soissons, 20 June 1789; adapted from Hardman, *French Revolution sourcebook* (1999)

Document-study questions

1   Study 3.1. Using this source and your own knowledge, explain the reference to the 'privileged order' (line 6).
2   Study 3.3. How useful is this source as evidence of the attitude of the noble deputies in the Estates-General?
3   Study 3.1 and 3.2. Compare these sources as evidence of the attitude of the Third Estate in the early months of 1789.
4   Study all the sources. Using these and your own knowledge, explain how far they show that the differences between the Third Estate and the nobility were too deep to be resolved.

4 The position of the Catholic church after 1789

Study these four sources on the impact of religious changes between 1789 and 1792 and answer all the questions that follow.

4.1 A contemporary cartoon about the confiscation of church property by the government

The original caption to this cartoon reads 'The Press [as in wine-press]: "Patience, sir, your turn will come."' You should look at the cartoon from left to right. The priests are being put in a press and squeezed before being released on the right.

Source: Photographie Bulloz, published in D. Richards, *An illustrated history of modern Europe 1789–1974* (1977)

4.2 A radical newspaper comments on the position of the clergy just after the National Assembly agreed the Civil Constitution of the Clergy in July 1790

If the clergy were less concerned with their past glory and wealth, if they did not wish to foment civil war at any possible price, they would no longer resist the lawful will of the nation. We would not see the majority of bishops of France, together with the parish priests, crying out that the Catholic religion is lost because they have been denied a display of wealth that is both insolent and absolutely opposed to the principles and spirit of the Gospel.

Source: *Les révolutions de Paris*; adapted from Jones and Cobb, *The French Revolution* (1988)

4.3 A royalist newspaper gives its summary of the two sides in the religious divide which appeared after the clergy were required to take the oath of allegiance to the Constitution in particular and the revolution more generally

France in division

Authorities who condemn the oath demanded of the clergy	Partisans of the oath demanded of the clergy
The pope and cardinals	Mirabeau
30 bishops in the National Assembly	Two bishops in the National Assembly
50,000 priests	7,000–8000 priests – ambitious, fanatical, ignorant
The right wing of the National Assembly	The left wing, and the monstrous assembly of the principal enemies of the church and of monarchy, Jews, Protestants, Deists
All good Frenchmen who love their country, their religion and the happiness of their brothers	All the brigands who burn chateaux, pillage mansions, set up gallows; all the scoundrels who have bathed France in blood
The will of our good king	The most detestable tyranny, which has taken his place

Source: *L'Ami du roi*, 22 March 1791; adapted from Cobb and Jones, *The French Revolution* (1988)

4.4 A modern historian comments on the significance of religious divisions in France

[The changes to the church] were imposed from outside and seemed to deny the fundamental nature of the Church as a divinely ordained institution. A refusal to swear the oath could easily be seen as a way of rejecting the whole progress of the Revolution and an attempt to rally opposition around an issue of great emotional force. There is little doubt that the schism [split] in the Church did indeed provide the issue around which the forces of counter-revolution could rally. Furthermore, the King's reluctant and grudging accept-ance of the Civil Constitution served only to deepen the suspicion which already existed concerning his attitudes and motives.

Source: L. Kekewich and S. Rose, *The French Revolution* (1990)

Document-study questions

1 Study 4.3. From this source and your own knowledge explain the reference to the 'oath demanded of the clergy' (lines 2–3).
2 Study 4.1. How useful is this source about French attitudes to the clergy?

3   Study 4.2 and 4.3. Compare these two sources as evidence of the attitudes of Frenchmen to the Catholic church in 1790–91.

4   Study all the sources. Using these and your own knowledge, explain how far you agree with the view that the changes imposed on the Catholic church in France were the major cause of division over the course of the French Revolution between 1789 and 1792.

Appendix
The Republican Calendar

The Republican Calendar was introduced by decree of the National Convention in October 1793 and designed by the actor, journalist and revolutionary Fabre d'Eglantine. The calendar was dated from the foundation of the French Republic on 22 September 1792. Year I ran from 22 September 1792 to 21 September 1793, Year II from 22 September 1793 to 21 September 1794, and so on.

There were 12 months of 30 days, at the end of which occurred 5 (6 in leap years) extra days or *sans-culottides*. Each month was made up of three 10-day weeks, or *décades*. The months were named in relation to nature and the agricultural cycle as follows:

Vendémiaire (22 September–21 October): the month of vintage (wine-making)

Brumaire (22 October–20 November): the month of fog

Frimaire (21 November–20 December): the month of frost

Nivôse (21 December–19 January): the month of snow

Pluviôse (20 January–18 February): the month of rain

Ventôse (19 February–20 March): the month of wind

Germinal (21 March–19 April): the month of germination (seeds growing)

Floréal (20 April–19 May): the month of flowering

Prairial (20 May–18 June): the month of meadows

Messidor (19 June–18 July): the month of harvest

Thermidor (19 July–17 August): the month of heat

Fructidor (18 August–16 September): the month of fruit

The calendar was in use until 1806.

Further reading

General surveys

There are few books that cover the whole period of this volume, as 1815 is often taken as a dividing line. A useful and readable account of the period 1780–1830 is *Europe 1780–1830* (Longman, 1989) by Franklin Ford. A thought-provoking and wide-ranging study is provided in *The age of revolution 1789–1848* (Abacus, 1977) by Eric J. Hobsbawm. This volume takes a world perspective and deals with social, cultural, economic and intellectual themes as well as political ones. Another useful and stimulating work is *Barricades and borders: Europe 1800–1914* by Robert Gildea (Oxford University Press, 1996). There are some useful summaries of key issues and themes in Stephen J. Lee's *Aspects of European history 1789–1980* (Routledge, 1982). The *Longman companion to European nationalism 1789–1920* by Raymond Pearson (Longman, 1994) is a mine of useful information.

In addition, some of the key issues and ideas that run through the period are considered in thematic books such as *Revolutions 1789–1917* (Cambridge University Press, 1998) by Allan Todd which deal with the causes and nature of revolutions. *Nationalism 1789–1945* by Andrew Matthews (Hodder & Stoughton, 2000) also provides a useful perspective on this key aspect.

The French Revolution

The French Revolution is the subject of a vast and ever-growing literature. Good, more thorough treatments include W. O. Doyle's *The Oxford history of the French Revolution* (Oxford University Press, 1989) and the narrative but very readable *Citizens* by S. Schama (Viking, 1989). More difficult to read but worth the effort is *France 1789–1815: revolution and counterrevolution* by D. M. G. Sutherland (Fontana, 1985). Another useful introduction is Duncan Townson's *France in revolution* (Hodder & Stoughton, 1990). *The Longman companion to the French Revolution* by Colin Jones (Longman, 1990) is an invaluable source of reference material.

On the debate on the nature of the revolution I would suggest William Doyle's *Origins of the French Revolution* (Oxford University Press, 1999), which begins with an assessment of the current state of historical writing before giving the author's own interpretation of the causes. Tim Blanning's *The French Revolution: class war or culture clash?* (Macmillan, 1997) is a shorter, punchier and very readable introduction to the historiography of the revolution.

Good sources of documentary material are: *The French Revolution*, edited by Richard Cobb and Colin Jones (Simon & Schuster, 1988), which also includes useful commentaries on various aspects of the revolution; *The French Revolution sourcebook*, edited by John Hardman (Arnold, 1999), which has key political issues as its focus and contains a useful commentary by the editor; *The French Revolution* by Leonard W. Cowie (Macmillan, 1987), which centres its selection of sources on issues of debate; and *The French Revolution 1789–99* by E. G. Rayner and R. F. Stapley (Hodder & Stoughton, 1995), which uses documents to illustrate key themes.

Napoleon

As with the French Revolution, the literature on Napoleon is vast and ever expanding. A readable recent biography can be found in *Napoleon* by Frank McLynn (Jonathan Cape, 1997). Also stimulating, critical and well written is Corelli Barnett's *Bonaparte* (Wordsworth, 1997). G. Ellis gives an overview of Napoleon and the nature of his regime in his volume *Napoleon* (Longman, 1997). It also has a useful section on the historiography of the period. Jean Tulard's *Napoleon: myth of the saviour* (Methuen, 1985), although poorly translated in places, is stimulating and gives a modern French perspective.

Good challenging overviews of Napoleon can also be found in Martyn Lyons, *Napoleon Bonaparte and the legacy of the French Revolution* (Macmillan, 1994); Charles J. Esdaile's *The wars of Napoleon* (Longman, 1995); Michael Broers, *Europe under Napoleon, 1799–1815* (Arnold, 1996); and Geoffrey Ellis, *The Napoleonic Empire* (Macmillan, 1991).

David Chandler's *The illustrated Napoleon* (Greenhill, 1991) gives a useful military history of the period by an expert in the field. Those who want to go further can move on to his mammoth *The campaigns of Napoleon* (Weidenfeld & Nicolson, 1993). Barnett, cited above, gives a critical account of the military history, as does Owen Connolly's *Blundering to glory* (Scholarly Resources, 1987).

The *Longman companion to Napoleonic Europe* by Clive Emsley (Longman, 1993) provides useful information on a wide variety of aspects of this period.

France, 1814–48

This period has relatively few readily accessible books apart from those whose treatment expands beyond the specific period. A useful introduction is K. Randell, *France: monarchy, republic and empire, 1814–1871* (Hodder & Stoughton, 1991). Two very good texts are J. P. T. Bury's *France 1814–1940* (Methuen, 1969), which gives a solid narrative account of the history; and Robert Tombs, *France 1814–1914* (Longman, 1996), which gives both a thematic and a chronological account of the period. The latter provides coverage of the social, economic and cultural developments as well as the political ones. There is a long account of the political history of the July Monarchy in H. A. C. Collingham's *The July Monarchy* (Longman, 1988). A. Cobban's *A history of modern France*, volume 2 (Penguin, 1965) is also useful.

Revolution and repression in Europe, 1815–49

A reasonably accessible account of Metternich and the Austrian Empire can be found in A. Sked, *The decline and fall of the Habsburg Empire, 1815–1918* (Longman, 1989). Another general account can be found in C. A. Macartney, *The Habsburg Empire, 1790–1918* (Weidenfeld & Nicolson, 1969). There are also relevant chapters on the development of nationalism amongst Magyars, Czechs, Austrians and Italians in M. Teich and R. Porter, *The national question in Europe in historical context* (Cambridge University Press, 1993).

Germany is well served with works in English. The relevant chapters of William Carr, *A history of Germany 1815–1990* (Arnold, 1991), and Mary Fulbrook, *German history since 1800* (Arnold, 1997), will provide sound narrative and analysis, as will *The course of German nationalism from Frederick the Great to Bismarck 1763–1867*, by Hagen Schulze (Cambridge University Press, 1991).

On Italy, a useful starting point is Andrina Stiles, *The unification of Italy 1815–1870* (Hodder & Stoughton, 1989). In addition, a sound blend of narrative and analysis is found in *The Italian Risorgimento*, by Martin Clark (Longman, 1998). H. Hearder, *Italy in the age of the Risorgimento* (Longman, 1983), is also useful.

On the 1848 revolutions there are two useful overviews in Roger Price, *The revolutions of 1848* (Macmillan, 1988), and Peter Jones, *The 1848 revolutions* (Longman, 1981). In addition, there is the more recently published and fuller account by Jonathan Sperber, *The European revolutions of 1848–51* (Cambridge University Press, 1994). Finally, *Europe after Napoleon: revolution, reaction and romanticism, 1814–1848* by Michael Broers (Macmillan, 1996) provides a very clear summary of the development of political ideas in this period.

Index

absolute monarchy, 1, 4, 172; in France, 10, 14, 26, 124; and Napoleon, 88–9; and the *philosophes*, 26; and revolutions, 5, 6

agriculture: crisis in (1840s), 174–5; in France, 145–6; and the urban economy, 173

American Declaration of Independence, 153

American War of Independence (1776–83), 4, 17, 53; and the French Revolution, 17, 25, 27, 29–30

Amiens, peace of (1802), 97

Anderson, Benedict, 155

armed forces: and Bonapartism, 133; and the Bourbon restoration in France, 124; and the 1848 revolutions, 188, 189; French revolutionary armies, 8, 49, 50, 60, 61, 99–102; and Napoleon, 76–7, 101, 102–7, 114–15, 116, 118–19; in Prussia, 117; and the success of revolutions, 8

Artois, comte d', *see* Charles X, king of France

Austerlitz, battle of (1805), 95, 98, 104–5, 106, 107

Austrian Empire: and the army, 189; and the Declaration of Pillnitz (1791), 48, 49; and economic crisis, 174–5; 1848 revolution in, 6, 7, 8, 171, 178–9, 183–4, 189–90; ethnic diversity in, 163, 170; French revolutionary war with the, 49–50, 52, 55, 56–7, 63, 66; and the German Confederation, 151, 156–7; and the German project, 182–3, 187; and the Holy Alliance, 167–9; and Hungary, 8, 164–6, 175, 177, 178, 185–6; and Italy, 160–2; and the July Monarchy in France, 137; liberal and nationalist ideas in the Austrian Empire, 163–6, 177; Metternich's government of the, 168–70, 187–8; and the Napoleonic wars, 96–7, 98, 99, 103, 104–5, 107, 109, 114, 116, 117, 119; and the Peninsular War, 110–11, 112

Balbo, Cesare, 162–3

Battle of the Nations (1813), 116, 117, 157

Belgium, and the Vienna Congress, 151

Berlin Decrees, 108

Bernadotte, Jean-Baptiste, 105

Berry, duc de, 127, 138

biens nationaux, and the Bourbon restoration in France, 124, 125, 133

Blanc, Louis, 148, 149

Blanqui, Auguste, 148

Borodino, battle of (1812), 114, 118

bourgeoisie in France: before 1789, 11–12; and the Enlightenment, 26; and the French Revolution, 32–3, 40; and the July Monarchy, 135–6, 145, 147; and the revolution of 1830, 132, 134

Britain: and the Eastern Question, 139; and the French revolutionary wars, 56, 63, 72; and the July Monarchy in France, 139, 140, 141; and the Napoleonic wars, 95–6, 97–8, 107, 108–9, 114, 120, 121

Buonarroti, Philippe, 148

Calonne, Alexandre de, 17–18, 19, 28, 44

Carbonari in Italy, 161

Carnot, Lazare, 59

Catherine the Great, empress of Russia, 26

Catholic Church in France, 10–11; and the Bourbon restoration, 125–6; and Charles X, 129, 130, 133; and the French Revolution, 44, 45–6, 62–3, 73, 200–2; and the July Monarchy, 135; and Napoleon, 80–1, 92; *see also* clergy

censorship, 25, 26; in Austria, 170; in France, 84, 89, 90, 91, 127, 131; in Prussia, 180

Charles Albert, king of Piedmont, 162, 176, 179, 186

Charles X, king of France, 6, 123, 128–34; abdication of, 131, 134; and Louis-Philippe, 143, 144; and the Ordinances of Saint-Cloud, 130–1, 132

Chartists, 5, 6

cholera epidemics, 9, 147

Chouannerie revolt in Brittany, 67, 83

cities, population growth in, 172–3

citizenship, and the French Revolution, 43

clergy in France, 10–11, 20, 21; anti-clericalism, 133; and the Bourbon restoration, 126; Civil Constitution of the, 45–6, 57, 62, 73, 80; refractory priests, 48–9, 50, 52, 53, 86

Cobbett, William, 5

communications, improvements in, 4

conservative ideology, 1, 2, 151

Constant, Benjamin, 83, 93

constitutional government, 4, 25, 30; and liberalism, 154

constitutional monarchy in France, 47; and Charles X, 132–3; and the Charter (1814), 124–5, 127–8; failure of, 51–2; and Louis-Philippe, 134–5

constitutions: in the Austrian Empire, 184, 191; in France, 77–9, 87, 91, 92, 93, 135; and the French Revolution, 37, 42, 43–6, 66, 77; in the German Confederation, 158, 159, 167–8; Germany (1849), 182, 188; Italy, 161, 178–9, 191; and liberalism, 153; Prussia, 191; Spain (1812), 153, 161

Corday, Charlotte, 53

Cordeliers Club, 48, 52, 64, 69, 71, 72

cultural nationalism, 156, 170

Czech nationalism, 166, 178, 182, 185, 187, 188

Danton, Georges, 48, 52, 53, 54, 55, 64, 69, 71

Davout, Louis-Nicolas, 105–6

Decazes, Elie, duc de, 126–7

Declaration of the Rights of Man and the Citizen, 24, 39, 40, 41, 42, 45, 153

Delacroix, Eugène, *Liberty leading the people*, 131

democracy, 4

demographic changes in Europe, 2, 3, 172

Desaix, General, 97, 106

Desmoulins, Camille, 22, 34

diseases, epidemics, 9, 147, 173

Dorset, earl of, 9

Du Teil, Chevalier, 100, 103

Dumouriez, General, 55, 56–7, 72

Eastern Question, 139

economic changes, 3–4; in France, 145–6